From Wade & Lynn

LAND OF FUR AND GOLD

AUTOBIOGRAPHY OF RAYMOND THOMPSON

Printed in the United States of America

ISBN 0-89716-068-1

Dedicated to my beloved wife Ruby

FOREWORD

At a time when the creative spirit in most men was being squelched, first by the Great Depression and later by the equally arduous World War II, Raymond Thompson never lost sight of his dreams. One of his dreams was to become a respected author, writing about this beloved Northwest where he trapped, mushed dogs, lived in the bush and acquired tons of writing material. Another of his dreams was to successfully manufacture a more humane concept of trapping, the Thompson Self-Locking Steel Snare.

Struck with multiple sclerosis while in his prime, this innovative individual overcame hardships that would have devastated a lesser man. With the love, support and fortitude of his wife Ruby, he survived to see these dreams realized.

Land of Fur and Gold is an autobiographical account of the undaunted pursuit of those dreams.

Robert A. Henning
Editor & Publisher
ALASKA magazine

ERNEST THOMPSON SETON
SETON VILLAGE
SANTA FE, NEW MEXICO

Seton refers to Raymond Thompson as a "field naturalist" in using Thompson material from "Forest and Stream" and "Wilderness Trapper" and other publications in "Lives of Wild Game".

FORTY YEARS AN AUTHOR AND EDITOR

OUTDOOR ADVENTURE FEATURES SYNDICATE
Raymond Thompson, Executive Editor
15815 SECOND PLACE WEST
ALDERWOOD MANOR, WASHINGTON (State)

FOR THE MAN WHO HUNTS AND FISHES:
"Forest and Outdoors" contains the pick of Canadian hunting and fishing narratives written by such noted authorities as Hamilton Laing, W. A. Parker, Ozark Ripley, Raymond Thompson and others.

PLAN LECTURES AT SPORT SHOW
Coeur d' Alene Idaho 1932
Thompson, Author, To Talk On Wild Game Life

SPORTS AFIELD
Along the Athabaska Trail
A Moose Hunt in That Almost Inaccessible Game Land North of Edmonton
By Raymond Thompson

. Raymond Thompson.

Wild Life by Raymond Thompson
Outdoor Editor — Detroit Daily

DOGS IN CANADA
FEBRUARY, 1958
SLED DOG RACING NOTES
by RAYMOND THOMPSON

BOY LIFE
Dogs of the Windfall Country
By RAYMOND THOMPSON

CATHOLIC BOY
ADVENTURE · ATHLETICS · OUTDOOR LIFE
SUBSTITUTE RIVERMAN, Trouble comes with rising waters.
By Raymond Thompson

August 17, 1930 THE HIGHROAD
On the Trail of the Moose
By Raymond Thompson

THE CANADIAN BOY
The Canyon Creek Scow
By RAYMOND THOMPSON

OUT-DOOR RECREATION
ROD — GUN — CAMPING
Edited by RAYMOND THOMPSON

THE PIONEER
May 16, 1931.
Where the Horse Is Still King
By Raymond Thompson

Fur Trade Journal of Canada, November 1946
TRADER AND TRAPPER
Edited By RAYMOND THOMPSON

THE TARGET
The Winter Camp
By Raymond Thompson
January 23, 1932

FOREST & Outdoors
MARCH 1959
Is the Canada Lynx Becoming Extinct?
Raymond Thompson

MUSKRAT RANCHING
BY
Raymond Thompson and A. C. McFadyen

FUR-FISH-GAME
TRAIL DOGS OF ATHABASCA
By Raymond Thompson

Fur - Fish - Game
Trapping in Northern Canada—Part IV
Raymond Thompson

HUNTER—TRADER—TRAPPER.
September, 1922
ADRIFT ON THE ATHABASCA
By RAYMOND THOMPSON

JOHNSON PUBLISHING COMPANY
ATLANTA — DALLAS — NEW YORK — CHICAGO
Raymond Thompson's stories used in the Sixth Reader by the Johnson Publishing Company.

August 23, 1931 THE HAVERSACK
Wild Animals Appreciate Kindness
By RAYMOND THOMPSON

LAND OF FUR AND GOLD

by Raymond Thompson

INTRODUCTION

This is an autobiography of sorts. It starts with the third year of my adventures in the Athabasca and Peace River areas of northern Canada, with an occasional flashback to my very early experiences in that vast wilderness. These flashbacks are pertinent as the various references make up important pieces of a jig-saw puzzle. I hope, too, that the reader will bear with me when I sometimes stray from the general course of this narrative, to delve even further back to the days of my boyhood.

My first published articles on the North Country appeared in 1918, in *Hunter-Trader-Trapper Magazine.* An adventure story, "A Winter in The North," brought a $12 check from *H-T-T,* when Otto Kuechler was editor. I recall only one rejection from Kuechler and that was for an article, "The High Cost of Trapping," in which I exposed some shady dealings of certain mail order fur houses. Two of the raw fur dealers I mentioned were regular advertisers in *Hunter-Trader-Trapper.* Kuechler wrote that one of these was being investigated by the Federal Government and that a woman who ran a country store in Colorado and also bought raw furs had taken practical steps to bring the crooked mail order house to justice. She had taken her sales records for a large number of coyote pelts, along with the fur grading lists that had accompanied the outrageously small checks from the raw fur dealer, directly to the authorities in Washington, D.C. The editor of *H-T-T* thought it unwise to publish anything that might have a bearing on that particular case while the Colorado woman's suit was pending in Federal courts.

I mentioned the above as similar incidents have had great influence in my early dealings with fur buyers and also in regard to their treatment of other trappers, including natives in remote areas where trappers had little knowledge of the true market value of their pelts.

Over these many years, I have had hundreds of articles published in such magazines as *Forest & Stream, Outing Magazine, Sportsman's Digest, Sports Afield, Rod & Gun in Canada, Fur Trade Journal of Canada, Fur News* and *Outdoor World* and since 1930, many of my stories have appeared in *Fur-Fish-Game.* For about 12 years, I was a contributor and department editor (Sled Dog Trails) in *Alaska Magazine* (formerly *Alaska Sportsman*) but much of my writings in this magazine had been slanted towards the breeding, training and actual racing of sled dogs.

One special reason for this book is that I now feel I had not previously covered my experiences with the Indians of northern Canada, sufficiently. In recent years, in travels through Canada and Alaska, via the Alaska Highway and to the Northwest Territory over the Mackenzie Highway, we passed through much of the territory covered in my early writings. But, I have come to realize that many of my former concepts of Indian and white man relations were based too much on my own experiences. It was not until the mid 1920's, when I was able to do serious research, in Edmonton and Alberta Provincial libraries, that I came to understand something of the real background, or heritage of both native and white trappers, traders, prospectors and homeseekers with whom I had been associating for over a decade.

Raymond, age 5

Chapter I

I was born in the state of Washington, May 5, 1896 on a ranch in the Big Bend (of the Columbia River) country. It was only twenty miles north of my birthplace to the Columbia River and this stream marked the southern boundary of a large Indian reservation. There were several cable ferries crossing the Columbia and a rural mail route from my home town Almira, to Nespelem, headquarters for the Colville Indian Reservation, included one of these river ferry crossings.

When my father built a house in Almira, I entered school there, on a standard course of from grade one through grade 12. During those years I had frequent contact with full blood Indians and several "breeds" of mixed white and Indian blood.

There were two families of the latter group who were substantial farmers. Their children went to the same school as we whites and I cannot recall a single incident in or out of school, where the slightest distinction with any racial overtones, was ever made. One of the Whitelaw boys lived in Wilson Creek Canyon and we hunted and fished together. A fleeting "puppy love" affair with Roy's sister, Dessie, was nipped in the bud when the Whitelaws moved. But I never did forget either of these fine youngsters, who were, according to reports, quarter-breed, or even more proportionately, "reservation" or "Status" Indians — that is, they could live on the Reserve as Indians, or be treated essentially as whites if they chose to farm or work ranches other than reservation land allotted to Indians.

Our home was on the outskirts of the town and my father owned land that extended for a mile east of the town. A neck of our property extended into the town itself and my father had fenced this for pasture as a creek named Corbett's Draw ran through it.

I recall how thrilled I was when in the late summer, the Indians came to set up their tepees on our pasture land, while they sold huckleberries to Almira residents.

My mother threatened to "give me to the squaws" if I didn't quit spending so much time there.

Another locality where I was in contact with Indians was in a fruit growing area about 25 miles northeast of our ranch. This spot called "Peach," boasted a Post Office, one store, a school and a church and extended two miles along the south bank of the Columbia River.

My uncle and aunt, John and Alice Hill, had grown sons and daughters and all of them were fruit growers. Although peach orchards predominated, many growers had strawberries, melons, etc., and during the peak of the berry harvesting season, Indians from the Reservation across the river, came to work for my relatives and others.

I often picked strawberries with Indian boys and girls. Most of them spoke English and were quite industrious and reliable, only one, a boy of about my own age, proved dishonest. I saw him putting berry-size clods of dirt in the "cubbies" (strawberry boxes) and then covering the clods with leaves and a layer of berries. As my uncle had assigned this particular lad and his sister to me, as helpers, I, of course, felt responsible. "My Uncle John will fire me if I take in dirt in place of berries," I told Charlie Mink.

Family home, Almira, Wn. 1902

I don't recall our exact exchange of words, but I do remember that Charlie left the berry patch in a huff. His sister and I filled Charlie's "caddy" (a carrier which held a dozen of the small boxes) with good strawberries and she took Charlie's share of pay to their tepee camp on the river bank.

Susie Mink also took my mouth harp with her — a highly prized possession. "Tell Charlie he can learn to play on it, but I want it back before he leaves the valley," I said. It was an impetuous gesture but one that paid real dividends. Charlie Mink came back and picked strawberries diligently and honestly. He also learned to play some weird tunes on my harmonica and I sold it to him for twenty-five cents. Charlie Mink and I spent many happy hours fishing in Hawk Creek and he showed me how his people made wooden traps for small game and birds, using a sort of figure 4 trigger, that when thrown, would let a sort of cage fall and trap the game.

I was a young boy when I started snaring animals and birds. First, I tried snaring suckers, a slow-moving bottom fish, clearly visible in the "Baptizing Hole," in Corbett Draw (creek) about three miles south of Almira. Using a small gauge brass wire, I made a noose, with the free end of the snare attached to a long fishing pole. On the rocks overlooking the pool, I would sit for an hour or more, manipulating the noose over a sucker and then, with a swift yank, close the brass wire noose around the fish and, hopefully, make a catch. It was a hit or miss method, to say the least, and the limpid waters of the "Baptizing Hole" were never much depleted of the sucker population!

Another method of snaring was to place a twine noose in the entrance to a ground squirrel den hole and to snare the rodent as he poked his head and shoulders up to look around. You had to give a quick yank to make it work. I improved the usual by attaching one end of the twine snare to a rubber band (made from a bicycle tire inner tube). I made a release that I could work with a pole and the rubber stretched, of course, gave a much faster pull on the noose. This device really worked! Ground squirrels were literally by the millions in the wheat farming country where I was raised. They destroyed thousands of dollars worth of grain on some large farms. In some sections, from one cent to five cents "bounty" was paid for ground squirrel tails.

My real progress in snaring commenced in 1908, when I obtained a copy of W. Hamilton Gibson's *Camp Life and the Tricks of Trapping.* The book contained excellent methods on how to make snares from materials easily obtained.

I nearly got into trouble with one of Gibson's spring pole methods. I rigged a set in our stable and enticed one of my mother's prized Plymouth Rock hens, with some chicken feed. The hen stepped on the willow limb release, the spring pole "power" worked, throwing the hen up against an overhead beam in the stable, killing the victim very quickly.

I was afraid, as any 12-year-old would be, to tell his mother what really happened to her fine Plymouth Rock hen! I "found" the hen dead later on, of assumed natural causes, used it as a bait, at an abandoned badger hole set and caught a coyote, which I later sold for $2.00. I learned one lesson from this incident — to be very careful where and how I made my trap, deadfall and snare sets.

During my high school years, I made several trips to Nespelem. Indians always treated me as a friend and looking back, I honestly believe it was

Hill family in Peach 1901

because I had the faculty of putting myself in their "shoes." There is an old Indian truism that warns anyone to "walk a mile in the other man's moccasins" before judging him.

While most of my early outdoor adventures had to do with fishing, hunting, and trapping, there was a current of "gold fever" coursing through my veins. One of my father's brothers disappeared in the Klondike, during the early 1900's. Our last word from Uncle Will was in a letter mailed in Dawson, Yukon Territory.

"Nothing for me here — returning south to the Peace River country in June or July. Guess I'd best settle down like my brothers!" he wrote.

Uncle Will never reached the Peace River district, as far as we ever learned, and by this time I was old enough to decide on my own future, man's search for gold, as evidenced in earlier "stampedes," was a thing of the past.

In spite of this general trend, the more I read of the Klondike gold rush, the deeper rooted became my own longing to follow in my uncle's footsteps and seek adventure in northern Canada — the Land of Fur and Gold. In our very modest high school library were a few books with sketchy references to prospecting in the west and north and by studying maps, I could pinpoint certain areas where gold had been discovered in quantities. Comparing such sections with the vast expanse of wilderness apparently untouched, was fascinating. "Surely," I said to myself, "there must be more gold in such an immense territory!"

My father was one of many wagon freighters who hauled supplies from Spokane Falls, Washington Territory, to the Coeur d'Alene mines in northern Idaho. The only concrete evidence I have left of his involvement in any mining enterprise is a certificate of shares in the Tom Hal Mines, which apparently were of no value. Possibly, my father had taken the mine stock in exchange for freighting bills. I remember when, some months after my father's death, in 1911, my mother showed me the fancy, engraved piece of paper, saying that she thought it of no value. The "hard-rock" Coeur d'Alene mines, mostly silver and lead, are still productive after nearly a hundred years, but my father was one of thousands who either worked in the mines or, as he did, in serving supply houses, none of whom ever made a "strike."

Hard rock mining, involving deep tunneling into the very heart of the mountains with drilling, blasting and back-breaking toil in loading and hoisting ore to the surface, never appealed to me. The search for a "mother lode" through constant samplings of outcroppings and the digging of "coyote holes" in ore-bearing rock was not my idea of how to wrestle a fortune from Mother Nature.

On the other hand, exploring streams with simple tools, such as pick, shovel and gold pan was my brand of "prospecting." I first learned something of placer mining for gold, while working for my uncle, John Hill, on the Columbia River. Uncle John's fruit orchard was on the river flats several miles below the spot where the Spokane River emptied into the Columbia.

About a mile downstream from the junction of the two rivers was a long island, never completely submerged even when the Columbia was at flood stage, and, by early September, when the river had subsided, we could reach the island on foot, over dry sand-and-gravel bars. This "dry" part of the river bed trapped a back channel of water that made a marvelous pool for swimming.

Single Copy 15¢

Official Newspaper For Lincoln County

The Wilbur Register

ESTABLISHED IN 1889 VOLUME 84 NUMBER 48

WILBUR, LINCOLN COUNTY, WASHINGTON 99185 THURSDAY, DECEMBER 27, 1973

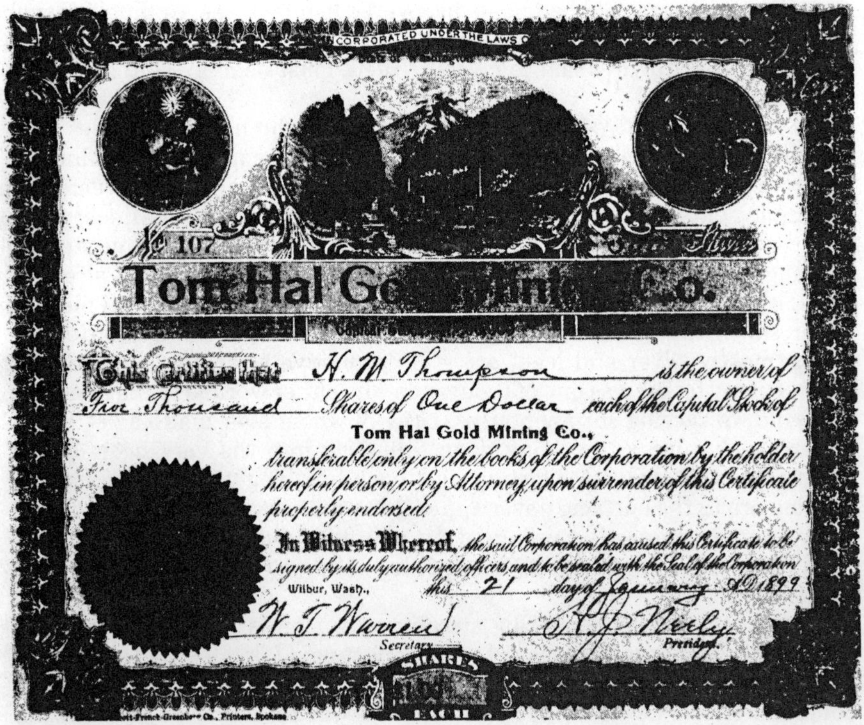

Incorporated under the laws of State of Washington

No 107 Shares

Tom Hal Gold Mining Co.

This Certifies that H. M. Thompson is the owner of Five Thousand Shares of One Dollar each of the Capital Stock of

Tom Hal Gold Mining Co.,

transferable only on the books of the Corporation by the holder hereof in person, or by Attorney upon surrender of this Certificate properly endorsed.

In Witness Whereof, the said Corporation has caused this Certificate to be signed by its duly authorized officers and to be sealed with the Seal of the Corporation

Wilbur, Wash., this 21 day of January AD 1899

W. T. Warren, Secretary

H. J. Neely, President

Shares ... Each

Hal Mining – $5,000 1899

Reprint Wilbur Register

On my first trip there, I learned why the spot was called "China Bar." It was named after early-day Chinese miners who often worked gravel bars scorned by white prospectors as low-grade. Thousands of Chinese were also brought into the western United States as soon as the Civil War ended to help build the railroads and interest in both mining and land settlement was renewed.

The early prospectors sought gold mainly along streams and in surface deposits. Placer mining required very little equipment and the gold collected was accepted as money in any reputable store or trading post.

A gold washing device known as a rocker (from a rocking motion used to facilitate the movement of coarse gravel through the device), was widely used, as were flumes made of boards with cross cleats designed to trap gold-bearing sand, while it was being washed through the flume.

I finally got around to a little prospecting in Canada, while operating the ferry at Baptiste River Crossing. As I had to be on duty, in case some traveler wanted to cross the river between 7 A.M. and 7 P.M., I confined my gold seeking efforts to a rather limited range up and down the stream itself.

With a shovel, pick, and gold pan, I soon discovered "flour gold" in (to me) exciting quantities. Fine and flaky, the tiny bits of precious yellow metal rarely exceeded a common pinhead in size. Along the river's edge, the exposed gravel yielded "color" in most every wash with the gold pan.

In the January, 1922 issue of *Hunter-Trader-Trapper* appeared my story, "Mining With A Grizzly," which related in some detail, the experience referred to. I thought it worth repeating here:

Thinking my fortune as good as made, I contrived this simple machine, or "grizzly" as they are termed by "sourdoughs" in this man's country. I secured the necessary boards from a discarded wagon-box. First, I made the bottom, four feet long by two feet in width. To this, I fastened the sides, supported by two cross bars six inches apart at either end, making an "endless" box four feet long, two feet wide and ten inches high. Next, I fashioned my sieve by making two gable ends out of two-inch by two-inch pieces joined at the top like ordinary house rafters with the bottom notched so as to set on the sides of the box. Between these two sets of rafters ran horizontal bars, two feet in length, made of half-inch iron with an intervening space of one inch. The idea of the bars was to act as a sieve. This arrangement was made separate from the box, hence, it could be lifted off for convenience.

To operate this crude machine, the only requisites, in my case at least, were a pick and shovel, an oblong piece of woolen blanket, about two feet by four feet, a gold pan, a tub for washing the blanket, water, gravel and a mighty good breakfast.

The woolen blanket, preferably one with a good nap, was stretched tightly on the bottom of the box and secured there with cleats. Then, the box was placed in the water near the shore at a sufficient depth for the current to wash the gravel off the blanket. The box was weighted down by flat stones placed on the cross bars at either end and the sieve placed in position, onto which the gravel was shoveled. The bars turned aside all but the very small stones and gravel. If the depth of the water was about right, the gravel would wash gradually off the blanket, leaving the gold and black sand clinging to it. In a short time, even through the water, one could see the larger flakes glistening on the blanket.

After this process had been carried on till the quantity of black sand on the blanket allowed no room for the gold to collect, it was necessary to lift the machine and wash the blanket in a tub. The weight of the gold had held it to the blanket, while being in a horizontal position, but the rinsing washed a percentage of the gold into the tub. Then "panned" with the gold pan, this process eliminated most of the sand. The final process involved the collecting of the "wash" with quicksilver.

I thought I was getting rich, but an old prospector, John Gregg, one of the pioneers of the Athabasca Country, happened along. He told me I might make a dollar a day if I worked hard enough. (End of excerpt from my story in *Hunter-Trader-Trapper.*)

John or "Jock" Gregg and his partner, "Frenchy" Duval, had stopped at the Baptiste crossing on their way upriver. They were prospecting for gold-bearing rock in outcroppings of ledges along the Baptiste and its tributaries. Placer mining with equipment, such as the crude "grizzly" I was working with, would never pay, in the old pioneer's opinion.

After a few weeks of hard work, with a very small amount of the flake gold collected, I put away my gold pan, pick and shovel. I did find one ore sample, in a deserted trapper's cabin, that was liberally sprinkled with flecks of gold.

A friend, Tom "Scotia" Murphy, who was operating the cable ferry at Little Smoky River Crossing, examined the ore and said that it unquestionably came from a quartz outcropping foreign to the vicinity where I had found it.

"Scotia" Murphy, himself, had discovered some gold-bearing rock near the mouth of a small creek that emptied into the Little Smoky River several miles below the wagon trail crossing. This had happened several years before and "Scotia" was so excited over his discovery that he returned to Calgary to form the "Lucky M Mining and Trading Company." His partner was named Morris and I remember very well when their outfit crossed the Baptiste River in the fall of 1916. Morris had a St. Bernard bitch that he expected to breed with a timber wolf and from the hoped-for litter, to build a strain of sled dogs.

Murphy and Morris failed in their "Lucky M Mining and Trading Company" enterprise and "Scotia" could not relocate the gold-bearing rock ledge. Morris and his dog went on further north and Murphy took over operation of the cable ferry on the Little Smoky Rover Crossing for the summer months.

Neither the "Lucky M" nor the Thompson and Knowles Baptiste River Post were feasible operations as straight trading posts, as Indians seldom strayed that far south and white trappers were too widely scattered.

Disillusioned over the general situation, quite early in the spring of 1917, I began to think seriously about leaving the Baptiste River Post. The choice was simple in one sense. I could either move south and give up my dream of Northern adventure, or head north, plunging deeper into the Canadian Wilderness.

CHAPTER II

In June, 1917, my partners and I were advised that the Alberta Government would no longer maintain and pay the operating costs of cable ferries that crossed several rivers on the Edson to Grande Prairie trail. Frank and Cliff Knowles and I were affected by this decision as we operated the two ferry scows at the Athabasca and Baptiste River crossings.

The reason for the closure of the pioneer trail to the Peace River was that the Edmonton, Dunvegan and British Columbia Railway had been completed to Grande Prairie in to the very heart of the Peace River Country. The 230-mile wagon road which had been hacked out of the wilderness, was short-lived, as it was first opened to major traffic in the winter of 1910-11. Home seekers enroute to the Peace River country left the Grand Trunk Pacific Railway in winter, at the town of Edson, mostly with sleds and horses, as by the end of December the streams were frozen over and they could be crossed readily. Several thousand pioneers entered the Peace River district during the four or five years the trail was in operation. It was a most difficult route to travel, as it crossed several mountain ranges with passes between 4,000 and 5,000 feet elevations and the downgrades into the valleys through which the Athabasca and Baptiste rivers flowed were steep and very dangerous. During the winter months, the heavily loaded sleds had to be rough-locked with chains on the slopes or slowed by chaining logs to the sled which, when dragged behind, acted as a brake.

Winter travel on the trail was actually less hazardous than during the summer months. The Athabasca River headed in the Canadian Rockies and during the June and July flood stage, was a formidable barrier for the small wagon trains. Because of the size of the Athabasca, the Baptiste, the Little and Big Smoky rivers, they could not be forded in summer and for that reason, the government built the ferry boats mentioned.

These ferry scows were long flatboats decked with heavy planks and were from 12 to 14 feet in width and from 30 to 40 feet long. Added to the scow itself was a hinged platform on either end. These served as ramps for teams and wagons to get on and off the scows. The hinged platform was called an "Apron." It was the same width as the ferry scow and extended from where it was hinged to the scow, another 6 or 8 feet. The hinge arrangement was necessary so that the outer end of the apron could be lowered to conform to the landing approach on the river bank. In loading, the outfit was driven onto the scow over one apron, and from the scow over the apron at the other end, when the landing was made on the opposite bank of the river, after each crossing. Ferry boats were installed where the trail crossed the Athabasca, the Baptiste (later called Berland) and the Little and Big Smoky rivers.

The Edson trail crossed the Athabasca River a few miles above where it was joined by the Berland and the trail cut across the divide between the two rivers and then continued on north toward the Little Smoky River. At the Little Smoky River crossing, or Mile 78 on the old trail, the river made a sharp bend to the north and from there the trail followed a course almost parallel to the stream until it came to another valley where the Tony River flowed in from the west to join the larger stream. At this point, or Mile 90 on the trail, there was a bridge across the river and on the south bank of the stream was one of the larger stopping houses on the entire trail. Mile 90 House was strategically located on some wild-hay meadows and the travelers could stop during the summer, graze their horses for a day or so before going on north on their long journey to the Peace River country.

I became interested in moving north and possibly to Mile 90, during the summer of 1917, while I was still in charge of the ferry boat at the Baptiste River crossing. One day, I had been upstream fishing for grayling, as the Baptiste was a wonderful grayling and trout stream. During this last year of operation by the Provincial Government, the river ferries were used very little on account of the new railway line, which made a wide loop from Edmonton north and west to the Peace River district. But, there were still a few land seekers traveling by wagons over the Edson-Grande Prairie Trail.

On this particular day, as I returned along the river flats and came onto the open meadows near the Baptiste stopping house, I saw two horses grazing and near the cabin was an improvised tent made by throwing a couple of blankets over some forked sticks in a sort of tepee.

Under this makeshift shelter, designed to escape from mosquitoes and a native fly we called "bull dog," was a trader from Mile 90 House. His name was Theodore (Ted) Walters. Walters was a medium-sized man, quite dark in complexion and although he never told me so himself, he was part Indian and today would be classified as a "Metis."

The man from Tony River, on which Mile 90 House was located, was also the Fire Ranger for the district between Sturgeon Lake and the Athabasca River and during the summer, he patroled not only the old wagon trail, but also many of the major trapline trails extending into the timbered country.

On this particular journey, Walters was on his way south to the Athabasca River crossing and was waiting for me to ferry him, his one-pack horse and a saddle horse, across the Baptiste River.

I had not seen another soul for several weeks, except one settler driving a four-horse team hitched to a heavy freight wagon. This man, with his wife and two children, was moving north from Montana to the Peace River country. Naturally, I was pleased to have Walters as a visitor, even for a short time, and we swapped trail yarns and renewed an acquaintance that had actually commenced two years before.

"What are your plans for this coming winter?" Walters wanted to know. This question was all I needed to explain the situation that had arisen in my partnership with Frank and Clifton Knowles, the father and son who were in with me in running the two "stopping houses" and operating the ferry boats at the Athabasca and Baptiste river crossings.

The younger Knowles with whom I had trapped the previous winter, had had his fill of that rigorous and often frustrating life and was moving with his father back to Edson, where he intended to work on the railroad.

When Cliff told me of his plan, it left me with a hard decision. I did not wish to remain on the Baptiste River alone and so when Walters offered me a partnership with him at the Mile 90 House, I was immediately interested. Walters said that I could trap where I wished, using Mile 90 as a headquarters and that there was untrapped territory both east and west of the trading post that had not been worked by either white or native trappers for two or three years. He also offered me a partnership in his trading post.

Ted Walters on Tony River – 1917

Cliff Knowles and R. T.

Another decision I had to make was whether I should remain in the wilderness or return south to my home in Washington State. In the last mail I had received from the "outside" was a letter from a sweetheart of my high school days, whom I had once thought to marry. In her letter, Isabel stated that she would not consent to move to Canada and that she thought we should wait until we were older. As I was already 21 and she only a few months younger, I thought this was nothing but a "Dear John" letter and my first reaction was the need to decide where I should spend the coming winter. For in spite of the bitterly cold winters and the many hardships I had endured on the trapline, I was still very much in love with the Canadian wilderness.

There were other considerations and developments that created problems for me. The United States was now in World War I. A few months before I met Walters at the Baptiste River crossing, I had registered with the American Consul in Edmonton, Alberta, but in May, 1917, that office could give me no definite information concerning the status of U.S. male citizens residing in Canada in connection with "War Service" responsibility. If the war lasted much longer, I was informed, there was a possibility that U.S. citizens living in Canada and eligible for draft in the U.S. Army, would either be returned to the U.S. or inducted into Canadian Armed Forces.

In June, 1916, a year earlier, I had enlisted in the 202nd Battalion, Canadian Expeditionary Force, but after a few months training in Sarcee Camp, near Calgary, Alberta, I was discharged because as a U.S. citizen under 21 years of age, the Canadian Government would not accept responsibility for sending me into the European war zone. My corporal, a man named Batson, who was also a U.S. citizen, around 30 years of age, told me that 200 American boys in army camps across Canada were released under like circumstances because of complaints from their parents in the U.S.

So now, a year later, with my own country at war with Germany and her Allies, I was torn between my desire to remain in Canada and the thought that I should return to my home. In talking with Walters, he had suggested that the war might be over shortly and that I would be foolish to leave Canada until more definite news from the war front came from overseas.

I mentioned previously that I had met Ted Walters two years before. This was on the trail at the Baptiste River crossing. On his way south, he had been bargaining with Bill Hare, a South African war veteran, for possession of Mile 90 Post.

At that time, I was running a trapline north from the Baptiste River crossing. It was in January and "Old John" Anderson who ran the Baptiste Post was running low on supplies including that vital item, flour. The previous October, a freighter had passed the Baptiste River Post with a heavy load of trade goods and food supplies for a man named Hugh McKinnon. McKinnon was opening a small trading post on Crooked Lake, at Mile 108 on the trail. In December, we heard that McKinnon was so discouraged in the amount of trading he had received from the Cree Indians at Isoegun Lakes, that he was trying to dispose of his outfit, supplies and trade goods.

I discussed this situation with Old John and he suggested that I take my sled dog and a small toboggan and go north to Crooked Lake, to see if I could

purchase some grub from Hugh McKinnon. This was a trip of around 55 miles each way and my reason for taking only one dog and a light toboggan was that we had heard by "Moccasin Telegraph" that McKinnon may have already either sold his trade goods or that it had been stolen from him. But I decided to take a chance and left the Baptiste one morning, reaching my trapline cabin at Jackfish Lake the same day. The next day I left before daylight with my empty toboggan hauled by a large Slave River Husky I called "Babe." This dog was a magnificent animal and could easily pull a toboggan load of 100 pounds herself, on a fair trail. On this particular trip, I had to break a snowshoe trail ahead of the dog for a good part of the distance between Jackfish Lake and Mile 90. In breaking fresh trails, we used a long, narrow snowshoe with an upturned "toe" of the frame made for that special purpose by Cree Indians, from birchwood.

The second day on leaving my cabin, I made it to Mile 90 Post, reaching there shortly after dark. At the time, it had been operated for a year by Bill Hare, the war veteran and his wife, Ritia. Mrs. Hare was a registered nurse originally from Boston, Massachusetts and had a reputation for being of great service to any injured traveler or trapper who might stop there for first aid. In one instance, she probably saved a man named John Fandrick from bleeding to death, as he had cut off his thumb accidentally with an axe, in his camp a few miles from the "stopping house."

At Mile 90, I ran into a real stroke of good fortune. When I explained the purpose of my trip, Bill Hare insisted on driving a team of horses and light bobsled to Crooked Lake, stating that he was also interested in what the situation was with Hugh McKinnon. This would save me a round trip of 36 miles and such a lift was rare in my trail travel experiences.

So, with plenty of grub, blankets, hay and oats for his team, Bill Hare and I left an hour before daybreak, the morning after my arrival at Mile 90. It was mid-January and the trading post thermometer registered 45° below zero.

It took about four hours for us to make the 18 miles from Tony River to Crooked Lake. Bill Hare never pushed his horses and the bobsled runners had a tendency to drag in the dry snow. I noted very few fresh tracks of furbearers and only two sets of moose tracks where a cow and yearling calf had crossed the trail.

"Wild animals are smarter than man," Bill observed. "They hole up in dens or keep in heavy woods cover where old Jack Frost and winds can't get at them and here we are bucking foul weather at 40 below!"

"Yeah, and don't say I forced you into it," I answered, noting a twinkle in Bill's eyes.

The truth was, my friend's curiosity over the situation at Crooked Lake was just as keen as mine. We were especially concerned over the possible grave consequences of Hugh McKinnon's rash act, if he had, as it was rumored, been living with a teen-age *Iskwa'sis* (Indian girl). A few weeks before, a Metis named Al Estelle, on his way south from Sturgeon Lake, had stopped overnight at Crooked Lake and the next day, at Mile 90 House, Estelle had told Bill and Ritia Hare that a Vic LaRonde (another Metis) and a full-Blood Cree Indian with a young *Iskwao* (Indian for woman) were also at McKinnon's cabin.

The Metis and Indian had bunked together, according to Estelle, while the

Bill Hare

Bob Hare, Bill's son

teen-age girl had slept alone, indicating that the girl was not LaRonde's "woman," but instead as Estelle learned the next morning, was a daughter of the Cree and apparently a full-blood native.

It was Ritia who had, by adroit questioning, obtained from Estelle, when he stopped at Mile 90 House, certain observations that hinted at real trouble for Hugh McKinnon.

"Sounded like LaRonde, with the Cree's consent, had pursuaded McKinnon that he needed a 'house-keeper'," Estelle had said. This meant that the Metis and Indian would leave the latter's daughter at Crooked Lake. If the so-called "trader" fell for this old trick, he would be at the mercy of LaRonde who could "blackmail" him for his supplies, trade goods, and even his outfit and furs, by threatening to inform the Mounted Police of the situation at Crooked Lake.

And now as Bill Hare and I left the main trail and took a side road into Crooked Lake, we were happy to see some smoke coming from one of the log cabins that had been a part of the stopping house at this point on the Edson-Grande Prairie Trail.

When I knocked on the door of the cabin, it was opened by a young Cree Indian woman and at first glance, I thought she was probably 16 years or so of age. She was very ordinary looking, as far as the general run of natives appeared, but had very compelling eyes and she looked me straight in the face.

"Is Hugh McKinnon around?" I asked.

"Mac has been away two days now on his trapline."

"When do you think he will be back?" I asked.

"Can't say, he may go for marten. Mac take grub for maybe one week."

In the meantime, Bill Hare had tied his horses to a fence rail and had come over to the cabin. I told him that McKinnon was gone and that the girl did not know when he would return. Bill, more outspoken than I, said, "We would like to come in and talk." The girl didn't answer, but opened the door wider and stepped inside. We followed.

With a natural curiosity, I saw that the interior of the old stopping house cabin was well kept and there was no sign of dirty dishes on the plank-topped table, or objects scattered around the clean, split-log floor. There were two bunks at one end of the room and both were apparently being used as they contained a number of blankets. There was little evidence of food in the cabin itself, something that Bill later admitted noticing. The Indian girl spoke English just as well as the average white girl of her age. Her raven hair was braided and her clothes were clean. She wore a Mackinaw shirt and it obviously belonged to McKinnon, as it was much too large for her. She also wore a pair of man's trousers and I wondered where her own clothes were.

Bill, who was much more familiar with the Crees and their habits than I, commenced questioning the girl, while I brought in our small grub box and prepared to make a lunch. There was a sheet iron stove, which undoubtedly had been brought in by McKinnon and on it was a kettle of boiling water, so I proceeded to make some tea.

After Bill's first few questions, the girl was on the defensive. "Mac good man, he says we will go and see Priest Father at Sturgeon Lake, soon. Mac says it is bad for us to be alone."

But Bill persisted, "Where is your home and why are you here?" he demanded. The girl, obviously annoyed, replied. "My father is Chief of Indian band at Lac Ste. Anne." "Why did he leave you here?" She answered, "I am big girl now, I like to marry. I like Mac and he likes me."

Bill and I decided not to press the girl with further questions, regarding her association with Hugh McKinnon. Neither of us knew enough about the white man to decide whether he actually intended to marry the girl, but her reference to his statement that "they would go see the priest at Sturgeon Lake," was in itself enough for the girl to assume that he really was honest in his intentions toward her.

As I had come all the way from the Baptiste River in a hope of buying some flour and other supplies from McKinnon in case he was selling out his stock, it was important that we at least find out whether he still had anything to sell.

"I am trapping on the Baptiste River and my grubstake is very poor. I came to buy some flour from Mac," I told the girl.

It was then that we noticed a really disturbed look in the girl's eyes. "Mac sell all his flour except for one sack. Here, I show you." She opened the door to a sort of store room at the cabin. It was as she stated, there was very little food left in the place. A 50-pound sack of flour, some cornmeal, oatmeal, a couple of cans of syrup and a small supply of essentials, such as sugar, salt, tea, coffee and so forth was all that remained of the two wagon loads of trade goods and supplies that had been freighted over the trail to McKinnon's "trading post" at Crooked Lake.

There was nothing for us to do, except to return south, empty-handed as far as any grub or food was concerned. We told the girl not to worry and that we were sure McKinnon would return from the Simonette River country in a few days.

It was after dark before we reached Mile 90, so I stayed there over night. Ritia Hare was all for returning to Crooked Lake the next day and to either bring the Indian girl back to Mile 90 or take her north to Sturgeon Lake where there was a Catholic Mission, but was not sure the girl would leave.

Mr. and Mrs. Hare knew quite a bit about Hugh McKinnon. In Edson, 90 miles to the south, Bill and his wife had been in charge of the Immigration Hall, when Hugh McKinnon first arrived there the previous fall. The Immigration Hall was a government operated institution established during the land rush to accommodate any settlers passing through Edson on their way north to the Peace River country. As Hugh McKinnon was a stranger, he was eligible for any help the Hares could provide. Hugh McKinnon appeared to have come from a good family and that he had ample funds.

His trade venture at Crooked Lake was merely a "stepping stone" to an expansion into a larger fur trading operation, as soon as he got the feel of the country and knew more about the business of dealing with Indians and the many white settlers further north.

McKinnon had left a large trunk with the Hares and said he would return for it the following spring. There was one thing that bothered Bill and Ritia and this was that McKinnon said he had been married, but that he thought his divorce was finalized after he had left Ontario.

Just before the Hares had closed the Immigration Hall, on notice that the government would no longer contribute toward its operation, a letter had arrived for Hugh McKinnon. It bore the return address of a barrister. The Hares had entrusted its delivery to a northbound trapper, but never had learned for certain whether the Crooked Lake trader had ever received it.

During the summer of 1917, Hugh McKinnon disappeared and neither he nor the girl was ever heard from again. The following fall, Bill and Ritia Hare had left the Tony River for good. In addition to selling what personal property they had at the Mile 90 Post, including household goods and so forth, the Hares also gave up their "squatters' rights" to the cabins there. Bill was also instrumental in securing the Fire Ranger job for Ted Walters, who would take over Mile 90.

Bill Hare, himself, hated to leave the Tony River, as he had hoped to build a trading post operation there with a man named Alex Parks. His wife, however, was adamant and threatened to leave him if he remained at Mile 90, so he returned with her to Edson and secured permission from the government to use the old Immigration Hall as a residence.

CHAPTER III

A short time after my meeting with Ted Walters, in the fall of 1917, I decided to move north to join the fur trader at Mile 90, on the Tony River. In September of that year, I had stayed at Greg Rapelje's horse ranch, while he made a trip with team and wagon to haul in supplies from Edson. He was located on some Baptiste River flats about three miles above the Baptiste River Crossing roadhouse, which Knowles and I had abandoned.

In exchange for my services, Rapelje had agreed to haul me and my small outfit north to Mile 90. So, early in October, we left Rapelje's ranch, northbound, fording the Baptiste River a mile or so below his cabin and stable.

A good eight inches of snow had fallen the night before we left, but Rapelje's two horses pulled the light buckboard type rig without difficulty. But when we climbed out of the valley, via the now deserted Edson-Grande Prairie Trail, we reached a higher plateau known as Fraser Mountain. There, the snow was twice as deep as in the valley we had just left.

"Guess I should have hitched Buck and Brownie to a bobsled," Rapelje said. "Think the snow will get any deeper, Ray?"

"I doubt it, but it's a good 15 miles across a high plateau to Mile 70 and the next shelter. One of the stopping-house cabins there is still in fair shape. Maybe we should turn back and wait for the weather to settle," I suggested.

Gregg Rapelje shook his head. He had pioneered in Manitoba but when settlers moved in on homestead claims, he too moved further west, in search of open range lands for his horses. The triangle formed by the Athabasca and Baptiste rivers on two sides and the abandoned wagon road which crossed between the two streams several miles above their junction, as the third side of the triangle, had seemed an ideal location.

"We'll go on — unless it starts snowing," the rancher said.

On the plateau, we crossed over my old traplines. I showed Rapelje where to turn off the trail to a small lake. We stopped there for lunch and a rest for the horses, while they fed on some wild hay and a few handfuls of oats.

We had to break an inch of ice on the pond to get at water for Buck and Brownie and to fill our water pail.

I pointed to a log sloping into the pond, just across from where we were boiling water for tea over a small campfire.

"It was on December 2nd, two years ago, that I caught my first silver fox, in a snow set on top of the ice where the log slopes into the lake," I reminisced. "I was on my way from our cabin at Jackfish Lake, bound for the Baptiste. When I rounded a corner in the trail and saw that black beauty in my trap, I literally fell on the fox — although after I killed it, I felt sad. But my partner and I owed 'Old John' Anderson for grub he had given us on credit!"

Gregg Rapelje was an understanding man and remained silent.

We left shortly and found the snow had settled a little and the horses seemed to have no further difficulty.

At Mile 70, where the abandoned trail crossed Marshead Creek, we examined the one remaining log house, but it didn't look very inviting.

"How far to your cabin at Jackfish Lake?" Rapelje asked.

"Two miles and I've got a fair stove there, a table, benches and a couple bunks."

Mamie Rapelje and Ruby, 1919

"Sounds great! Brownie, Buck, let's move on!"

Back of my trapline cabin was a log shelter closed on three sides. We watered the horses at nearby Jackfish Lake, fed them and Rapelje also strapped some heavy horse blankets on the pair.

We left Jackfish Lake under a pale moon quite early the next morning. Six miles further on the trail, we crossed the Little Smoky River without incident, as the water was low and the ford was no obstacle for Buck and Brownie.

"Only 12 more miles to Tony River, Gregg," I remarked, "with the good start this morning, we ought to make it with an hour of daylight to spare."

My prediction proved correct and when we came out of the timber at the start of a steep grade into the Tony River flats, I could see the old trading post in the distance.

I immediately noticed a big change in the general appearance of Mile 90. The meadow in front of the large log building that Walters had converted into a store or trading post, had been cleared and many of the old corral log fences had been removed.

After leaving the hill overlooking the valley, the trail dipped down onto the meadow and we came to a row of cabins that Walters had renovated and, as I learned later, were to be occupied by several people he would bring in to help operate the Post itself.

Walters was not at home when we arrived and the Post was locked up. We took care of Rapelje's horses and put them in a log stable and then started to look around. In one of the cabins not far from the main building, we found a Cree Indian woman and a boy of about 10 years old, who appeared to be at least three-quarters white. When I asked the woman about Ted Walters, she turned to the boy and he answered, "My grandmother Natoka, does not speak English much." The boy drew himself up proudly and stated, "I speak English, French and Cree; I go to Mission School at Lac Ste. Anne. Walters should be back soon, he went to Buck Lake to see about fish nets."

It was almost dark by then and Rapelje and I were undecided what to do, when we heard a dog bark. Shortly after, Walters appeared, riding a horse on the meadow trail below the trading post. He apologized for not returning sooner, as he had half expected us to arrive that very day.

"Hope you like our setup, Ray," Walters said, as we entered the trading post. Compared to the makeshift cabins I had been living in, during the previous winter, Mile 90 House was a mansion. Entering the log building, one came into a large room about 20 x 30 feet. Along one wall was a row of shelves on which was an impressive amount of supplies that Walters had freighted in during the previous summer. In one corner of the room was a large cook stove, the likes I had never seen, except in logging camps in the west. It had been brought in by an English family who stayed one year at the Tony River, after they built the stopping house there. This stove had a huge oven and a large fire box, which would take wood at least two feet in length. I had learned to bake sourdough bread from Old John Anderson and I am sure that the stove impressed me more than any other single item in the whole room.

The Post itself was actually a number of separate log buildings that had been constructed in sections. Immediately back of the 20 foot by 30 foot main room was another about 20 feet square, which contained several bunkbeds and a large sheet iron heating stove commonly called an "air tight."

Behind this second log building were two additional rooms used for storing supplies that would not freeze and one was also used as a fur cache. The windows in any of these buildings were very small and heavily barred to keep out bears in summer and dogs the year around.

Only small amounts of perishable foods were used in the North country, during the period that I write about, but Walters had brought in a few vegetables, such as potatoes, onions and rutabagas. These were kept in a cellar under the floor of the living quarters. Staple foods, such as tea, coffee, sugar, cornmeal, oatmeal, rice and pot barley, were kept in small packages or tins and stored where the mice could not get to them. Dried fruits including raisins, prunes and apples, were packed in substantial boxes. Flour was in 25, 50 and 100 lb. sacks.

There was no store counter for dealing with customers, but I learned later that when the Indians came to trade, Walters would place their purchases on a big table and then bargain over the price. Some of the Indians were very shrewd in bargaining and others were indifferent and Walters told me that those who questioned his prices were usually familiar with the cost of similar goods or foods at the Sturgeon Lake trading posts, almost 100 miles to the north.

One thing I admired about my partner at the Tony River was that he would not deal in whiskey or alcohol with the Crees. He did keep some for his own use in emergencies, as those items were often stocked by the pioneers for "medicinal" purposes, in moderate quantities.

Walters also stocked quite a bit of dry goods, such as ginghams, flannels and muslin. I was surprised when he showed me several men's suits and I wondered if he would have success in selling them to Indians. I asked him about the price he would have to get for a suit.

"Louie Abraham from Iosegun Lake ordered a blue serge suit last summer and he was sure some others in his band would also be interested. I think I can get $90 in trade for a suit."

I asked Walters what they cost in Edmonton and he said that he had paid $18.00 for each suit and at first, I thought that his price was rather stiff.

"Sounds like a pretty high price, Ray," my partner said, as if reading my mind, "but just consider these few facts. First, the rail freight on our goods from Edmonton to a point 200 miles west was quite high. The nearest I could get to the Athabasca River was about 2 miles, by unloading at the small station called Dalehurst. There, I hired a homesteader to haul my goods and food supplies to the river, and it took two trips as the road down a creek valley was very steep and rough. Also, the homesteader had to haul my lumber for the river scow, which took two additional trips with his wagon and two-horse team. Then, I hired him to help build my scow, which took almost a week and, as you know, the run from that point on the river down through Goose Neck Rapids and northeast to the trail crossing at Mile 53, is a winding 150 miles of river and a real rough experience in itself. I sold the scow to Gregg Rapelje at the Athabasca River crossing, so I didn't lose any money on the cost of the lumber. But, it is nearly 40 miles from there north over the old trail, by wagon, to Mile 90. Now, Ray, do you still think that $90 is too much for a suit of men's clothing?"

But to show what kind of man Walters really was, when I later bought a suit for myself, he was adamant in charging me the Edmonton price, $18.00 for it.

Two years before I joined Walters, when I was running traplines between Jackfish Lake and the Baptiste River Post (Mile 60 or Old John's Stopping Place), I had my first experience in fur trading. Early in November, a white man with three sons by an Indian woman, came upriver and stopped to see what Old John Anderson had in the way of supplies.

Nels Anders, the white trapper, wore a heavy black beard, liberally sprinkled with gray. He was tall, lean and wiry and when he spoke Cree to his sons, his voice was full of respect and he gave no inkling that he thought himself in any way superior to his boys. In fact, although I could not understand when he spoke Cree, Old John told me later that Anders always asked for his boys' opinions on practically every item on which a price was quoted.

"We have enough grub for six weeks and we'll be back before Christmas," Anders said, adding, "My boys are the best lynx snaresmen in the bush." ("Bush" was the general term used to describe the vast stretches of wilderness, such as that drained by the Athabasca and Peace river systems.)

In mid-December of the same year, Old John received a letter by "moccasin telegraph," concerning a matter that required his consulting an attorney in Edmonton. He asked me to stay at the Baptiste River Post for an estimated two weeks while he made the trip "outside." I, of course, agreed as the pioneer trader had been very good to me.

Old John was past 70, but he was as hardy and agile as a man half his age. The fact that he had to snowshoe over 35-Mile Pass on the trail to Edson (the nearest railroad point 60 miles south of the Baptiste River crossing) didn't bother him at all.

"I'll make it to the 35-Mile cabin in one day," the old timer told me in a matter-of-fact tone.

"The next day I should reach Carl Olsen's at 10-Mile where he usually has n extra bunk. The third day will be an easy one into Edson. The trip to Edmonton and return to Edson takes two days over the railroad (the Grand Trunk Pacific) so my total travel time wouldn't be more than 10 days at the most. I'll be back in two weeks for sure. Make yourself at home, 'Boy' (old John generally called me that), and you can run some 'lines' up and down the river from here. I've seen silvers, red and cross fox several times this fall."

After Old John was gone, I did some washing and mending of my pitifully inadequate clothing. The knee-high stubs of poplar left by snowshoe rabbits in the woods along my lynx traplines had torn my corduroy trousers badly. I was pretty handy with a needle, sewing awl and thread. I also made some badly needed repairs on my moccasins, snowshoes, dog harness and toboggan. Anyone who thinks a wilderness trapper is lazy should spend a winter with one!

A few days after Old John left, two Swede trappers came upriver with a lynx and two red fox pelts. They were fully prime and I exchanged flour, tea, sugar, and pipe tobacco for the skins.

Strand and Johannson stayed one night and left with their dogs, toboggan, and purchases on a bitterly cold December morning. I did not know it but they had put out some poison (strychnine) baits alongside their toboggan trail on the way upriver, hoping to pick up a fox or wolf on the return trip. This practice was followed by some trappers, and, in fact, Old John had instructed me in the preparation of the poison baits, which are lard and tallow balls impregnated with strychnine. I didn't approve of the method and it has long since been outlawed in both the United States and Canada.

The two Swede trappers, on their way back to their own trapline, had failed to pick up one of the poison baits and a few days afterward, I missed my best sled dog, a big yellow Husky I called "Babe." Following her tracks downriver, I discovered my sled dog dead in the trail and on my way back to the post, found the slender branch on which the poison bait that killed her, had been impaled.

This was a shaking experience and, had I not been entrusted with conducting trade for Old John and looking after the Baptiste River Post, I probably would have left on the trail south, myself.

I dared not leave the Post for any length of time so confined my trapping to short lines up and down the river. A Norwegian trapper named Ole Aasen was due any day from the south and Old John had rather expected Nels Anders and his sons from Hay River (a tributary of the Baptiste, later renamed Wildhay River when the Baptiste was also renamed the "Berlund River").

Old Aasen showed up with a silver fox, but Old John had strictly warned me against trying to buy, or accept in trade, such a pelt. Canada was already deeply involved in World War One and the market value of "luxury" furs, such as silver or black foxes was most unpredictable. So I told Old Aasen that I couldn't deal and he was quite understanding. He had one marten pelt in his pack and we traded, with the fur being valued at $10.00.

Nels Anders and his boys came in a couple days after Ole Aasen was at the Post. They were down to a few handfuls of flour and a little tea. Their dogs had been fed nothing but snowshoe rabbits and lynx meat for a month. I mixed up a batch of oatmeal and dried fish heads and the Huskies devoured it in a few minutes.

The Hay River trappers had some fine lynx pelts, but Anders thought Old John's prices for fur were too low.

"We'll take a couple cat's worth of grub from you and hope we can do better at a trader's in Whitecourt," Anders decided.

It was about three days' travel down the frozen Baptiste, on past its junction with the Athabasca River on to Whitecourt, so I could see the reasoning back of Anders' decision.

They stayed overnight and the trapper gave me a section of "deer" ribs to roast in Old John's cookstove oven. I learned, afterward, that I had eaten my first wild cat, as Anders told me the ribs were from a fat Canadian lynx.

"We and the dogs did pretty well on rabbits and lynx, with now and then a fool hen (local name for the Spruce Grouse), but a week or so ago the lynx 'run' quit and my boys said they'd had enough," Anders told me, adding, "We're past the fur cycle peak for lynx and rabbits are dying off by the thousands. If you trap next year, you'll get mighty few lynx. Maybe some foxes and, if you can get up west between the Baptiste and Little Smoky, you should find marten in the high country."

My customers headed downriver the next morning and, a couple days later, Old John returned. He thought I had done all right except for one "lynx" that Anders traded in, as it proved to be a small, well-furred brush wolf, minus a tail. It was worth a few dollars less than the other pelt, a genuine Canadian lynx.

I told Old John that I was disappointed in not being able to converse with Anders' Indian sons.

"The Crees are pretty scarce around here. You've seen their tepee poles on the river flats a few miles upstream. Two or three small bands used to hunt moose here in the fall and beaver in the spring, but they've moved north, nearer the Sturgeon Lake Reservation or east to Lac Ste. Anne. Some mighty fine looking young women in their bands." Old John surprised me by saying, "And if I were young again and loved the wilderness life, I'd do what Nels Anders did and marry a Cree."

I was to recall Old John's words many times in later years. The next spring, I made a deal to buy him out, then went "outside," enlisted in a Canadian Overseas Expeditionary force, trained for several months at Sarcee Camp, was released because I was an American citizen under 21 and the Canadian Army could not take me overseas. Returning north with a new partner, Cliff Knowles, I concluded my deal with Old John, and Knowles trapped with me that winter.

The next summer, we operated the Baptiste and Athabasca river ferries (Cliff's father having joined us) and then dissolving our partnership that fall, we parted, I eventually heading north to join Ted Walters at Mile 90 House, as already related.

I might mention before resuming my story with my arrival at Mile 90, that during the summer I was training at Sarcee Camp, near Calgary, Alberta, we were stationed just across the Bow River from the Sarcee Indian Reserve. We were sternly warned by our C.O. that if any soldier made himself obnoxious to the Sarcees he would be in immediate and serious trouble.

In my battalion, there was an Irishman who should never have been allowed in uniform on account of his age. He said he was 42, but I would have added another 20 years for his real age. I don't remember exactly how we got acquainted, but Casey and I became friends. He was real dark in complexion and I was not surprised when one day he told me he was "part Indian," could speak Sarcee and wanted to know if I'd like to "cross the river and pow-wow with the natives."

I hesitated and asked my Lance Corporal what he thought of Casey's invitation. Corporal Batson said it would be okay, as long as I stayed with Casey, as he knew that the Irishman was, in fact, part Indian.

One particular trip to the Indian camp sticks in my memory. In a "long house" or canvas and hide tent, the Sarcees were celebrating a wedding. It was a warm day and the tent wall was rolled up in several places. There was a solid wall of braves around the two entrances and Indian women were just as solidly jammed in the spaces where the canvas was rolled up.

What Casey did, or said to the squaws, I never knew for sure, but he got them to squeeze together tightly enough to let Casey and me, separately, to ease in between them and watch the proceedings. It was most fascinating. Apparently, it was some sort of "wedding shower" where a few braves would dance and cavort, displaying gifts and depositing them in a common pile, accompanied by the beating of drums and the never ceasing chant from a hundred or more lusty voices.

Athabasca crossing

Cabin at Athabasca Crossing

Line cabin – 1919

I remarked to Casey afterward, that if this ceremony was indicative of the seriousness with which Indians regarded matrimony, bigamy, adultery and separation must be minor problems in their culture.

CHAPTER IV

A serious student of the North American Indians and their culture must necessarily resort to histories, such as journals of early explorers, fur trade reports, letters, maps and a miscellany of historical data and material in libraries and museums that house collections of artifacts, such as native hunting and fishing tools, equipment, etc.

At the time of the white man's first contact with the American Indian, very few Europeans attached any importance to the historical impact of their early adventures. With the discovery of fabulous wealth in fur resources, particularly in beaver, the sole purpose of the several organized groups of traders was simply to explore to the limit of their capacities; first, for territorial control and then to harvest the fur resources within that territory.

A third, and most important effect from the white man's conquest of North American wilds, involved people native to the invaded territory, the Indians.

The early fur traders or so-called Canadian "Beaver Men" included: The French, 1604-1760; The Hudson's Bay Company, 1670-1834; Montreal (Quebec) Traders, 1760-1784 and the North West Company, 1784-1821. In the United States, starting in the first colonies, the fur trade era ran from 1668 to 1834; also, in what was then Louisiana and in New Mexico from 1598 to 1834.

For two hundred and fifty years, the fur trade was the principal industry in most of Canada and a large portion of the upper United States. The last 40 years of this period was particularly crucial, as by then, the white traders had armed their Indian hunters and supplied many of them with steel traps.

The beaver was threatened with extinction and stringent laws were eventually passed in the effort to save this valuable fur bearer.

In the early 1900's, beaver hunting as a means of livelihood, was a thing of the past. Only comparatively small colonies of beaver existed in any part of the Athabasca-Peace River watersheds by the time I ventured north.

Trappers had worked the streams and lakes adjacent to Edson Trail, including the Tony River, which crossed the trail at Mile 90, for a few years preceding World War I, but Walters had made an agreement with the native trappers, who still hunted beaver in that area, which guaranteed the Tony River trader certain "territorial" rights.

Walters drew a map and since he expected to have little time for trapping himself, said that I could run "lines" (trapper's term for "traplines") in the areas shown, without interfering with the Indians.

"The beaver are scattered," Walters said, marking locations for me, both on the Little Smoky River and its tributary the Tony, "but you can trap enough for making lynx and fox scent." The fur trader had made reference to the use of beaver castors in making lures for trapping other species of animals, especially lynx.

The areas Walters showed on his sketch were roughly in the shape of a cross. One section extended north to Crooked Lake or Mile 108 on the Edson Trail and south to Mile 70. This elongated stretch of wilderness was 48 miles in length and 10 miles wide in average width.

The other part of the "Cross" was marked by a somewhat narrower strip down the Tony River, east from Mile 90 and across the Little Smoky River to Buck Lake where Walters had a cabin and fish camp.

Westward from Mile 90, or up the Tony River, that area covered a somewhat more limited section of Walters' territory, as small parties of Indians sometimes trapped the headwaters of the Tony River.

"If you get too far west, you might meet up with trouble," Walters cautioned.

But it all sounded fascinating to me. The prospect of learning to know the native trappers and to see how they managed to exist in such a hostile environment had been one of my main reasons for moving to Mile 90.

"I won't trespass on any Indian trapping grounds," I assured Walters.

The first order of business was to build a good supply of wild game and fish and store it in the food cache (a log building near the trading post). This meant that we should concentrate on ducks and geese at Buck Lake, as the time was near for the last fight south of migratory waterfowl.

Walters had two all-purpose horses he called "Preacher" and "Parson." They may have been classed as typical Indian ponies, although they were probably a couple hundred pounds heavier than most. Certainly, they were much stronger than any owned by the Crooked Lake and Iosegun band Crees, perhaps because they were well fed, as Walters had cut several tons of wild hay along the Tony River and, he had also hauled in oats from Sturgeon Lake.

Preacher and Parson were fantastic trail horses, whether used as saddle ponies, or in carrying dead weight packs, or when driven as a span, hitched to a wagon or bob-sled.

On my first trip with my new partner, we rode the horses to Buck Lake, about 10 trail miles east of the trading post, which included the crossing of a series of muskegs.

The early snow had completely disappeared, except for patches lying on the north slope of Tony River valley. We rode down through the meadows on a well-worn trail and Walters dismounted at one point to indicate a big game crossing. There were some moose tracks in the frozen mud, several days old.

"Not many moose in this valley," my companion said. "They were hunted real hard when the Edson Trail traffic was heavy. I heard of one hunter who made a grubstake selling moose where they were killed for 15¢ a pound, or delivered to certain points on the trail for considerably more. But, I guess you've heard of this going on further south."

I nodded. "Yeah! As a matter of fact, a wagon freighter offered my first partner and me 8¢ a pound for all the moose we could deliver to him on the trail. This was in October, 1915 and we were building a cabin some 30 miles north of the freighter's chosen pick-up point. But, this being illegal, we passed it up!"

The game trail Walters had examined for tracks, paralleled the Little Smoky River and followed the west bank of the stream. The pack trail we were on crossed the Little Smoky near where the Tony River emptied into the larger stream.

When we reached the Little Smoky, Walters had some beaver traps on a back channel of the river, so we tied Preacher and Parson to a cottonwood tree and proceeded on foot.

Except for a very rare flooding from heavy fall rains, the flow of rivers in the north country is stable from October, on through the winter months, with a gradual slowing of the stream and a corresponding drop in the water level. Following this pattern, the Little Smoky was now quite shallow at the point where Walters stopped, just below a beaver dam.

Here the river was split by an island, with the larger channel on the east side of the poplar-covered strip of land. The other channel, carrying much less water, had been dammed by a small colony of beaver, after the summer flow had subsided. The dam extended from the west bank of the river to the island. It was only a few feet in height, but sufficient to hold back the river and form a pond, seven or eight feet in depth. There was no mound-shaped house of sticks and mud on the dam, as this particular family of amphibians were called "bank beaver." Their winter home was a den in the river bank itself, with a tunnel entrance several feet below the surface of the water on the pond.

Walters led the way up along the west bank and we soon came to the beaver cache, or the winter food supply. Cottonwood, poplar, willow and birch limbs had been cut on both the main bank of the river and the island and floated to the site selected for the cache. In building the food storage pile, the first sticks are lodged in the mud and held permanently in place (or until they are finally removed for food) by the weight of other limbs placed on top of them.

The beaver selects only choice limbs, as the bark from them is his principal food, during the several months that he is imprisoned by two or more feet of ice on the pond. His den is high and dry above the pond level, as the tunnel, even though having its entrance near the bottom of the pond, slopes upward to the den.

The beaver does not really hibernate, although he sleeps a great deal of the time. But whenever hunger dictates, this amazing fellow leaves his den by way of the tunnel, swims to the food cache, selects his "dinner" and drags it back through the passageway to the den. There, he eats the bark by chiseling it off the limb with his set of sharp (two upper and two lower) incisors. When the limb is completely stripped of the nutritious bark, the beaver takes it back to the pond and discards it. Such is the incredible instinct of the beaver, these same sticks settling to the bottom of the pond, may be used again to reinforce a dam or beaver lodge.

Walters had a beaver caught and drowned in a heavy cord snare, at the food cache. The animal, caught below the surface, had become entangled in his own food cache.

I shall never forget the thrill of my experiences with men like Ted Walters and the resulting contacts with his Indian trappers and fishermen. It was a way of life fast disappearing. I learned some valuable lessons in compassion for both the natives and the many animals and other species of wild life, that were in a constant struggle for survival.

Like the beaver colony, I write about, surely a lesson in persistence. With each summer flood, their dam would be destroyed, but unwilling to move permanently, the beaver would return in September, to rebuild their dam and make another stockpile or cache of green limbs, to supply them with food through the winter months.

INDIAN HUNTER'S PRAYER

Me old trapper from Hay River,
Indian praying to Great Spirit
(White man calls his God — "The Giver")
Both are same or very near it.
When I lay me down to sleeping,
With the night about me creeping,
Then I lay my weary head
On my swamp grass feather bed,
Spruce poles for a sort of springs —
Where in dreams, I spread my wings.

But just before I close my eyes
I pray for days of cloudless skies,
With other days of rain between
To keep Great Spirit's forest Green,
For good hunting, forgiveness too,
For all killing I must do,
To feed and shelter ones I love,
Guard them while I am away
Until I return — please set the day.
Great Spirit judge me from above —
For I am just a lowly man.
I only know this simple plan,
To live and let live when we can!

—Raymond Thompson

CHAPTER V

The days were already getting shorter when I joined Walters at Mile 90 Trading Post. But my partner had everything well in hand, except for seasonal projects, such as setting nets in Buck Lake to harvest enough fish for dog feed. The heavy and more serious netting of whitefish for sale to traders at Sturgeon Lake, would not commence until mid-December.

The wild hay, cut and stacked in the meadows below Mile 90, would be hauled as needed later when the Tony River was frozen, so that Walters could use his hay rack on a bob sled.

Upstream about a quarter of a mile was a stand of fire-killed spruce that provided all the fuel needed for the stoves, including the logging-camp-size cook stove.

"We might drag in some more logs — just in case a heavy snow might foul us up," Walters suggested. So, we spent a day falling the spruce and hauling the logs to the cabins, using Preacher and Parson hitched to a "stone boat." This was a sled with two runners made of logs and planks for the top. In the logging operation two or three spruce trees would be chained at the larger or butt end, to the "stone boat" with the top end of the tree logs trailing behind on the ground. With a little snow on the ground, Walters' two horses could easily drag the logs to the "wood lot" back of the trading post.

Early in October, some of Walters' native customers came to Mile 90, usually two or three at a time. They all wanted credit, but Walters knowing most of the Indians and Metis in that section, was very selective in trusting trappers wanting to purchase grub or trade goods.

"Indians are like whites — some good, some bad," Walters commented one evening as I helped him take a new inventory. "Another thing we have to watch is the fur cycle. A trapper who doesn't have fur to trap, can't pay for a grubstake! Take the Goodswimmer boys, Al and Louie, for example. They asked me today for a two-months grubstake for their marten line west of here. That territory has been over-trapped, the population cycle for marten is at the low stage and I figure that Al and Louie couldn't catch enough fur to pay for supplies they'd need. So, I had to cut them down to a two-weeks supply and advised them to trap beaver around lakes and streams northwest of Crooked Lake."

"What about Isaac Abraham's trappers?" I asked, noting that the trader had extended considerable credit to a few Indians from the Iosegun Lakes region, to the northeast of Mile 90 and north of Buck Lake, which Walters claimed (by agreement with the Crees) as his territory for both fishing and trapping.

"Ike Abraham and his trappers are my best customers. They are in a fine fox trapping section and they'll be bringing in enough red fox, crosses and silvers to settle their account, by the end of November."

Walters knew what he was talking about, as later events proved.

Natoka, the old Indian woman and Petite Napa ("little boy" in a combination of French and Cree), stayed in one of the several log cabins, a hundred yards or so below the main buildings at Mile 90.

Natoka kept our moccasins and snowshoes in repair, but her hands were slowed down with advancing age and Walters did not ask the old "'*Iskwao*" to help us make whitefish nets for later use at Buck Lake.

Raymond, taken by Walters at Mile 90, Dec. 1917

We had finished two nets, 300 feet long and 6 feet in depth, when Walters asked me to stay at the Post, while he drove up toward Sturgeon Lake to meet Dan MacMillar at House River. An Indian had brought a note from "Mac," who had hired a freighter at Sturgeon Lake to haul some supplies that Walters had bought from the Hudson's Bay Company. If Walters would drive his team north, with the bob-sled, he could meet Mac and the freighter and save about $40 on the freight bill.

I was glad to "man the fort" for a couple days, so Walters hitched Preacher and Parson to a sled and left early the next morning.

Old John Anderson, the Baptiste River ferry operator, had taught me how to make sourdough bread, using salt as a starter, but Walters had a good supply of dry yeast cakes, so I baked several loaves, using the yeast to make the dough "rise."

I had taken the loaves from the big logging camp stove oven and placed them on a table when "Petite-Napa," the boy staying with Natoka, came in to visit me.

"*Meywa-ayukonaw*," he said, pointing to the loaves.

Not able to understand, I hesitated in making any remark. The young Metis grinned and added, "Good bread," so I laughed and cut a slice for each of us.

Petite-Napa, Petite Jean, or just "Little John," as I called him, was as "sharp as a tack" and I became real fond of him in the few weeks he was at Mile 90 with his grandmother, Natoka.

During the two days I was alone at the Post, Little John followed me around constantly, always eager to help in any way he could. He was neatly dressed with made-over trousers and a khaki shirt that Natoka had made for him, plus a moose-hide jacket with fringed sleeves and a little bead work on the sleeve cuffs. Natoka had made some toggles out of willow sticks that served as buttons on the jacket.

Also, Little John was clean — a rare condition among most young native boys with whom I had come in contact.

Little John's idol was Ted Walters. "When I am man I become trader, too," he said.

This remark gave me the opening I had been waiting for. "To be a good fur trader you have to know how to spell and write, and add up trade bills, Little John. That means you should be in school!"

"This I know, my father will be here soon to take me back to Lac Ste. Anne. I will go again to Mission School there."

"I am glad, Little John. Now, maybe you can teach me some more Cree words."

The lad and I caught some grayling in the Tony River just behind the trading post. Walters had warned me against leaving the Post for any length of time, so I locked it up, even though we were fishing only a few rods away from the north end of the log building.

The second day of Walters' absence, Little John and I came in from the river to find a Metis (mixed-blood) sitting on a bench in front of the store.

"*Utmus-Kao, Jean*," the newcomer said, looking toward the boy.

"This is Victor LaRocque, from House River, Ray," Little John said, and, speaking to the Metis, I heard my name mentioned, but as the lad spoke in

Left-John Abraham
Right- Vic La Rocque

Cree, I didn't know what other information he had offered the man who was a stranger to me.

"Jean says Walters will be back tomorrow. Natoka will let me stay in her cabin tonight," LaRocque said, aware of my inability to understand their conversation.

Little John then left with the Metis. LaRocque was an average-sized, swarthy-complexioned man with several scars on his cheeks that, I later learned from Walters, had resulted from smallpox.

About an hour later, Little John returned from Natoka's cabin. He was quiet and seemed disturbed.

"Something wrong, Little John?"

"I do not like Vic; he is what we call '*muchatisew*' — bad medicine. Some say he knows what happened to Crooked Lake trader, McKinnon. He has traps with white man's mark on them. Walters will want to know about this."

The Metis that Little John didn't like did have a bad reputation and I remembered that both Walters and Bill Hare were suspicious of the man who went by two different names, "LaRocque" and "Plante".

I asked Little John about "Vic" and his using two names.

"His woman, Marie, goes by name of Plante. So does Vic, around Iosegun Lakes. Maybe the Mounties are watching him, so he uses these names in different places."

Then Petite Jean surprised me with, "Walters says you have no woman, Ray. He hopes you find good '*Iskwao*' and stay at Mile 90. Vic has real fine sister — not like Vic at all. They have same mother, part Cree and Iroquois, from Lac Ste. Anne, but different white man for father. Vic's wife — named Marie, also his sister — same name. Natoka says they both be here soon and will take cabin next to ours. Maybe you like Vic's sister — she good girl — no man yet!"

I smiled. "You're good friend, Little John. I left a '*netomis*' (sweetheart) back in the States. My country is at war, too, now. I will leave Mile 90 before spring. So, for now, I just need woman for mending moccasins and your grandma, Natoka, takes care of that."

Later, I was to recall that conversation with Little John. With the direct and unclouded view of the situation as he saw it, I, a single man, would probably be looking for an "*Iskwao*" and, since there was no white woman around, Little John had thought I would be interested in Marie LaRocque, a girl whose mother was a Metis (of mixed white and native blood, with a French father). I was a bit curious over the fact that Walters had told Natoka and Little John that he hoped I might "settle down" and possibly marry a certain Metis woman.

Walters and Dan MacMillar drove in late the next night and we had to unload the provisions and trade goods by lantern light.

MacMillar or plain "Mac," as Walters introduced him, was a wiry Scotsman, about 60 years of age. He, like Walters, had lived in the Peace River country most of his life and was an experienced fur trader. He proved a valuable addition to our trading post staff at Mile 90. Mac knew most of the village chiefs of the Indian bands in Walters' trading territory and the owner of Mile 90 trusted him implicitly.

Among the items Walters had ordered through an "Independent" trading

Vic's wife, Marie, their children and "Preacher"

post at Sturgeon Lake, was enough twine, backing cord, floats and lead weights to make several more whitefish nets.

"Vic's woman, Marie, will be along next week to help make our nets," Walters told me.

This gave me an opportunity to question the trader about Vic LaRocque and his presence at Mile 90.

"LaRocque is one of the very best fishermen in the whole area between here and Slave Lake. The whitefish run doesn't start until mid-December and peaks in January. Sturgeon Lake is almost fished out and the traders there and at Slave Lake will take all the whitefish we can deliver," Walters said.

"Little John tells me that Vic LaRocque is 'bad medicine'," I countered. "Isn't it risky to have him around?"

"In a way, yes. But, if we keep him busy with the nets at Buck Lake and loan him a few traps and cord for lynx snares, we can keep track of the rascal. I talked with the Mounties at Grande Prairie in August. They are very suspicious about LaRocque or "Plante" as he sometimes calls himself, but they do not have enough on Vic to charge him with any crime! The Mounties did welcome my idea of giving the Metis some work."

Walters and I had already set two nets at Buck Lake, which had "netted" us a good supply of whitefish and jackfish (Northern Pike) for two distinct needs. The whitefish was filleted and smoked for our own use, while the jackfish was smoked for dog feed.

"I'll get LaRocque fixed up with grub and an outfit at our Buck Lake cabin, Ray. This will take a few days, as I want to check up on the layout at Ike Abraham's camp at Iosegun Lakes, before I return. Mac will stay here and I thought it would be a good time for you to head up the Tony toward the Simonette. If there are marten in that section, it might pay you to spend a day fixing up a dugout cabin about 15 miles from here, on the Tony. The camp stove in it should be okay and I left some small kettles and a fry pan hanging out of any pack rat's reach."

I welcomed the trader's words and made my plans accordingly. Then, in the midst of my preparation for the fur prospecting trip, Little John showed up.

"Ray, can I go along? I can help in camp and snare rabbits. I can read fur sign, too! I —"

"Wait a minute, Little John, what about Lac Ste. Anne?"

The lad showed me a piece of paper. "Read — it is from my father."

"Petite Jean," the note (in English) stated, "I have been delayed but will be at the Tony two weeks from today. Your father, Jean Fortier."

I made a quick calculation, based on the date of Fortier's note and concluded that Little John wouldn't be leaving Mile 90, for at least a week. But, I hesitated taking the responsibility for such a young lad.

Hurriedly, I consulted Walters. "The boy would be good company, Ray, and he sure won't slow you up. I've been on the trail with that 12-year-old kid."

So, I told Little John I would be glad to have him as a "partner" and the lad's dark eyes really sparkled when I so informed him. I was pleased, too, when I learned that he was two years older than I had thought.

The early snow had melted down to a few inches in depth around Mile 90, but knowing that we would be in a snow belt in the foothills of the Canadian Rockies as we hiked westward, we added snowshoes to our camp gear. I carried a medium size Cree-made pair and Little John had his own, made by his grandmother Natoka, during the previous summer.

Two pack dogs carried our blankets, a "tarp" or canvas sheet and some of our food supplies. If we had been on a longer trip, I would not have let the dogs carry such vital necessities as flour, sugar, lard, tea, etc. On two occasions, a year earlier, my dogs had lost their packs while chasing a bear; one losing several beaver pelts and the other a blanket and canvas tarp, plus of course, their pack sacks.

CHAPTER VI

Fur prospecting is a science and its pursuit is particularly important in wilderness trapping. Generally, a successful survey depends on (A) the trapper's ability to scout unknown or strange territory, (B) his knowledge of furbearers and their habits and, (C) weather conditions while making the survey.

I was fairly well qualified in the categories (A) and (B) and, fortunately, the weather was ideal for our trip up the Tony River valley. Little John's enthusiasm was enough in itself to make our expedition exciting.

Ted Walters was my third full-time partner in the Canadian wilds. But, having Little John as a trail companion, took me back down memory lane to my very early experience as a young hunter and trapper. I remembered, when I was about 10, being with two older boys, on a jackrabbit hunt and they allowed me to carry a .22 caliber rifle for a short distance. Only a born "Nimrod" can appreciate the thrill of such an experience.

NIMROD

by Raymond Thompson

When I was just a barefoot lad,
My mountains only haystack high,
A wooden gun was all I had,
To aim at wild geese passing by.

And when I'd grown to man's estate,
And trophies decked my floor and wall,
How oft' I'd sit and contemplate,
On memories cherished most of all.

But this I know — throughout the span,
That changed a boy into a man,
No mountains ever grew as tall,
As haystacks loomed when I was small,
Nor ever have I had such fun,
As with my homemade, wooden gun!

Then there was Bill Perkins, a rancher's son, also several years older than I, who taught me how to locate and mark muskrat runways on the shores of a lake on the Perkins' ranch, for trapping later.

A light snowfall two days before Little John and I left the Tony River Post, made for ideal tracking conditions. Also, the ice on the slow-running stretches of the river, made it possible to cross the stream without having to ford it.

Little John could read "fur sign," as well as many much older trappers I had known.

"Not many beaver here," he said, pointing to a small cache of poplar limbs on a beaver dam we reached about noon.

"Right, Little John. Walters trapped one beaver here and asked me to pass this dam up for this winter. I figure that he hopes a pair is left on the dam and that, come spring, they'll have some kits."

The beaver cache, to which my companion had pointed, was the work apparently, of a small family of the amphibians, judging by its size. The food supply would not have lasted even four or five beavers through the long winter, with their movements restricted to the ice-bound pond.

One lynx had crossed the frozen beaver pond and seeing the tracks, Little John said, "Lynx bad for beaver kits — this cat will be around for sure next spring."

"You're right, partner. I'll come back up here and set a No. 3 trap and a few snares, maybe next week. Right now, let's track this cat. If I remember right, Walters said there were a couple of lynx snare cubby sets near this dam."

We followed the lynx tracks from where the cat had left the snow-covered ice, on into the woods and, sure enough, there were two weathered cage sets, minus the cord snares, located under spruce trees bordering a jackpine thicket.

It took us perhaps 10 minutes to place new cord snares in the "door" of the narrow cages, Little John making one set and I, the other.

A bait or lure stick, smeared with a foul-smelling concoction of beaver castor, rotted rabbit liver and fish oil, was thrust on a bait stick into the ground at the back of the cage. The objective of the lure was to induce the lynx to poke his head through the 7-inch diameter snare noose, while attempting to reach the lure. In such an attempt, the lynx would tighten the snare as he moved into the cage and would find a real "hangman's noose" around his neck as he backed out.

The snare noose, fastened to a toggle pole propped against the "doorway" of the cage, would be dragged free and the snared cat, heading for the bush, or even trying to escape by instinctively climbing a tree, would soon choke himself to death.

"Cats plenty dumb. Fox or wolf have to starve before they mess with lure in cage," Little John remarked, standing back and looking over his work with the critical eye of an expert.

I nodded in agreement and told my companion that, when I first heard of snaring lynx with a hard, twisted cord of less than a quarter-inch in diameter, I was very skeptical. I also admitted that I had later been converted to the idea that snares were very efficient, when properly used.

Looking back, I can credit my experience with Walters that winter, for encouraging me to continue experiments that later resulted in my invention and manufacture, of the self-locking steel snare.

"Hungry?" I asked, noting that it was past noon, when we made the snare sets.

"Maybe — a little," my buddy replied. "I make fire for tea." Little John obviously was ready for the lunch of left-over hotcakes, jam and peanut butter I had prepared that morning, before we left Mile 90. My companion produced, from his own pack sack, some smoked fish his grandmother had given him.

While Little John was making a small fire, I had gone to the beaver pond to cut a hole in the ice, so I could fill a small pail with water for our tea. Just as I broke the ice, a muskrat swam out from its bank den, under a small section of transparent ice, in a runway that had been kept open a night or so after the last snowfall.

I told Little John about the 'rat. "Sure, Ray," he said, "muskrats and beaver get along together very good. Mink and otter bad for 'rats—specially kits."

While we were eating our lunch, a pair of "Whisky Jacks," Canadian Jays, visited us. Little John threw a bit of food on the ground and the birds made a dive for it. Also called "Moose Bird," this hardy winged denizen of the Canadian North seems to appear out of nowhere, whenever a trapper or hunter stops for lunch on the trail. The Whisky Jack also "winters" around any trapper's cabin. This persistent visitor is also a skilled "bait robber," often ending tragically for the bird itself, when attempting to steal the trapper's bait left in sets for squirrel, weasel (ermine), and marten.

"Whisky Jack very tough," Little John observed. "Other birds leave and fly south in winter. Some eagles, hawks and owls with big ears, stay here, too."

"You're a good woods watcher, partner. Maybe you should learn in Lac Ste. Anne Mission School how to write about wild animals and birds."

"Indians and good white trappers already know," Little John countered. "I read some in newspapers — not much about all this," he said, making a sweeping gesture with his arm, as if to encompass the whole vast wilderness around us.

"Many books in Edmonton libraries," I remarked, "about Indians, Hudson's Bay Company and Northwest Company fur traders and trappers. Maybe the Mission people could get some for you to read."

Little John and I went on up the valley, which, just above the beaver dam, suddenly narrowed, making travel much more difficult and the Indian trail became much harder to follow.

CHAPTER VII

Little John and I were now in what Walters had described as "marten country." Jackpine thickets had become scarce, with spruce-clad slopes taking over. Poplar (or cottonwood), willow and birch lined the banks of the Tony River, but the stream itself was much smaller than at Mile 90.

We checked Walters' map again. He had marked an area to the southwest of the beaver dam, where Little John and I had stopped for lunch. "A creek heads out of a marsh, on a plateau about a couple miles from the river (Tony) valley," Walters had pointed out, when drawing the map for me, adding, "On the north side of the marsh, is a caribou and moose trail you can't miss. I made some blazes on a cottonwood, marking the start of a trail through five or six miles of spruce, that will take you back to the Tony and the line cabin I told you about."

I repeated Walters' instructions to Little John, while we studied our map. "Which side of creek we take to reach marsh?" he asked.

"Your guess is as good as mine, Partner. You take this side of creek and I'll scout the other. First one to find trail sign, holler," I suggested.

A sandstone cliff, maybe 50 feet in height, formed the east bank of the small stream just above its confluence with the Tony. The water in the creek was low enough to expose a narrow strip of sand and gravel, making an easy "trail" for Little John.

I had to cross the frozen stream to look for sign of a trail leading up and out of the canyon. I had barely entered a wooded slope when Little John yelled, "Ray, come quick! Big bear tracks, real fresh!"

Sure enough, a grizzly had gone up the creek canyon and his tracks along the snow-covered gravel bar had indeed been made within the past few hours.

"I bet grizzly travel same way we must go to reach marsh and trail Walters showed us," Little John said, his dark eyes fairly dancing. "You should have brought .280, Ray!"

"H-m-m, maybe so. But I doubt if a grizzly would be very scrappy this time of year. This fellow is probably headed for higher ground and his winter den. Most likely, he's been scrounging for the odd Bull Trout (Dolly Varden) that might get trapped in shallow water along these high country streams."

Incidentally, the lad, when referring to my ".280," was talking about my Ross, big game rifle, of that caliber. I had left this rifle at Mile 90, on purpose, as we were not on a big game hunt. The only firearm I carried on our fur prospecting trip was a .22 caliber rifle, for shooting rabbits and grouse, to supplement the grubstake we, including the dogs, were packing.

"Well, I'm not afraid of grizzly if you're not!" Little John commented. "I think we follow bear tracks and find game trail leading out of canyon."

"Okay, Trapper, lead on," I agreed. So we went on up the creek canyon, taking the same general route the grizzly had selected.

Within a mile or so, we came to a break in the canyon wall. Following what appeared to be mostly a big game trail, with here and there an axe blaze on a tree to indicate a trapper had also used that route, we reached the marsh shown on Walters' map.

Enroute, we crossed the grizzly's tracks twice and, at a beaver pond created by a dam the wilderness engineers had thrown across the small stream emerging from the marsh, we saw the last bear sign.

The grizzly had crossed the ice, from the shore of the pond to a large beaver house and after inspecting the frozen mud-and-limb impregnable mound, had returned to the nearby shore and disappeared in the woods.

"Big family here," Little John remarked, noting a sizable amount of poplar limbs protruding through the ice, in the winter cache near the beaver house.

The young trapper was right again and I was about to warn him not to go near the cache, when he said, "Grizzly too smart to look at cache. Ice plenty tricky there!"

In later years, reading notes I had made during that winter at Mile 90, I kept thinking of the change in Indian life-styles, and attitudes, that had taken place in the last 70 years.

Today, in all the Indians and Metis that I have learned to know, there is a sad lack of interest in traditional skills, such as my companion, Petite Jean Fortier, possessed — those 60 long years ago.

In most Indian villages, during the past 15 years or so, I have noted an indifference on the part of teen-age boys, in learning any of the traditional native skills, that is sad to behold. Of course, this indifference applies to white boys, too. But, being by nature, a sort of "Indian" myself, I deplore the dependency of both Indian and Eskimo youth, especially, on modern equipment, such as outboard motors; snowmobiles; harpoon guns; aluminum canoes, etc., etc. Not for a moment would I suggest that Indians throw away their guns, traps and other modern equipment, but I do regret that, as an example, very few young Indians bother to learn how to make primitive "survival" tools, such as bone fish-hooks, deadfalls, and snares.

I wonder, too, how many Indian boys that spend most of their "idle" hours at any convenient tavern, would know, as Little John knew, the danger of breaking through the ice, near a beaver cache, in early winter.

To resume our journey — my companion spotted a sizable blaze on a tree, on the north side of the marsh. This, according to our map, indicated the start of a trail Walters had blazed between the marsh and a cabin on the Tony River.

We followed the trail without too much difficulty, losing it once where it crossed a dry marsh, where Walters had not bothered to plant a blazed pole in the long marsh grass, now flattened by early frosts.

The trouble was that, instead of crossing the marsh, Walters apparently had made a detour (probably horseback in summer), and then continued his trail marking at the extreme western end of the wildhay marsh.

We found the blazes, but, losing the time involved in the search, resulted in our reaching the river and locating Walters' cabin, just before nightfall.

The cabin was already "occupied" — by a family of pack rats! I shot one particularly bold critter, while Little John held a couple of lighted candles. We located a fry pan, small kettle, a granite plate, cup, saucer, knives and forks, in a four sack suspended by wire from a log roof beam.

A sheet-iron camp stove and several lengths of stovepipe, seemed in good condition and by candlelight, we had the cabin habitable — at least, from a wilderness trapper's viewpoint.

The dogs were chained outside — at opposite corners of the combination log-and-dugout line cabin.

CHAPTER VIII

Thoroughly exhausted from the travel through unfamiliar stretches of spruce, windfall (downed timber), muskeg, and frozen marsh grass, Little John and I ate a cold lunch of dried moose meat and bannock, along with several cups of tea and hit the bunk.

But, even in the poor light from two candles, I saw that the dugout cabin had recently been occupied. There was fresh-cut, dry marsh grass on the lower of the two bunk beds. Marsh grass was often used for a "mattress" in trap-line cabins in that part of the north country.

Some recently split birch wood, in lengths suited to the fire box in the camp stove and some strips of birch bark for tinder in starting a fire, was further proof that some trapper, or possibly an Indian caribou hunter, had used Walters' cabin not long before our arrival.

Little John and I used the lower bunk together, as we didn't have enough blankets for two separate beds. I can remember my companion saying, "May be Al or Louie Goodswimmer were here. They had a trapline between the Tony and Simonette."

"Uh-huh, Walters told me about them. He turned them down for a grubstake on credit — said they'd never take enough marten to settle their bill." Then, I went to sleep.

That young Metis lad was surely a real woodsman, and more than willing to do his share. It seemed like I had barely closed my eyes, when the sound of a clattering fry pan woke me. Little John had made a fire in the stove and was already stirring up the bannock or hotcake mix. We had slept with our trousers on, so it didn't take long for me to join him.

"Look what I found," Little John said, pointing to something behind him. What proved to be a single-shot .22 caliber Stevens rifle was leaning against a bench.

The rifle was empty and in good condition. Who had left it in that out-of-the-way place? Thinking back and recalling Walters' remarks, concerning the Goodswimmer boys and in particular, their wanting to buy ammunition from the Tony River trader, I doubted that the .22 caliber rifle was left by them. They had asked specifically for .30-30 caliber shells only.

"Big puzzle, Ray," my partner said, after we had discussed the mystery of the rifle he had discovered.

"You're right, and no trapper leaves his rifle in a spot like this, unless —"

"Unless what, Ray?"

"Maybe the owner was traveling light, ran out of .22 shells and didn't want to pack a useless gun!"

The mystery deepened when Little John, on examining the contents, or lack of contents, of some cans on a split-log shelf, came across the upper portion of a Royal North West Mounted Police letterhead. The body of an apparent communication was missing, but on a separate piece of brown wrapping paper was a map. The map was a crude sketch of a route or trail apparently crossing about three hundred miles of wilderness.

Several lines, presumably indicating river courses, with broken lines (perhaps trails) between the streams, had possibly been made by someone who had either traveled these routes, or was intending to, when he stopped at the dugout cabin on the upper stretches of the Tony River.

Only one identifiable clue was shown on the map and that was a good portion of the mighty Peace River. At the fartherest extent of the line showing that watercourse, was the one word "FORT."

"Walters might figure out more of the details," I said, pointing to our approximate location on the map. "Anyway, we'll take the rifle along, too."

And so, that curious incident was temporarily forgotten, while Little John and I prepared for a trip into more marten country, southwest of the dugout cabin.

Walters, as a fire ranger during the summer months, was supposed to "cover" several hundred square miles of wilderness, a large portion of which was the territory between the Simonette and Little Smoky Rivers.

The fire ranger's job was not to fight fires, unless he happened across a small one just started by lightning, but rather to assess the damage already done by fire, along with the location of heavy concentrations of downed timber or windfall. Walters was a very conscientious ranger and a most excellent woodsman. With his pack and saddle ponies, Parson and Preacher, he explored areas between rivers that I am certain had never been traveled by a white man before.

The Indian blood in Walters caused him to leave very little sign and consequently one could depend on only a few trail markers, such as blazes on trees.

So it was that the "marten country" map Walters had sketched for me, was very skimpy in detail.

Little John and I had reached the dugout cabin by following directions on one of Walters' maps, so we knew, in a general way, how and where to look for trail signs.

"You go south and west for a couple miles or so, up a creek that empties into the Tony about a quarter mile above the cabin," Walters had explained. "This is a new trail I marked a couple years ago. You'll find some deadfalls for marten, minus the triggers, on this trail. You should take a few triggers along, bait and set the deadfalls and if there are any marten on that spruce slope, you might take a few."

We had left our pack dogs chained to trees near the cabin, carrying only some tea, a small pail to brew it in, plus some leftover hotcakes and several pieces of stewed rabbit. I had my own .22 rifle and Little John carried the one left by some unknown party at the cabin. The two rifles were chambered for .22 L.R. (Long Range) cartridges. We also included several deadfall triggers.

Both snowshoe rabbits (Varying Hare) and grouse were at a low population cycle, but we were lucky enough to shoot three spruce (Franklin) grouse, and two rabbits.

We used the "innards", head and feathers to bait four deadfalls that we found on Walters' trail, using the triggers we had brought along.

One surprising development, during our entire trip, was the lack of snow encountered. On this last day, at the highest elevation, there was barely six inches of snow out in the open and, of course, much less under the largest trees.

About a month earlier, in late October, there would have been at least two feet of snow where Little John and I explored Walters' "marten country."

Shortly after noon, we came to a brush shelter near a small spring. Walters hadn't mentioned this campsite.

"I think we'll eat our lunch and call it quits, Pal — not much use going further."

"Guess so," Little John replied. "Bad winter for marten. They catch pine squirrels easy and we saw only two bushy tails all day."

I thought my companion looked as tired as I felt, so after a lunch and a good rest, we started back down the trail.

Nearing the next to the last marten deadfall set we had made on the way up the slope, Little John, ahead of me, hollered, "Ray, a marten!"

Sure enough, there was a big, rather light-brown, male marten, killed in our primitive trap during the hour or so since we had made the set.

There was no other marten sign in the vicinity of our deadfall, so we reset the trap and hurried on down the creek valley to our cozy dugout cabin.

CHAPTER IX

The capture of a big marten, within a short time after setting our deadfall, was not in itself an unusual experience. This tree-climbing furbearer belongs to the weasel family and has no equal, when it comes to killing pine squirrels, flying squirrels and any species of grouse that inhabits its hunting territory.

The marten often hunts during the day and can actually outrun a pine squirrel trying to escape by seeking refuge in trees.

"This is good *wapistan*," Little John said, when, after feeding the dogs and ourselves, we turned to the skinning and stretching of our catch.

The lad wanted to do this task and while he removed the pelt from the "*wapistan*" (Cree for marten) I looked for fur stretcher material.

"Walters should have some stretchers around," I said.

"Look in that top bunk," Little John suggested. I looked and, sure enough, I discovered three wooden frames, two of the size used for drying marten pelts, and one larger, that I assumed was made for the fisher, a fairly rare "cousin" of the marten.

"You little rascal," I said, "Is there anyuthing else in this cabin I don't know about?"

Little John answered with a wide grin and I was sure he knew how his keen observations and sharp eyes really pleased me. Nor was I surprised when, without a single word, he lifted the wild hay lying on the poles that made the bed slats for the top bunk and handed me a small miner's pick.

"Maybe someone look for gold on these creeks, Ray!"

I nodded. "Walters may have done a little prospecting." Then, I told Little John about my attempt to separate fine "flour gold" from the black sands near the Baptiste River crossing.

"Indians not care about gold before white man show up," my partner said, in his matter-of-fact way. "My father told me about the Yukon gold sickness."

I couldn't argue with the boy over his use of the word "sickness" instead of "fever." I did tell Little John that an uncle had disappeared in the Klondike shortly after the gold rush reached its peak, only 20 years or so before.

While caring for the marten pelt, which although not really dark, had a fine, bushy tail and a beautiful silky coat, we discussed our plans.

"Could be a few more marten where we were today," Little John observed.

"Could be, but I'm wondering if we might delay your father. He might reach the Tony before you expect him."

"Father would wait," my little friend replied firmly. "Grandmother Natoka would see to that."

I mulled over the situation, undecided, until, on stepping outside, I saw that it was snowing.

"If it doesn't snow more than a few inches over night, we could make a quick trip back up the slope and see if any animals have moved across our trail."

"Good!" agreed Little John. "I'll make bannock before we turn in, that way we get early start."

Luckily, less than two inches of snow fell at the cabin, during the night, so much to Little John's delight, we started over our deadfall trapline just at daybreak.

Our trail, made the previous day, was easy to follow, as the light snowfall had not obliterated our moccasin tracks. It was lucky for us that we didn't have to wear snowshoes.

We reached the first deadfall set, which had not been disturbed, without seeing much game or fur sign. A lynx had followed our tracks for a short distance. The tracks were as big as those made by a timber wolf, but easily identified by their rounder shape.

"Big cats scarce," Little John remarked, and I nodded. Rabbits were very scarce, too, and we saw but a few signs of this denizen of the wilderness, which in the peak years of its cycle, is preyed upon by a host of carnivores, ranging in size from weasel to wolverine, as well as being the principal food in the diet of great horned owls, eagles, and hawks.

"Guess that marten we got yesterday was truly a loner," I said, as we approached the last deadfall set. Moments later, Little John let out a whoop!

There was a small, but very dark marten, in our wooden trap.

"Maybe my ancestor was a marten medicine-man," the lad exulted.

I was about to question Little John, concerning his obvious reference to Indian legendary hunters' medicine powers, when the snapping of underbrush caused us to look toward a small, frozen marsh a hundred yards or so behind us, on the trail we had just covered.

"Caribou!" Little John whispered.

He was right. A small band of this scarce member of the deer family, crossed the marsh and disappeared in less than a minute, leaving us standing there, finding it hard to believe that we had actually seen the stately, antlered creatures.

"Too bad you didn't have your rifle, Ray," my companion said.

"It would be a long trip with the pack horses," I answered. "Woodland caribou like those, average three to four hundred pounds."

A short distance beyond the last deadfall set, we came to the brush shelter where we had lunched the day before. Although it was early, we decided to make a fire for boiling tea water, and to eat the bannock and dried fish sandwiches Little John had prepared.

"What about this marten medicine-man stuff, Partner?"

"Indian legend, boy hunter sleeps under a tree and dreams of girl from his tribe. Girl turns into a marten. The marten leaps from another tree and soars through the air, toward hunter, like a big flying squirrel. Hunter wakes up, tries to grab marten. All at once, marten turns back into girl and boy hunter is happy. He calls marten his very good medicine and never sets deadfall for marten ever after. This is story Grandmother Natoka told me. Maybe she tell stories for you, Ray."

"This, I would like very much, Little John. But, if your ancestor got good medicine from marten and never killed marten again — how would this help you now?"

The lad answered promptly, "That bothers me. Old native customs have changed with white man's coming. But, I guess we still have to kill to eat."

Not sure of my ground when it came to discussing the truth, or fantasy, in native "legends," I didn't question Little John further, and we started back to the cabin.

We reached the frozen marsh and stopped to examine the caribou tracks and, to our surprise, saw wolf tracks, made by predators on the trail of the caribou. I guessed that not more than a half hour had passed since we had seen the small band crossing the marsh.

"I wish, too, that I had brought my rifle," I half whispered to my companion.

We figured that at least three wolves were after the caribou, but it would have been very foolish for us, in turn, to try and track down the killers.

So, we continued on past the marsh and on to higher ground.

Our trail skirted a "hog back," or small section of elevated forest land and here, Little John said, "I'll climb a tree — maybe wolves still in sight."

That lad was a real climber. He chose a tall, rather sparsely limbed pine and, before I could caution him to be careful, he was a good 20 feet above the ground.

"Ray," he shouted, "I see one caribou and four wolves, on bare hill. Caribou backed into windfall. Big bull — big antlers. Now bull make run for better cover — out of sight now. Poor caribou — no escape from wolves — that for sure!"

"It seems wolves have to eat, too," I said rather lamely.

A few minutes later, Little John left his perch and we continued on down the slope, reaching our cabin just before dark.

CHAPTER X

About an inch of new snow had fallen, during our last night spent in the dugout cabin on the headwaters of Tony River.

Our pack dogs howled once, just before daylight and Little John thought he also had heard a wolf.

We left as soon as there was light enough to travel and we made much better time returning to Mile 90. In several places on the way up the valley, Little John had broken off willow and cottonwood branches, once remarking, "Good hunter always leaves sign for back trail."

It had turned cold and this accounted for the light snowfall and, because of the sudden change, we saw very little sign of wildlife all day. At one beaver dam, a persistent amphibian had broken the ice, gone ashore, cut a small poplar and dragged it back down through the hole in the ice.

With an hour or so of daylight to spare, we reached Mile 90. The plank door, and main entrance to the trading post, was locked or barred on the inside.

Someone was sawing wood on the east side of the long building and I assumed it was Dan MacMillar.

"You go on to your grandmother's cabin," I told Little John. "I'll unpack the dogs and get into the store through another door. See you later — maybe Natoka has word from your father."

My recent "partner" grinned and ran toward the small cabin Walters had allowed the old native woman to occupy, in exchange for her services in keeping our moccasins and snowshoes in repair. I would have liked to hear Little John bragging about his woodcraft skills to his beloved Natoka.

The trading post was a combination of log buildings, evidently added in sections, one behind the other. The main store, kitchen and two rooms used as sleeping quarters, was the nucleus for the additions and immediately back of this, was a sort of utility room and fur shed. Here, we stretched and dried pelts, made small sections of gill nets and did our "laundry."

Bill and Ritia Hare, when turning over Mile 90 to Walters, had left most of their household furnishings with the new owner. Among these was a large galvanized wash tub, the nearest thing to a bath tub one could find in that part of the North. There was a large "air-tight" sheet iron stove in the utility room and I had already washed my clothes there on several occasions. Along with the tub Ritia Hare had left a wash-board and I knew, from personal experience, as a farm boy, the value of this household tool.

There were two doors for entry into the fur shed — one opening from the store and the other from the west side of the building. Since the main entrance to the trading post was barred, I had to either go around the east side where I heard Mac making firewood, or choose the nearer entrance on the west side of the building.

I was about to ask Mac for his key, when a dog I did not recognize, appeared out of nowhere.

It was a big Husky and seemed ready to tackle my own dogs, so I quickly snapped chains, already secured to the west wall, onto the collars of my Huskies and grabbed a beaver stretching frame leaning against the wall.

The dog backed off, snarling. I unpacked my Huskies and quieted them down for a moment. But, the instant I turned, to unlock the door to the fur shed, the three renewed their growling. I decided on putting my own pack and those carried by my dogs, inside the fur shed and then see who owned the belligerent one that was looking for a fight.

I unlocked and opened the door and, seconds later, stared in astonishment, at a sight I was never to forget.

Standing in Ritia Hare's big wash tub was a young woman, entirely naked, except for a towel over one shoulder.

The girl, no doubt just as surprised as I, screamed, and as I later concluded, cursed me in both French and Indian terms and ordered me out of the place. I said, "I'm sorry," and backed away, closing the door behind me.

That was my first encounter, one could hardly call it an introduction, with Marie LaRocque-LaPlante, half sister of "Vic" the Metis, Walters had hired to help in our whitefish netting operation.

I was young and animalistic enough to appreciate the beauty of any young woman, clothed or unclothed, and this particular Metis female would certainly have qualified, as a model, for any artist.

Marie was tall and rather slender, compared to the native "*Iskwaos*" I had seen in the North. She, apparently, had been washing her long black tresses, when I so rudely, though accidentally, invaded her privacy. Her skin was actually only a shade darker than my own. Old John Anderson had told me there were attractive native women in that area and Marie LaRocque was certainly a living example of what he was talking about.

Outside, I chased the strange dog with a well-aimed throw of the beaver fur stretcher and went on around the front of the trading post, to where Dan MacMillar was sawing firewood.

Mac grinned when I told him what had happened, but when he saw that I was really disturbed, said, "Don't worry, Ray, Vic's sister is a fine, sensible girl. She and Vic's wife are in the cabin next to Natoka's. That was her pack dog — he's scrappy and over-protective of Marie. You'll have to win Mookun over before you can get anywhere with her. Anyway, I'll be down to their cabin with some wood shortly and set things right for you."

Then, Mac pointed behind me. The girl I had just seen without a bit of clothing, was now wearing a moose hide jacket, a skirt of blue cloth, reaching just below her knees, canvas leggings and stout leather boots. She was already half way between the store and Natoka's cabin. Her hair was still flowing over her shoulders and she carried a fur cap in one hand.

The dog my Huskies and I had encountered on the west side of the Post, followed her, looking back once as if he were still looking for a fight.

Marie LaRocque had barred the store door on the inside. Mac had told her to do this, as he was expecting some of the Abraham boys to come in from Iosegun Lakes.

When Mac and I entered the store, I went on into the utility room and out to my chained dogs.

"I'll take some wood down to the cabins, Ray, but I'd better borrow one of your dogs — some bare spots make for poor sledding," Mac said. So, I got a dog harness from the fur shed, hitched my Husky, Kiskio, to a sort of stone boat, and helped Mac load the firewood.

A good fire was in the big cookstove and I made some tea and ate a quick lunch.

Mac returned in a half hour or so. "Marie is still mad. She says Little John would have recognized her dog and should have told you that she must be in the store. Little John is quite unhappy. Not only over the way Marie is acting, but because Vic's wife brought no word from Jean Fortier, Little John's father."

"I'm sorry, too, especially for the boy. I'll miss him, but he's too bright to be out of school. As far as Marie LaRocque is concerned, I doubt if it would do any good for me to apologize again."

At dark, Walters showed up, with two trappers he had met on the trail. One could speak English and I heard him ask, "What cabin for Vic's wife?"

I was a little curious about this fellow, a rather handsome breed, or Metis, and the more so when he also mentioned Marie LaRocque, and insinuated that he hoped to persuade her not to return to Lac Ste. Anne and enter the convent there. "Marie make some man, maybe me, very good wife. She is fool to think of wasting away for white man's religion."

Mac called this breed "Ike" and I learned from Walters that he was related to Isaac Abraham, the Iosegun band's chief.

Then, for the time being, events of the past two hours were forgotten, while I told Walters about my trip with Little John.

"The .22 rifle — (I had brought it back from the Tony River cabin) is a puzzle. Never saw it before," Walters said, adding, "I agree with you. Whoever left the rifle was a stranger, as he could have hiked down here and traded the .22 for grub or bought shells from me."

So, the matter was dropped. Walters said there was enough snow for his bobsled and that he'd be glad to haul me and some grub, for my trapline cabin at Jackfish Lake, about 18 miles south on the old wagon trail.

CHAPTER XI

Twelve miles south of the Tony River crossing, was an abandoned road house or "Stopping Place" where the Edson-Grande Prairie Trail crossed the Little Smoky River. The original owner was Joe Purcy, but he had "pulled out" in the fall of 1916, as soon as the cable ferry was dry-docked at the end of the season, when travel by wagon was no longer possible.

A trapper named Bert Peterson had a cabin on the south bank of the Little Smoky River, a few hundred yards downstream from the river trail crossing. Peterson also left for parts unknown, in the spring of 1917.

The Alberta Provincial Government had authorized, for one more year's operation, the river cable ferries on the trail at the Athabasca, Baptiste and Little Smoky River crossings. I have already mentioned that my partner, Cliff Knowles, his father Frank Knowles and I, ran the Athabasca and Baptiste river ferry scows that final season.

Our friend, Tom "Scotia" Murphy ran the Little Smoky River ferry during 1917. His wife, Gertie, and two little boys stayed with him. "Scotia" was a "dreamer," something like this writer. He had trapped, prospected and worked in Nova Scotia, Ontario and Manitoba, after several years at sea from the age of 13. Now, in 1917, he was looking for gold on the Little Smoky, following a previous summer (1910), of prospecting in that area.

Tom "Scotia" Murphy, had returned to the Little Smoky Rover country in the fall of 1916, leaving his family in Edson during the following winter. A man named Morris had joined Murphy in a prospecting and fur trade enterprise called the "Lucky M Mining & Trading Company." The operation was supposed to be adequately financed by a Mrs. Campbell, who had a substantial interest in a Calgary, Alberta newspaper. It developed that her main interest was in Morris, Tom's partner.

By mid-winter, their financial backer having withdrawn support, the "Lucky M" operation folded. Morris returned to southern Alberta and Murphy came back down the Edson Trail to the Athabasca Crossing and wintered there in Jim Hindmarsh's cabin. There, Murphy's wife and two boys joined him, leaving the Athabasca for the Little Smoky Crossing and the ferry job, in the spring of 1917.

Actually, the old Joe Purcy cabins had been vacated for only a short period, by the time I had joined Walters. One sizable room was quite livable, with a still usable cook stove, a sheet-iron heater, two bunks and a table and chairs made from sawed lumber.

Walters and I made a lunch, after taking care of his horses, Parson and Preacher.

"You could run a good line up-river from here," my companion observed, "that is if you want to build a real operation."

"Guess so," I said, rather noncommittally. Recent happenings had caused me to have reservations about "settling down" in the North Country. Just the night before we left Mile 90, a bootlegger stopped by and left a letter for me, from my ex-partner, Cliff Knowles. "You'd better come to town. I got a job as fireman already and the pay is good. Dad (his father, Frank Knowles) is working for a blacksmith. We've rented a big house and have lots of room. Your girl friend and her mother have moved to Edmonton, but Diddy Griggs was asking about you. Another thing, we're in this war, too, now and Uncle

Ruby and Tom Murphy - 1923

Sam will probably be calling for us. No letter for you from Isabel and I think you'd better forget your high school gal."

The reference to an Edson "girl friend" was about Ruby Millar. I had met her twice in that frontier town, the first time only briefly and again in June, 1917, while on a trip to Edson with Greg Rapelje's team and "democrat," after supplies. My partners and I were then still operating the river ferries.

Ruby's brother, George, did some wagon freighting out of Edson and he had hauled the Murphy and Morris outfit and supplies over the trail to Half-Way House, about 120 miles north of Edson. I became acquainted with George Millar when, on that trip, he crossed the Baptiste River. I also saw him on the return trip, driving a four-horse team hitched to a heavy freight wagon. The Baptiste River ferry had already been dry-docked, but the river could be forded in the fall.

"Be sure and stop at our house the next time you come down the trail," young Millar had said.

Curiously, my first brief meeting with his sister, Ruby, also had something to do with firewood. After reaching Edson on a June evening, I left Rapelje's horses in an Edson stable. Then, I set out to locate the Millar residence. No one answered my knock on the door, but I heard someone splitting wood in the back yard. There, I came upon a young girl swinging an axe like a veteran woodsman. Though we had met but briefly once before, I recognized her at once.

"That tamarack is plenty tough — may I tackle it?" I said, adding, "You might remember me — one of the Griggs girls introduced us last winter."

"I remember," the girl said, handing me the axe. "George thought you might be down from the Athabasca." Turning, she went inside to call George.

And now, even farther north, at the Little Smoky Crossing, I was thinking back to an incident when, all at once, while Walters and I were inside Joe Purcy's abandoned cabin, I told him about the letter "Smitty" the bootlegger had delivered and confided in my partner with, "I told you about meeting George Millar a year ago. Well, I met his sister last June and, darn it, Ted, I must have fallen for her — maybe I'll hear from her yet — Cliff Knowles wrote that Ruby and her mother were in Edmonton, staying with relatives, but that he understood they were due back in Edson."

Walters said, "Don't remember meeting George's sister, except once, a few years ago, when she was helping an older brother, Will, in his Edson hardware. I did hear that Ruby Millar can break ponies as good as most men. But," here my companion hesitated, "She might turn you down in a hurry if you tried to make a trapper's wife out of a city bred gal!"

"Maybe so — then, too, there's the war. Last summer, I registered with the U.S. Consul in Edmonton, and my registration must be renewed on or before next June 1st."

Early the following day we packed up, hitched Walters' team to the bob-sled, drove the eight miles to my Jackfish Lake cabin, unloaded my supplies there, and headed north again back to Mile 90.

It was real dark when we arrived. The dogs, including Marie LaRocque's Husky, announced our arrival. Mac met us with two lighted kerosene lanterns and Little John came out of his grandmother's cabin to greet us.

"Vic came for some flour and lard," MacMillar said. "The fall run is poor

— mostly jackfish — but he's started to smoke some for dog feed. Guess he could use some help."

We entered the trading post and the aroma of fresh baked bread filled the big kitchen. "Marie is a darned good cook," Mac said. "I had to order that Ike character out of here while she baked and, wait 'til you sample the moose stew!"

Mac was right — that girl was an excellent cook and no wonder — she had been trained in the culinary art, at Lac Ste. Anne Mission School.

In spite of myself, I kept hoping Marie LaRocque would come up from her cabin — out of a woman's natural curiosity, if for no other reason.

But Marie didn't appear and, after a brief discussion of plans for the next day, we all "hit the bunks."

I dreamed about Ruby Millar that night. Walters' inference that he doubted any young white woman would marry a wilderness trapper, must have permeated my subconscious thoughts, for, in my dream Ruby had laughed when I did propose, answering, "I've been on that trail — afraid it wouldn't work out — marrying a trapper. And, my folks would think I'd gone crazy!"

That dream was to haunt me for a long, long time and I was feeling low the next morning, when I left Mile 90.

I had offered to hike over to Buck Lake, to help Vic LaRocque with the gill net fishing. Any time now, the lake would freeze over for the winter and we would then have to resort to setting nets under the ice, a cold, miserable operation.

CHAPTER XII

LaRocque had said that more snow was due on the higher plateau beyond the Little Smoky River, on the trail to the fish camp at Buck Lake.

So, I hitched three of my dogs to a small toboggan, loaded it with blankets, a small tent and camp stove, some camping utensils and left Mile 90 an hour before daybreak. As LaRocque had predicted, it had snowed during the night.

While passing the LaRocque cabin, I saw no sign of Marie's Husky and decided she must have taken the dog inside overnight, not wanting to risk a confrontation with my Huskies.

Even at that early hour someone was ahead of me, for there were fresh moccasin tracks in the trail along the Tony River flats. Here the snowfall had been comparatively light and whoever the traveler might be, hadn't bothered to put on snowshoes. I thought it possible that "Ike" — the trapper who was staying overnight with old Natoka and Little John, was on his way to Iosegun Lakes. The trail, about a mile from Walters' place forked, the northeast route leading to Iosegun Lakes and the easterly route, to Buck Lake.

It was still poor light when I reached the forks, but the party ahead of me had kept on the Buck Lake trail. And suddenly, I noticed dog tracks, along with those left by someone wearing rather small moccasins.

After crossing the Little Smoky River, about two miles east of Mile 90, the trail led up a long gradual slope, through jackpine and spruce.

Nearing the plateau, my "trail breaker" had taken to snowshoes and my dogs made better time hauling the toboggan. Then abruptly, the new snowshoe trail ended.

By then, it was quite light. My dogs started whining, and instinctively, I sensed that something unusual had happened. No one wearing snowshoes, would leave a trail, well blazed and easily followed in spite of new snow — except for a very compelling reason.

Chaining my lead dog to a tree, I commenced searching for some clue to the mystery. It took but a few minutes to discover that a moose had crossed the trail and the fish-camp-bound traveler's dog had taken off after it, with the owner in pursuit.

And that's how I met Marie LaRocque the second time. For, a hundred yards off the Buck Lake trail, I found her sitting propped against a tree, trying hard to conceal the fact that she was suffering considerable pain, possibly from an injury.

For a moment, I thought Vic LaRocque's sister was going to blame me for her obvious predicament. She grimaced and said something like "*Osi-Kew*" and when I asked, "May I help?" she replied, in English, "Little John says you do not speak very much Cree — so — I fell and twisted an ankle. Yes, you can help me back to the trail. I'll wait for Ike — he's sure to come after me."

It was a real struggle. Marie had sprained an ankle and also broken the frame of one snowshoe. We had to detour around a small jackpine thicket, as it was virtually impossible for me to half carry her through the tangle of pine and bush.

One encouraging development resulted from this second, and bizarre like the first, encounter. Marie LaRocque suddenly started laughing and for a few anxious moments, I thought she was becoming hysterical. "I can't wait to tell the Sisters about Ray Thompson!" she fairly screamed.

This was too much for me. I commenced laughing, too, and if someone had happened along about that time, we both would probably have been considered "*wooninau*" (crazy in Cree!).

But, we both calmed down and at an agonizing pace, finally made it back to the trail where my dogs were tied.

I removed the mocassin from Marie's sprained ankle and saw that it was swollen. She winced and muttered something like "*nanipoo-utem*". This, Walters told me later, indicated that Marie LaRocque had obviously been cursing her dog. I think she was saying, in Cree, 'damned dog!' But at the moment, I tried to help and said, "I'd better take you back to Mile 90."

Marie's dark eyes flashed and she jammed her muskrat fur cap tighter over black tresses, apparently done in a "bun" on top of her head — a style of hairdressing practiced by pioneer white women.

"I cannot go back to Mile 90," she snapped. "Chief Abraham will pick me up at Vic's cabin and take me to Lac Ste. Anne, if Little John's father does not get there first."

"Well, maybe we should try to reach the Buck Lake cabin," I countered.

"You can make a fire and leave wood. Ike will be along anytime — he can track my dog. I must not lose that dog pack," the girl insisted.

Marie's remark concerning Ike puzzled me. How could he help the injured girl? I had neither seen nor heard any sign of a dog team around Natoka's cabin, where the Iosegun Lakes trapper had spent the previous night.

But, I decided not to question my "uninvited" companion on that score. Instead, I offered to track Marie's dog, saying, "Can't see how your Husky could go far without losing the pack."

"You can try — but —," here Marie forced herself to a more upright position, with her back against a tree trunk, "Do not expect any favor from me — if you find the pack!"

For a moment, I thought of answering her implied insinuation with some caustic remarks of my own. But, I held my tongue, built a fire and took off after the girl's runaway Husky.

Well-trained pack dogs can maneuver through bush and tree stands in a remarkable manner, twisting and turning through or around obstacles, without losing their packs, often in most difficult situations. I knew this from my own experience. I tracked the dog "Mookun" into a windfall where the moose being chased had left signs of being hampered by the fallen spruce. I concluded that the Husky could not have made it through the windfall wearing a dog pack.

I looked at my pocket watch and noted, with dismay, that it was past one o'clock and only a couple hours of light remained.

Then, back-tracking, I was within a hundred yards or so of the Buck Lake trail, when, on making a slight detour, I discovered Marie's dog pack, lying in a clump of knee-high bushes. Here snowshoe rabbits had "topped" a clump of small poplars and when Mookun tried to force his way through, the stiff stubs of brush had hooked into the dog's pack straps and relieved him of his load.

Marie had been crying and she shed a few more tears when I dropped the dog pack beside her.

"Should have found it sooner," I said, rather lamely. "How's the ankle?"

"Not good — if you get some moss —."

"Of course," I said and remembering passing through some spruce a short distance down the trail, added, "Keep your chin up," and left to search for some moss.

When I returned, Marie had made some bandage strips, apparently from a shirt that had been in the dog pack. Between us, we managed a compress of the moss and bound it tightly to her ankle.

"Well, Miss LaRocque," I said firimly, "we've got to make camp here — this trail — either going back to Mile 90, or on to the fish camp, would be mighty dangerous at night. My dogs can carry you in the toboggan all right, but I can't risk the chance of breaking your pretty neck!" I was surprised when she remained silent.

It was sheer good fortune that the small tent and camp stove were on my toboggan. I was going to help Vic LaRocque set up the tent, on a light frame, with the two side poles on the bottom of the frame, for makeshift sled runners. The tent would be used while being skidded from one hole in the ice at Buck Lake to another hole, for setting the nets and in removing the catch. The small camp stove would provide enough heat to prevent the net from freezing in below zero weather.

Using a snowshoe for a scoop, I cleared away the snow, spread some spruce boughs on the ground and set up the tent. The camp stove, placed just inside, was ready as soon as I installed the several sections of stove pipe.

Then, as I was carrying Marie through the tent flap, we both started laughing again, but Marie ended up sobbing.

"A priest told me I'd pay for my sins," she cried, "I broke a vow to be a Sister — maybe the Father was right!" This really shook me.

It happened that I was raised as a Protestant and almost had enrolled in a university where I would have majored in theology. Instead, I had gone to a business college and although still considering myself a Christian, after migrating to Canada (and a taste of wilderness living), much of my earlier enthusiasm for the ministry was lost. I had read about the role of the Catholic Priests and Sisters on Canada's frontier and had considerable admiration for their work in the Far North, especially in the field of medicine. But, the more I learned from the Indians, about their simple beliefs, the weaker became my conviction that the white man had all the answers where "religion" was concerned.

"I'm sure you'll do what you think best and please stop crying — things will look better — come morning."

Shortly after, Marie calmed down. She took some bannock and pickled bear meat from the dog pack and I also had carried a lunch. A small pail from her own pack sack, along with my own, was filled with snow. Melted down, it made enough water for a cup of tea each.

From the dog pack, she then removed a rather skimpy piece of a "Hudson's Bay" blanket and a small tarp, or canvas and insisted on making her own bed at the far end of the tent. I dragged in several long, dry spruce poles and placed them just outside the tent flap, to be cut into stove lengths for fire wood, as needed. Finally, I spread my blankets alongside the stove and tried to get some sleep.

On several occasions, I had been forced to "camp out" in the wilderness, but that night, in the emergency bivouac on the Buck Lake Trail, had to register as the most bizarre experienced to that date.

I slept fitfully, fully clothed, even to my heavy, mackinaw coat. The camp stove afforded a fairly good heat level, as long as I kept on stoking it. But, the minute the fire died down — the near-zero temperature outside penetrated the tent canvas as though it did not exist.

Once, when I was sure she slept, I placed my mackinaw coat over Marie's shoulders. She had refused an earlier offer of a blanket from my bed-roll.

It was around midnight, when my dogs started a furious uproar.

Marie roused and said, "That must be Mookun. If he starts a fight, take a club, or axe and do what you have to!" My "guest" was obviously still very angry with her Husky. Later, she told me that, in her hurry making up her packs at Natoka's cabin, she had placed a cherished Bible (a gift from a Father) in Mookun's pack, instead of carrying it herself.

But Marie's Husky didn't press his luck and the next morning, we saw his tracks, heading west, back to Mile 90.

So ended the unexpected campout. At daybreak, I left the tent standing, loaded Marie LaRocque on the toboggan and set out on the return to Mile 90, leaving Marie at the La Rocque cabin shortly after noon.

Then, hastily explaining to Walters the cause for the delay, I again drove my dogs east, on the trail to the Buck Lake fish camp.

CHAPTER XIII

Luckily, Vic LaRocque had broken the trail open since the last snowfall, with his dog team and toboggan, from the Buck Lake cabin across the lake. This made the last two miles of my trip from Mile 90, much easier, especially since I was traveling in the light of a waning moon toward the end of my journey.

LaRocque's dogs welcomed my team and me, with fierce howls. Vic came outside with a lantern and grabbed a club, cursing his Huskies.

I drove my own dogs to the far side of the cabin and chained them. Vic helped me unload and feed my dogs. Finally settled for the night, I surely enjoyed Vic's coffee and a mixture of beans and dried moose meat.

The next day, Vic and I set two more 100 ft. long gill nets, under the ice. Walters and I had already marked the location for each net by "staking" long poles, each pair a little over 100 feet apart, anchored by forcing the lower end of each pole into the lake bottom. To set the net, a hole was chopped through the ice at the stake nearest to the shore. Then, with a stout line tied to one end of a long slender pole, it was shoved through the hole in the ice and slanted toward the opposite stake. When completely submerged, this "lining" pole, carrying the setting cord, would automatically float up against the ice.

At a pre-determined distance (the length of the net-setting pole), a second hole was chopped through the ice. Next, the pole, shoved under the ice, still carrying the long set-line, was extended toward the second stake its entire length. Then another hole was chopped and the process repeated until the set-line reached the second stake.

Once the set-line reached from stake to stake, the fish net, complete with floats and weights, was shoved down through the hole at one stake and hauled under the ice to be anchored at the second stake. Set-lines, each a little over 100 ft. in length, were tied to the fish net ends, so that the net could then be set, or pulled out by simply reversing the hauling operation.

Later, when fishing with nets started in earnest, the small tent, set up on a pole frame and skids, would be in place over the hole in the ice where the net would be pulled, for retrieving the catch.

Though gill net fishing under ice in the North Country is a cold, miserable job, it still is fascinating.

Isaac Abraham's sons had shown Walters where the whitefish runs were located in Buck Lake. Without that knowledge, a great deal of time and effort could be wasted in experimental setting of the gill nets.

While netting the marketable whitefish, averaging three or four pounds each, the nets could also be seriously damaged if Northern Pike, a long snouted species, got entangled in the net. Even one pike could twist it into a sort of rope.

The secret of whitefish netting was in knowing when and where to place the nets in the whitefish runs that were not used extensively by the voracious "Jackfish" or Northern Pike.

Vic LaRocque was a good fisherman, trapper and hunter, but somewhere, he had gone wrong, turning to devious ways of making a living by theft, cheating at cards, whiskey running, etc. Walters was one of a very few traders who knew what to expect from the 'breed' or Metis, and how to deal with him.

The one night I stayed with Vic in the fish camp cabin, we played cards, but because Walters had warned me, I refused to play with "stakes" other than matches. Vic let me win a few hands, then wanted to use money instead of matches. I refused, saying I needed to replace some webbing in my snowshoes.

Suddenly, LaRocque asked, "You like my sister?"

"Don't know Marie very well," I countered.

"You spend one long night, in small tent alone with girl and not know her!"

"That's right, Vic. Your sister wasn't in the mood for talking — even if I'd wanted to. She really suffered with a sprained ankle."

"You told me about that — Marie is unhappy. A young buck in the Iosegun band wants to marry her, but she don't like him enough."

"She said something like a Cree named Ike following her on the trail. I thought she was afraid of him."

"My sister trusts no man, white or native. She wants to go back to Lac Ste. Anne, where we lived before, but I think she is afraid of a young priest there," Vic said.

Turning to my bunk, I ended the conversation with, "Walters tells that Marie is a good girl, with a mind of her own. I'm sure things will work out for her."

But, I wondered, there in the dark after Vic had snuffed out the candle, about his half-sister's future. Especially disturbing, the more I thought of it, was Vic's reference to the young priest at Lac Ste. Anne and Marie's fear of him.

Then, just before the sandman came, I was thinking about Ruby Millar, the Edson girl I had met in that frontier town, a few months earlier. Smitty, the bootlegger was due at Mile 90, any day now on his last trip for the winter from Edson to Grande Prairie.

Smitty, well known along the Edson Trail, always brought mail, addressed to anyone he knew, from the Edson Post Office.

Maybe he'd arrived at Mile 90 and brought me a letter from Ruby. . . .

I reached Mile 90, around noon the next day. Smitty had passed through with his two horses, one saddled and the other carrying Smitty's pack, bed roll and camp gear. Walters told me there was a thousand dollars' worth of illicit whiskey and alcohol (when peddled to the Indians at Sturgeon Lake) in the bootlegger's pack.

Smitty had delivered some mail, including a letter and small package from my mother, but there was no word from Ruby Millar.

"Smitty told us there was smoke coming from the stovepipe in the Little Smoky cabin," Walters said. "He didn't stop, not wanting to risk meeting some stranger. Maybe you'd better investigate!"

"Beats me," I agreed, "I'll get set for tomorrow. I —," just then, Little John burst in with, "Sure glad to see you, Ray," and with a big smile, "Marie has made a cake today — maybe she isn't mad at Ray, any more!"

Sure enough, Marie LaRocque had been using Walter's big cookstove. Shortly after Little John's arrival, she came in, said, "We meet again, Mr. Ray," and went to the stove, to remove some loaves of bread. She walked with a crutch someone had made for her.

"Hope your ankle is better," I said. She thanked me, took two of the loaves and started for the door. "There's some stew on the back of the stove," she said. Then, this girl already an enigma and now more of a puzzle than ever, was gone again. I had wanted to ask, "What about the cake?" but thought better of it.

Marie LaRocque was dressed in a fringed and beaded deerskin, or caribou jacket. Her black hair, rather short for the way of the average native, was worn in two braids, their beauty accentuated by a headband of muskrat fur, artistically adorned with vari-colored bead work. I suddenly realized that I wanted to talk to her — about her suitor, Ike, the Iosegun Lakes trapper and about her plans for reaching Lac Ste. Anne, a good 150 toboggan trail miles from the Tony River Post.

I was feeling low in spirit, and although my mother did not mention it directly in her letter, I felt that she was worried about me and what might happen if the war in Europe continued. I knew that I must renew my registration with the U.S. Consul in Edmonton by June 1st of the next year — now only months away.

An *Edmonton Bulletin*, Smitty had left with Walters, carried grim news of casualties in the fierce war overseas. I later learned that Chuck Adair and "Tiny" Stewart, two soldiers I had chummed with at Sarcee Camp in 1916, had both been killed, only a few weeks after many Canadian foot soldiers entered the War Zone.

I told myself that it was "crazy" for me to think about either Ruby Millar or Marie LaRocque.

I was tired and wanted to call it quits for the day. But, three of the Iosegun Lakes trappers showed up with several fine beaver pelts, wanting to trade and play poker.

"You'll make a hit if you stay up and play a few rounds," Walters said.

While I hesitated, Ike, one of the trio, said something in Cree that I didn't understand. It was a good thing, as Little John (my shadow) told me next day the Cree had said, "Indian girl too much for white trapper — (he) didn't get much sleep in tent, two nights ago." I would have been furious, had I understood Ike and the laughter of his companions at his remark.

So, we played poker and although a novice in a card game, I managed to end up with enough "credit" to buy a pair of moccasins from one of the Indians.

It wasn't real late, but Walters said no when Ike wanted to continue the card game. A few minutes before the last deal, Walters had whispered to Little John and he left. I yelled, "Good night," he waved back with, "See you soon, Ray."

I didn't realize just "how soon" until Little John returned, accompanied by Marie LaRocque.

"Maybe you like some cake and coffee," she said, looking at Walters. "You bet," the trader replied and Marie went to a cupboard near the cookstove and brought out a big frosted cake. That strange girl could really cook.

There already was a big pot of coffee on the stove, so we thanked Marie and waited while Walters cut the cake. "I'll share mine with Natoka," Marie said and started to leave again.

"You stay — eat!" Ike demanded, grabbing Marie by the arm. He spoke in English, obviously for my benefit.

But the girl shook his hold, retorting sharply in Cree and started for the door.

The trapper tried to follow, but Walters blocked his way, while more sharp words were exchanged in Cree.

Ike calmed down, ate his cake, along with the rest of us and a potentially dangerous confrontation, between the Indian and me, was averted.

The trapper left, so Walters and I settled down for the night.

Dan MacMillar, away on a scouting trip to Crooked Lake, where some trappers were expected to have furs for trade, came in during the night. This meant I was free to run my trapline to the south and see who was "holed up" in the old Purcy cabin at Smoky River crossing.

CHAPTER XIV

It was noon, on a late November day, when I reached the Little Smoky River Crossing. My trapline yielded a couple foxes and one lynx on that 12-mile stretch of the abandoned Edson-Grande Prairie Trail.

My dogs started whining as we neared the old stopping place. A wisp of smoke came form the stovepipe of the log cabin last used as living quarters by Tom Murphy and his family, while he operated the river ferry the season just past.

I halted my dog team and, by way of caution, drew my rifle from its moosehide cover and yelled, "Hello, the cabin," as I approached the building.

There was no reply. I waited a few minutes, then chained my dogs and opened the heavy, plank door. Small dry branches near the stove had been broken, not cut with an axe, into short pieces and a smoldering fire indicated that the builder had not been absent for very long. A pair of moosehide moccasins I had left there on a previous trip, were missing, also, some cornmeal, sugar and tea.

Outside, I found moccasin tracks that showed the wearer had left that morning, headed west, or upstream on the frozen Little Smoky River.

All this was puzzling, to say the least, but, after some deliberation, I decided to try and cover the eight miles south on the trail, to my Jackfish Lake cabin and return to the Little Smoky for my overnight stay.

I took two more lynx on the way to Jackfish Lake. There was no sign of anyone having stopped at my cabin, and after a late lunch, I hit the trail with my dog team on the way back.

Memories of my first two winters in the North, when Jackfish Lake was my trapline headquarters, haunted me. I felt really depressed and thought seriously of continuing on into the night, not stopping at the Little Smoky. If I pushed my dogs a little, we could make Mile 90 by midnight, a total of 40 miles for the day. There was one drawback — it had turned colder during the afternoon and, although there was enough moonlight for safe travel on a broken trail, I knew that below zero weather would make hard going for my Huskies, on account of the toboggan "drag" created by dry snow.

Then fate stepped into the picture when, an hour after daylight had vanished, I reached the Little Smoky and saw that the cabin was again occupied. Apparently, on hearing my dogs, a man opened the cabin door. I could see only a shadowy form in the candle light.

"I'm Jim Brown — this your cabin?" The stranger's words were barely audible, his voice hoarse, as if he were suffering from asthma or a heavy cold.

I gave him my name, adding, "I use this place as a stopover camp — my headquarters are at Mile 90, on the Tony River, 12 miles north of here. You'd better get back inside. I'll take care of my dogs and come in soon!"

While unharnessing, chaining and feeding my dogs, I suddenly recalled that a trapper named Jim Brown, on his way "outside" from a trapline on the headwaters of the Little Smoky, had stopped overnight at my Jackfish Lake cabin, in May, 1916, a year and a half previously. But, *that* Jim Brown would surely have remembered me, as we had swapped rifles and I had bought some beaver pelts from him.

I thought, too, of a mysterious and fatal accident that had taken place, early in March, 1917, only a few miles up the valley from the Little Smoky River Crossing. While returning to his trapline cabin, Bert Peterson had been forced to take a seldom-used "short cut," to avoid an overflow on the ice, in the bend of the Little Smoky River. On this trail, he had discovered a rifle resting against a tree trunk and, on looking closer, found the remains of a human skeleton near the ashes of a campfire. The identity of the unfortunate man was never established.

Now, on the spur of the moment, I led one of my Huskies with me, when returning to the cabin. A wilderness trapper learns that "the survival of the fittest" is more than a clever quotation. An instinct, in many respects like that of his wild neighbor, the wolf, prompts him to move cautiously in situations that border on the mysterious or unusual. Maybe the stranger's name was really Jim Brown and maybe not.

Inside the cabin, I was due for a real shock. The slight, bearded, emaciated creature, eyes sunken deep in their sockets, wearing trousers and shirt so tattered and stained, one could only guess at their original shape and color, was obviously starving.

He was sitting on a bench, shivering and started to rise.

"Stay put, Jim. I'll build up the fire and get us a bite!"

One of the log stables afforded dry wood from stalls still standing. I knocked a couple planks off the posts and carried them back to the cabin, chopped them into stovelength pieces and soon had a good fire going.

Jim Brown sat so close to the stove I was afraid his ragged shirt might take fire. He hardly spoke while I made some tea and warmed up some baked beans I had brought from Mile 90.

Although darkness had fallen several hours by the time we were through with the lunch, it was not late, so I brought in a lynx from my toboggan and started to remove the beautiful, gray, silky coat.

"I like cat — can I have some?" my uninvited guest asked, his voice much stronger than when he had first spoken.

"Help yourself," I replied, handing him my hunting knife.

He sliced some strips of lean meat from the cat's flank, poured a little water into a fry pan and watched impatiently while his "dessert" simmered. After it was a few minutes in the boiling water, he proceeded to cut the lynx meat into chunks and literally devoured the pieces, one by one. That man had one physical asset — good teeth, but he didn't waste much time in chewing.

"First meat I've had for a week," he blurted. "Had some rabbit snares out, but the snowshoes are mighty scarce."

"Right you are, Jim," I remarked. "I shot a couple of fool hens (common name for Spruce Grouse) today. I'll boil them later, with some pot barley. That will do for our breakfast. Then, we'll head back north to Walters' place at Mile 90."

I spoke in a matter-of-fact tone, waiting for the stranger's reaction. This wasn't long in coming.

"I've heard of Walters — good man. Who else is at Mile 90?"

Jim Brown seemed relieved and his shoulders straightened a little, as I finished naming the people in, or near the Mile 90 post.

My job with removing the lynx pelt completed, I went out to my toboggan for the grouse. Just as I re-entered the cabin, Jim Brown rose, pointed to one of the crude, homemade chairs and with a fixed stare, exclaimed, "I knew it — that thing has feelin's — I can't place it but I believe it might be a man from Fort Vermillion. They found him stiff frozen in an ice overflow!"

For a moment, I could hardly keep from laughing, but quickly restrained myself. The man's sudden outburst was no laughing matter and I remained silent as Jim Brown pointed to several objects in the cabin, giving them names of persons he must have known — all of them "reincarnated" in his view.

Only once did this bizarre character let slip part of a name that aroused my suspicion. "This," pointing to the stove, "would be that son-of-a-bitch Mountie, Constable Jack —," here he paused, as if suddenly afraid that it might be unwise to name any certain Mounted Police officer. He sat down again, his shoulders sagging, as he sought warmth from the fire. Maybe, in his wild imagining, Jim Brown was gloating over the demise and reincarnation of his enemy, in the shape of a stove that now gave him comfort.

I nodded now and then with a, "Could be — strange things do happen," and hoped Jim Brown would think I agreed with him.

But, taking no chances that the man might suddenly decide I was "Constable Jack," I let my Husky stay inside the cabin with us that night.

I gave nearly all of my skimpy bedroll to the believer in reincarnation and kept the fire going most of the night. I heard Jim Brown moaning once and wondered if he suffered from bolting his food, or some more serious ailment, like, for example, permanent injury to his lungs and respiratory system.

Altogether, it was a wild, weird and generally bad night for me.

CHAPTER XV

That 12-mile journey, in sub-zero weather back to Mile 90, is still vivid in my memory as I write this, 60 years later. We had never heard of such terms then, as "chill factor." But, we knew when it was cold enough to be foolhardy to venture out on the trail.

It wouldn't have been so bad, traveling alone with my dogs. Wearing a silk scarf over my mouth, fur cap flaps down, I could walk or half trot, even though encumbered by a heavy sweater and mackinaw coat, behind the toboggan and sustain some circulation. But with this derelict along, I had a real fight on my hands.

Before leaving the Little Smoky, I had cut a piece of blanket into strips and wound them spirally around Jim Brown's legs from ankle to knee. I had learned how to apply "puttees," or cloth-leggings, while in the Canadian Army. I also gave my mackinaw to my fellow traveler and made a sort of cape or poncho, for myself, out of a piece of canvas.

The first two miles on the climb out of the river valley, wasn't too bad, as we traveled through fairly heavy timber. But, once on the higher plateau, where scattered pines and poplars afforded little protection from the wind, I had a real problem.

Jim Brown wanted either to ride the toboggan and risk freezing to death, or stop every few minutes and have me build a fire. Several times, I had literally to drag him off the toboggan and force him to walk. Twice, in despair, I built a fire and let him "roast," while I melted snow and made tea. My passenger rarely spoke on that hazardous trip. Hunkered down in my mackinaw, with the collar stiff from his frozen breath, Jim Brown was surely a pitiful sight.

At long last, we had crossed the plateau and entered timber again. Now, with the killing cross winds behind us, I wrapped Jim Brown in a blanket and tarp, lashed him to the toboggan and ordered my dogs to "Hyap!" I caught up with them twice, where the toboggan had veered from the trail and side-swiped a tree. On the last mile or so, across the Tony River flats, my dogs increased their lead.

When I finally reached Mile 90, Dan MacMillar and Marie LaRocque had already carried the half-conscious Jim Brown into the cabin. And, of course, Little John was there to see who had "run away with Ray's dogs!"

I was too groggy myself, to take much notice at first, but Dan and Marie knew how to treat frostbite. Within the hour, they had Jim Brown up in a chair, eating and drinking coffee. I told Mac, aside while Marie was busy with the "man of mystery," how I'd met the stranger and the condition he was in.

"Good enough, Ray," Mac said. "Now, you try some of Marie's stew and hit the hay. We'll look after this fellow and take care of your dogs. Walters will be back tonight and he'll know now to handle things."

"Mac very much right," Little John said, adding, with a sly grin, "Marie make good breakfast for you — she stay with us down in cabin and Walters have her cook for two days now. She be back in morning."

I was too tired and sleepy to object and Mac's words made sense. A little later, I went to bed and didn't even hear Walters when he came to retire in his own bed, in the room we shared as sleeping quarters.

Walters had the only spring beds with comfortable mattresses, north of the

Athabasca, for a stretch of over a hundred trail miles. Bill and Ritia Hare had sold them to him when leaving Mile 90.

I was barely awake, when that irrepressible Little John banged on the door and yelled, "Hot cakes and sow belly! Marie says hurry before Jim Brown cleans up!"

It didn't take Walters and me long to dress, dab some cold water on our faces and join Mac, Marie and our mysterious guest.

Jim Brown looked almost human, in some clean clothes Mac had managed to locate. Only his sunken eyes and their darting glances, reminded me of the disciple of reincarnation I had met at the Little Smoky. The man did possess amazing powers of recuperation and seemed quite steady on his feet.

When we had our fill of Marie's hot cakes and fried salt pork or "sow belly," Walters asked Mac to show the stranger around the Post and he also told Little John to "go along, kid." This left Walters, Marie and me alone. "We've got a problem in this Jim Brown," the trader said. "Look at this!" Walters placed a piece of brown paper on the table. A rough sketch showed a map with four locations marked on as many rivers and a trail between each point. A spot on the Wapiti River was designated "Rowe"; one on the Simonette, "Olson"; the third, on the Tony River, "Goodswimmer"; and the fourth, on the Little Smoky, was marked "Jim Brown."

I whistled, amazed at the clue to the stranger's identity, or lack of identity, disclosed by the map Walters had found in the man's ragged shirt.

"Looks like our man took the last name on his map — 'Jim Brown,' a trapper who had a cabin about 20 miles upstream from Bert Peterson's place near the Little Smoky Crossing," Walters declared.

"Sure," I agreed. "The real Jim Brown stopped at my Jackfish Lake cabin, a year ago last May. What next — 'Mr. Feelin's' is one queer character!"

Marie spoke, directing her words to me, "I think you did right, Ray," then, turning to Walters, "Maybe he could help Vic at the fish camp!"

"Smart girl," Walters said. "Mac can take him over to Buck Lake. Don't think he's dangerous — just a little nutty. We've been treated to his wild ideas that things like stoves, chairs, and even snowshoes and toboggans had 'feelin's' and were live people or animals once."

So Walters, who of course had to make any decision about the man who called himself, Jim Brown, told Mac to take the newcomer along when he left, shortly, for the Fish Camp.

Two days after Mac had brought a toboggan load of jackfish (for dog feed) from Buck Lake, Vic LaRocque followed him to Mile 90. Mr. Feelin's, or Jim Brown, had stayed two nights in the fish camp, then, during a blizzard, had disappeared. LaRocque, a good woodsman and tracker, lost the wanderer's trail when one of Isaac Abraham's trappers had covered earlier signs, with a dog team and toboggan.

Marie LaRocque was really shaken. "Poor soul — he must be lost for keeps this time. Can't we do something?" She looked from Walters to me.

"We can look for tracks on the trails out of here — that's about all," Walters promised the distraught girl.

"No use looking for sign north of here," Vic LaRocque said.

"Why?" Walters quizzed.

"He told me that the Mounties, from Fort Vermillion were after him. Was real shook up when I said there was a Mounted Police detachment at Sturgeon Lake — only a couple days dog team travel, north from here!"

Walters shook his head. "Fort Vermillion is a good 300 miles away, downstream from Peace River Crossing. That poor devil must have run like a scared rabbit!"

Fate decreed that, since I was the one to "rescue" the man I called Mr. Feelin's, I was to be the last to see any sign of him. The next day, after LaRocque had told us of "Jim Brown's" disappearance, I made a trip south again to the Little Smoky.

The old Purcy cabin was not occuped this time. But, I was positive that the pseudo Jim Brown had been there. A foul smelling whitefish was hanging by a wire alongside the stove. The ashes in the stove were dead and cold.

Vic LaRocque had told us that the only thing missing at Buck Lake, when the stranger disappeared, was a whitefish Vic had suspended by a wire, to "ripen" for trapline bait. Beset by fear of punishment for some real, or imagined crime, the mysterious stranger had disappeared, this time for keeps.

When I returned to Mile 90 and gave an account of my meager findings, Marie LaRocque wept. "It's so unfair," she sobbed, adding words that oddly disturbed and puzzled me. "I could maybe have helped by taking him to the Mission!"

Curiously, it was two years after this incident that, meeting Walters at the Athabasca River Crossing, I learned that a man answering "Jim Brown's" description had been paroled at Fort Vermillion, after being suspected of taking part in a wood camp brawl on the Peace River, during which a Mounted Police officer was wounded.

Walters had heard that our Jim Brown, snowbound in the camp where they cut wood for the river steamboats to use during the summer and evidently afraid of reporting late to his parole officer, had taken off on trails leading south. Walters had concluded, too, that the .22 rifle Little John and I had found in the Tony River cabin, had been stolen by Jim Brown and left in the cabin, when the fugitive had run out of ammunition.

Walters and I were in agreement when, on our last meeting at the Athabasca Crossing, two years later, he summed it up with, "Guess no one will ever know what happened to Jim Brown!"

CHAPTER XVI

Walters and I took time out to cut a winter trail down Buck Creek, from its outlet at Buck Lake to where it emptied into the Little Smoky River. The stream was real low at that time of year, and several inches of ice made it safe for travel with Walters' team hitched to a bobsled. Clearing the trail consisted primarily in cutting logs that had lodged crosswise of the current during high water or flood stage. Walters' purpose was to make it easier to haul whitefish from Buck Lake, down to Mile 90, and from the trading post on north to the Sturgeon Lake market.

Then for a couple weeks, Mac and I trapped marten on a trapline extending east from Buck Lake to higher country called "Swan Hills." During that period we had a run-in with some natives who had violated the agreement between Walters and the Iosegun Lakes band, over trapping territories. Ike, the Indian who wanted Marie LaRocque to marry him, and with whom I had trouble previously, at Mile 90, was teamed up with a Metis (mixed blood native) and, but for Mac's timely arrival, I might have been in serious trouble. The pair had stopped me, on my own trapline, and were threatening to shoot me (assuming I was alone), when Dan MacMillar came along.

Walters was furious when I told him what had happened. He rode over to Iosegun Lakes and reported the incident to Isaac Abraham.

I never learned what happened to "Ike," Marie LaRocque's would-be suitor, but he never showed up at either Mile 90, or at the Buck Lake fish camp, where he had visited with Vic LaRocque.

Vic's half-sister, Marie, was still at Mile 90, staying with Vic's wife in one of Walters' small cabins. She had not heard from the Jesuit priest, who was supposed to stop at Mile 90, with a dog team, on his way to Whitecourt, and on to the Catholic Mission at Lac Ste. Anne, a journey of 200 trail miles.

Marie baked bread for us, and sometimes cooked moose roasts, and baked whitefish in our logging-camp-size oven. This was a real treat when we came in from the trail, cold, weary, and ravenously hungry.

Petite Jean (Little John) Fortier was still with his Cree grandmother, Natoka, living in a cabin next to that occupied by Marie LaRocque, and Vic's wife. One evening Little John invited me over to Natoka's cabin, "Grandmother will tell legends, Ray. You said when we stay in Tony River trapline cabin — you like to hear Indian stories." So, I walked down the trail with Little John and Natoka seemed real pleased with my visit. She could speak very little English, so Little John was our interpreter.

In the telling of a legend dealing with the lynx and beaver "people," Little John suddenly appeared to be confused, shaking his head when his Indian grandmother, repeated several times, words that apparently had something to do with Pisew's (the lynx) ego in admiring the reflection of his long beard and tufted ears, in the mirrored surface of a beaver pond.

"I'm not for sure, Ray," Little John said, adding, "Wait one minute!"

And before I realized what he was really up to, the 12-year-old had left the cabin. Natoka was obviously puzzled, too, but not for long. Just when I had decided to see where Little John had gone, the cabin door reopened, and in walked the lad, accompanied by Marie LaRocque.

"Petite Jean says you are interested in Indian legends. Why?" The girl's dark eyes seemed to flash a warning, as if she were prepared to question my motives, and purpose for visiting Natoka.

"Why?" I countered, "Simply because I'm interested in anything to do with wild animals, and remember," I added, "I told you the night we camped in the tent, on the Buck Lake trail, that I've lived near Indians most of my life. Anyway, sorry to have bothered you — and, I didn't send Little John to get you!"

I picked up my cap, tablet and pencil, and started for the door.

"Wait, Ray, I'm sorry," Marie said, adding, when I was lifting the wooden latch, "Please, please stay — I want to tell you a story — and not a legend either."

The compassion I had felt for this distraught girl, almost from our first encounter, welled stronger than ever. I sat down, hardly noticing when Little John and his grandmother left the cabin to visit next door.

"I was raised in a Catholic Mission. My father, Louis LaRocque, is a full-blood Frenchman, my mother only one-fourth Indian, which means I am seven-eighths French. But maybe Mac has told you this?"

"No, Marie, neither Mac nor Walters has, but, Little John worships you and has often spoken for you. I've felt that you did not wish me to know what was really troubling you, although you did say, several times, that you must go back to the Mission at Lac Ste. Anne. So, please go on, I would like to help, if I can." I put some more wood in the cabin stove, and sat down again on the bunk.

Marie remained silent for several minutes and when she looked up from a bench near the stove, I could see she had been weeping. An almost overwhelming desire to take this really beautiful girl in my arms, came over me. Had my compassion changed to a much deeper emotion?

A dog's howling in the distance seemed to arouse the girl from her despondency. She shook her head, her raven tresses falling about her shoulders.

"Sorry, Ray, I shouldn't bother you with my troubles. Mac tells me you have problems, too, like you must go back to your home in United States?"

"That's right, but maybe it's good to talk to someone who really cares. If you wish to confide in me, I assure you, I'm here to listen."

Then, pausing only briefly now and then, Marie LaRocque told me about her early life, and how she happened to be at Mile 90. Her mother had died during childbirth, and her father, Louis LaRocque, had left her at the Lac Ste. Anne Mission, where she received a very good education, learning both French and English, and some Cree, as well as cooking, sewing, and nursing. When only 13 she had been raped by an itinerant "preacher" who passed himself off as a priest.

Speaking of this she said, "I was afraid to tell anyone — the fake priest said he would kill me if I did tell. But, after he left the Mission, I confessed to a Jesuit Priest, Father Johns. That was a big mistake — the Father said I must have lured the man and that I would have to make confession often and do penance as the Father directed, and he would then pray for absolution of my great sin. I did what Father Johns said I must do! Then, a year ago last summer, I could take the Father's abuse no longer, so I ran away from the Lac

Ste. Anne Mission, hoping to be with my real father, at Grouard, on Lesser Slave Lake. He —."

"Just a minute, please," I interrupted, "what happened to the fake priest? Didn't the real Jesuit do anything about him?"

"I never knew — that terrible man left when Father Johns came to the Mission."

Marie's answer puzzled me, but when I questioned her further on the confrontation that must have taken place between the two missionaries, she was visibly disturbed. So I changed the subject.

"Did you find your father at Grouard?"

"Yes," she replied, regaining her composure, "but he works for a big trader supply house in Edmonton and travels by riverboat in summer and dog team in winter. He and Dan MacMillar were good friends and Mac let me travel with his pack train from Grouard to Sturgeon Lake, and later, on down to Mile 90. Father should be along soon, to take me to Lac Ste. Anne. I am supposed to be a Sister."

Marie's occasional reference to "Mac" included the comment, "He (MacMillar) has been a real friend. We were on the Grouard Trail for over a week, and Mac never once laid a hand on me, and often we were alone in a tent camp, when his packer was rounding up the horses. Mac had some oats for feed, but one horse would be staked out in a meadow at night, and the pack horses were hobbled and left to range. I remember one morning when it took several hours for our packer to bring in a couple strays."

Marie's pack dog was pawing at the door. She voiced a sharp command, in Cree, and the big Husky apparently gave up on any attempt to join his mistress.

"Maybe your dog was checking up on me," I said lightly, adding, "Mookun doesn't like white men too much."

My "visitor's" face flushed. "You, Ray, are trying to — like you say, 'rub it in.' I have already said I am sorry for not knowing what you are really like — that night in the tent on the Buck Lake trail proved that — I —" Suddenly she started weeping again and started for the cabin door. "I — I think this must be au revoir."

Instinctively, my arms reached out and drew Marie's trembling form close to me. She offered no resistance, and for several moments I was tormented with desire to possess her. But, afraid that she would then be able to class me with other white men who had taken advantage of her, I said good night, without even trying to kiss her.

"Tell Little John, I'll see him soon," I called over my shoulder, as I walked away toward the trading post.

CHAPTER XVII

I was halfway between Natoka's cabin and the trading post when the sound of dogs barking caused me to look back. In the pale moonlight, I saw a dog team, toboggan and two men nearing the cabin occupied by Vic LaRocque's wife. Assuming it was a couple trappers who would spend the night in a vacant cabin near the others, I went on to the post.

The heavy door at the main entrance was barred, so I went on around to the side of the building and entered the fur shed, by using my key for the padlock. Inside, I put some green birch wood in the fire in the heater, to keep a slow fire going as we had several beaver hides drying, while being stretched in hoop frames.

There were some bunks in the fur shed and I had told Walters I would sleep there that night. "Good deal, Ray," he had said, "we'll need all the pelts we can collect, for our trip south."

The sheet-iron heater stoked and the beaver pelts rearranged, I sat on a bench and had started taking off my moccasins, when someone knocked on the fur shed door.

"Ray, Ray, let me in, let me in!" There was a genuine fear in the outcry and I quickly unbarred the door. Marie LaRocque to whom I had said good night only a short time before, almost fell into my arms.

"Ike and Louie Goodswimmer! Ike is drunk — he won't leave our cabin!" she sobbed.

"Calm down — you're safe here. I'll call Walters," I said, leading the girl to a bench, then hastily barring the fur shed door.

"Ike will look for me — he is mean!"

"I know, I remember I had a run-in with him on the Swan Hills trail. But I doubt if he'll come near the trading post this time of night."

"May-be so — but what about morning? Louie says that my father, traveling with a fur trader and Little John's father, three dog teams in all, are camped at Iosegun Lakes tonight and due here in the tomorrow by noon. Louie says that Ike will try to take me away, before my father comes."

I sat beside Marie and held her hands. They were ice-cold. She had quit sobbing and no longer trembled. Rather, she suddenly seemed dazed and resigned.

"If only things had been different," she half whispered.

Hesitating to ask what she meant, I said, "Everything will be all right. I'll get Mac to bunk in here and you can sleep in his room. I've got to leave early tomorrow morning, to meet some trappers west of here at Walters' Tony River line cabin. You'll be safe here with Walters and Mac, until your father shows up."

I started for the inside door that led to the main quarters of the post. "Wait, Ray," Marie said. "This must be goodbye for us. Don't call Mac! I can stay here," and she pointed to a bunk bed above the one I had been about to occupy.

I remained silent, trying to think clearly. The attraction I felt for this fascinating girl was swiftly driving me to the point of no return. I was sure, then, that Marie, in spite of the wide barrier of race and religion between us, would be as helpless as I, were we to remain together and alone in the very room where we had so strangely met, only weeks before.

"Are you sure, Marie?" I managed.

"Very sure, Ray. I will just have one more confession to make when I join the Sisters at Lac Ste. Anne."

Impulsively, I turned to lock the door that led to the living quarters, just as it was opened and Walters came in to the fur shed. I started to speak, but he cut in, "It's all right, Ray. Little John slipped away from Ike and says that dirty son-of-a-bitch is trying to get hold of a gun. But Louie Goodswimmer has their two rifles hidden. Marie can stay with us tonight. Her father is sure to be here by noon tomorrow. You two had better say good-bye. I'll send Mac in and Marie can have his room."

Walters left and the French-Indian girl and I were alone briefly. All the wild emotion that had welled in me, was gone. Nothing but an indescribable sense of compassion and futility remained. I held her briefly in my arms and kissed her trembling lips.

"Good-bye, Ray," she whispered, as Mac appeared, adding those enigmatic words, for the second and last time, "If only things had been different."

I never saw Marie LaRocque again. Leaving for the rendezvous with trappers at the upper Tony River cabin, early the next morning, I had hoped to get back to Mile 90 the same day and that Marie's father would stay over night at the post. But one of the trappers didn't arrive with a fine catch of marten furs, until late in the evening, which forced me to lay over at the trapline cabin.

When I did return to Mile 90, the three dog teams had left several hours before. For a few wild moments, I thought of following them. Half hysterically, I confessed as much to Walters.

"Don't blame you, Ray," the Mile 90 trader commented. "There was a time when I thought you and that girl would make a fine team. But something Marie's father said, really riled me."

"That was?"

"Louis LaRocque at first believed some of the wild stories Ike had told, about you and Marie. He called you a damned Englishman and swore he'd get even with you — if you ever met. Of course, I told him you were an American and I think he decided that the Iosegun Lakes trapper stories were lies."

What might have happened, had I left Mile 90 for the "outside world," by way of Lac Ste. Anne, I was never to know. For, after further discussions, Walters agreed to a trip south over the Edson Trail, about five days travel with his team and bobsled. We would sell our furs in Edson and I could take the train to Edmonton, another day's journey, and contact the American consul.

In the meantime, the war news from Europe was very bad. Jack Spaner, a fur trader on his way south over the trail to Edson, had left some newspapers at Mile 90, only the week before.

The counter-offensive by the British and the French, had failed with heavy losses for our Allies. The U.S. involvement in the war had not reached the proportion where the American forces would have been of substantial benefit. One historian wrote, "Up until late 1917, U.S. aid to the Allies had remained more or less as a promissory note, except in the economic sphere."

Optimists, especially war correspondents, at that time, had hoped that the U.S. Treasury aid to the Allies, about 2½ million a month, would have had such an impact on Germany that the enemy would want an early settlement in the war. These optimists were, of course, wrong, as it was over a year later that Germany finally surrendered.

On our reading the various dispatches from Europe in the *Herald* and *Weekly Star*, we realized that newsmen had concluded in early November, 1917, that there was little chance Germany would accept an armistice or other attempt to end the war. The really bad news was that Russia had withdrawn their support of the Allies, leaving the eastern route practically at a stalemate and allowing Germany to withdraw large numbers of their troops from that area to serve on the western front, where the pressure was mounting.

Russia's part in the war effort actually commenced to slow down in March, 1917, when revolutionists forced the Czar to abdicate and, finally, after several attempts to rally the Russian people, in support of the Allies war effort, the Bolsheviks concluded an armistice with Germany in November, 1917.

It was now late December, 1917 and in fairness to Walters, I had to make a decision, one way or the other. If I remained in Canada, I would certainly be subject to being drafted in the Canadian Army or forced to register as an alien and subject to deportation if I did not join the Canadian war effort. I was now several months past 21 and, of course, although an American citizen, I had no special protection in Canada, a country with over three years involvement in World War I. So, early in the morning of December 21, 1917, Walters and I headed south over the winter trail, to Edson.

Walters drove Preacher and Parson, hitched to alight bobsled. Our sled was loaded with hay and oats for the horses, our own grub, blankets, etc., and several thousand dollars' worth of choice furs — beaver, lynx, fox and marten, principally.

CHAPTER XVIII

In all my years in the Canadian North, I have never met a more resourceful woodsman than Theodore (Ted) Walters. He was an expert hunter and trapper, combining the know-how of both Indian and white man when it came to knowledge of wild animals and game birds and the use of both native and modern skills and equipment in their capture.

There was a two-day-old "tracking snow" on top of a foot or so of packed snow, on the trail, as we reached a plateau about five miles south of Mile 90. The thermometer had registered 10 degrees above zero when we left the trading post — ideal weather for traveling with a bobsled with steel-shod runners. Parson had worked up a sweat on the climb out of the Tony River Valley. When we stopped to pick up a snared lynx in one of our sets, just off the trail, Walters put blankets on the horses. This was typical of the man, as on previous trips with him, I had noted that his first concern, when making camp, was for either dogs or horses.

We had observed very few Varying Hare (snowshoe rabbit) tracks, on the trail, so far.

"Snowshoes scarce," Walters commented, when I mentioned that only a very few lynx tracks had crossed the trail.

"Fox fare better than lynx when the rabbits die off," Walters remarked, adding, "They (foxes) are fine mousers."

"Yeah," I replied, "Lots of mice in the meadows, still." I checked a marten cubby house set, a hundred feet or so into the bordering woods. The trap had remained undisturbed, so I returned to the sled, just as Walters was removing the blankets from Parson and Preacher.

We drove on across the plateau and down into the Little Smoky River Valley. Here in the abandoned ferry-crossing cabins, we stopped for lunch and a break for the horses. Remembering my harrowing experience with the parole violator (Mr. Feelings — alias Jim Brown), I was glad that Walters was there, too.

"Sure a lot of ghosts around," I said, pointing to the bench where the derelict had sat near the stove and explaining in detail the actions of the pseudo "Jim Brown."

"This old trail has taken a heavy toll — men, horses, cattle and gear — may be a lot more than you or I, Ray, know about.'

We reminisced, wondering about Purcy, the original squatter and ferry boat operator at the Little Smoky River Crossing; about Bert Peterson, the trapper who found the charred bones of a man around a campfire on Peterson's trapline. And, last, we talked about Tom and Gertie Murphy, who had operated the cable ferry, the summer of 1917, moving to Edson in late September, where Tom had landed a job as foreman of a railroad "paint crew."

It was another eight miles to my Jackfish Lake cabin and on reaching it, we called it a day. There was a makeshift shelter for the horses back of the cabin and only a short distance to the lake, where we cut a hole in the ice so that Parson and Preacher could have their fill of good, clean water.

"Look, Ray. Lots of jackfish (Northern Pike) and bony mullet, but no whitefish, like at Buck Lake."

I was to recall, many times in later years, my conversations with the Mile 90 trader and others, comparing actual experiences and personal observations, with those of college trained "experts" in ecology (a term never heard of in my youth), conservation, environment, etc. Their knowledge was invaluable.

On our second day, we continued on south across a wide plateau to the Baptiste (Berland) River Valley. Here at the old river crossing, were the log cabins originally owned by "Old John" Anderson and for two seasons occupied by J. C. "Cliff" Knowles and myself. We had abandoned operation of the trading post and cable ferry, the previous fall, shortly before I joined Walters at Mile 90.

The river was frozen over and we drove across without incident.

The abandoned wagon road made a crescent-shaped loop across a height of land between the Baptiste and Athabasca rivers.

"Another dream shot," I told Walters, explaining how Knowles and I had thought of fencing the valleys and high land separating the two rivers, as the start of a horse ranch.

"Could have been a good deal, Ray. Still a good market for horses further north."

Walters was referring to the need for more horses, in the Peace River country, now that settlers were coming in by the thousands.

There still was an hour of daylight left when we reached the break in the hills bordering the Athabasca River valley. We were due for a real shock! In the distance below, we could see a dark ribbon of open water separating the ice that extended from opposite banks. The open channel wasn't wide, but there was no possible means of getting the horses across.

Gregg Rapelje, to whom we had sold our Athabasca crossing interests, had moved from the Baptiste River and had built a new log home, during the summer and fall of 1917. There was a flat-bottom skiff on the south side shore ice of the river, apparently used by Rapelje in crossing back and forth to reach hay stacks where he was feeding a small band of horses.

I fired my rifle once, waited a few moments and fired the weapon twice, in rapid succession. This was a standard "distress" signal used in the north. A disturbing silence prevailed for several minutes. "Rapelje may be out feeding stock on that side of the river," I suggested.

"Could be. But, he should have a rifle and for sure he'd hear our shots. We'll wait a little longer and try again," my partner replied.

I was about to say that Gregg Rapelje, for some unknown reason, seldom carried a rifle and that I had never known him to kill a deer, moose, or bear. But, just as I turned toward Walters, he exclaimed, "There he is!"

Sure enough, the pioneer rancher was on his way down to the ferry boat landing and was soon out on the ice, where his skiff was anchored.

Walters and I hurried out on the north shore ice and discussed the situation with Rapelje. The Athabasca rancher told us that he had been crossing the stream, with his small boat and that the open channel was narrowing slowly. "I'd guess it will take another week," he said.

Walters then asked Rapelje if he had horses, on the south side of the river, that we could borrow. The answer was in the negative, all of the rancher's horses were on the north side, where there was still some grazing on the hillsides and where Rapelje had mowed and stacked the bulk of his winter feed, consisting of wild peavine and vetch.

It was getting dark, but luckily a waning moon gave us enough light to follow the only course open to us, other than to turn back to Walters' trading post at Mile 90.

Back in a grove of spruce, a few rods from the north shore landing, was an abandoned log stable. We left Parson and Preacher there, with hay and oats for the night, and then proceeded to move our outfit across the open channel.

First, we separated the bobsled runners and light boards that made up the body of the sled, and ferried them across in the skiff. Next, our blankets, camping outfit, etc., then our bundles of fur were moved to the south shore.

It was cold, miserable work, but I don't recall any really unpleasant memories of that ferrying operation. To survive in the North Country, a man had to face and overcome obstacles, that later seemed unsurmountable.

The old Jim Hindmarsh cabin, a short distance from Rapelje's new log house, was unoccupied, so Walters and I, after a wonderful feed in the Rapelje home, spread several beaver hides on the Hindmarsh cabin floor and enjoyed a well-earned rest.

Further proof of Walters' woodcraft, came the next morning. We followed the trail, alongside the river and downstream, to a point where the Athabasca widened.

"The current is slow about a mile below the old cable ferry," Walters had explained. "Could be the river's frozen over."

My partner's speculation proved correct. But on examining the ice, Walters shook his head and, much to my relief, said it was too risky to attempt leading his horses across the newly formed ice "bridge."

"Maybe a few more days?" I quizzed.

"We haven't got a few days to spare, Ray. Heavy snows may block the 35-mile pass any day. We've got to get into Edson and back! I've got an idea — let's try it."

Walters' plan was simple. We cut a number of small spruce and pine trees and tossed them into the open channel of the river, just above the spot where ice had formed from shore to shore. Sure enough, this action, through the slowing of the current, allowed the ice below (in the bridged area) to freeze and increase in thickness much faster.

"Come morning, we'll see!" Walters said.

We spent a most enjoyable evening at Rapelje's. Mamie, Gregg's wife, was a marvelous cook, preparing tasty dishes from the most ordinary food ingredients, along with "extras" prepared with her own recipes, from blueberries, cranberries, strawberries and other wild fruits.

It was cold the night of December 22, 1917, for which we were thankful. Rapelje's thermometer registered about 15 degrees below zero. The next morning, on inspecting the proposed river crossing downstream from Rapelje's, Walters was convinced we could safely lead his horses across the ice.

Today, many years later, I can easily work myself into a sort of shock, by merely recalling that hazardous part of our mid-winter journey, south on the abandoned Edson-Peace River Trail.

Rapelje ferried us across in his skiff. Then, we led Parson and Preacher down the valley on the north side of the river, to the point where the crossing on the ice was to be attempted. Walters' horses were "sharp shod" with calks on the horseshoes that might crack the ice and cause a tragic disaster. But my partner had prepared for this, by tying grain sacks onto his horses' hooves.

Walters went across first, leading Parson. I followed with Preacher. The new ice was crystal clear and I remember the chill that ran up and down my spine, as I looked into the depths of that ice-cold water. We carried long poles, but I doubt if either man or beast could have survived, had we broken through that ice bridge. But, no ice gave way and a short time later, we reached Rapelje's, much to their relief.

Sarah, Gregg Rapelje's 70-year-old sister, blind since a young girl, had been crying. She was a very special friend of mine and I was humbled when she said, "I was scared, Ray, but I prayed for you!"

CHAPTER XIX

Walters and I left Rapelje's the morning of December 24th and, shortly afternoon, had reached Beaver Creek and the start of the long trail to the plateau bordering Breakneck Pass (also known as 35-Mile Summit).

Breakneck Hill proved quite passable as the old wagon road was not yet blocked by snow drifts. On the high plateau, nearing the summit, we had trouble. There was about two feet of hard-packed snow underneath a fresh blanket of the white stuff and our horses frequently broke through the hard crust. At times, it seemed we would never make it through. We stopped once to let Parson and Preacher rest and eat a few handfuls of oats. Their stamina was truly remarkable.

On reaching the old 35-Mile stopping place, we ran into good luck. A party of three men, judging by the tracks, had camped there recently and apparently, moose hunters, had broken a trail with a team and bobsled, from the south. This was indeed, a break for us. We watered the horses at a spring just above the cabins and then decided to try for 27-Mile, eight miles further on.

"Joe Kerr will put us up for the night," Walters remarked.

But 27-Mile was deserted and only a battered sheet-iron heater had been left by the last occupant. We learned later that Joe Kerr (an immigrant from Ireland), his wife and several small children, had moved to Edson, where Joe was lucky as he got a job as night fireman for the boilers in the railroad roundhouse.

Walters stabled his horses in a log barn and, when he returned to the cabin we had decided to occupy, I could see he was worried, so I asked him why.

"Parson is lame — I think he twisted a hind leg. If he isn't better come morning, I may have to hike into 10-Mile and borrow a horse from Carl Olson."

I, of course, expressed my concern, offering to hike on down the trail that night. "It's only 17 miles," I suggested.

"Let's wait 'til morning, Ray. I'll heat some water and make a hot pack — that Parson is tough as they come!"

Walters "doctored" his faithful equine and when we hitched up the team the next morning, Parson seemed much improved. But my companion, taking no chances, tied Preacher's single tree back to the sled, so that Parson had scarcely any load to pull. Even with this precaution, Parson became noticeably more lame, as we traveled south. We reached Carl Olson's homestead at 10-Mile with very little daylight remaining.

Olson, an irrepressible bachelor, wanted us to stay overnight at 10-Mile, but after making a deal for the loan of a horse, to replace Parson, we headed on south toward Edson. It was almost midnight of Christmas Day, when we finished caring for the team and unloading our gear and fur, at Alexander's Dray and Livery.

For the past several days, in spite of the hardships experienced on the trip from Mile 90, I had been thinking more and more about the few friends I had made in Edson. Then, too, there was my ex-partner, Cliff Knowles, his father and family, all of whom had moved into Edson. But, most important to me was whether Ruby Millar and her mother had returned from Edmonton. Casually, I asked the liveryman about both the Knowles and the Millars.

Alexander showed me where my ex-partner and his folks lived and I already had visited Ruby in the Millar home the previous summer.

"If I don't show up, I'll be staying at the Knowles' place," I told Walters.

"Sure, Ray — see you in the morning."

But the Knowles' home was dark, which was really no surprise, as it was midnight.

I started back to Alexander's, then suddenly decided on a detour of a few blocks. I knew that George, Ruby Millar's brother, worked on the railroad and might still not have retired. Sure enough, there was light in the front room of the Millar home. I stopped on the porch and knocked on the door. A muffled scream sounded and two pajama-clad figures made pictures on the window shades and someone called out, "Go around to the side door — George will let you in!"

I almost turned away. "These people will think you're nuts," I told myself.

But, I went to the side door and, sure enough, George was still up, drinking coffee and eating candy and popcorn. I joined young Millar and he called Ruby. She visited briefly and then returned to join a friend, Dagmar Beaupre.

It was two o'clock when George and I got through reminiscing over trail adventures and then, at his insistence, I spent the rest of the night on a couch, in the living room of the Millar home. Mixed emotions kept me from sleeping. I thought that Ruby might have shown a little more interest in my arrival, even at that late hour.

And the next day, after concluding some business with Walters and returning to visit the Millars, I wondered why Ruby had not asked her friend to join her, when she came into the room where George and I were chatting.

Dagmar Beaupre, part Cree Indian, was a beautiful girl. She was darker than Marie LaRocque, but their actions, carriage and general appearance, were quite similar. I learned shortly that she was George's "girl."

There was no mail from my hometown, except a brief note from Isabel, my high school sweetheart, reiterating her "polite" position, regarding marriage. She was going on a trip to Pennsylvania and would maybe stay in or near her childhood home. Isabel thought we were foolish to think of marrying until we were at least 27!

I made arrangements to room and board with the Knowles family, for the time being. It was urgent that I learn as soon as possible, just where I stood in regard to the war in Europe.

I settled my affairs with Walters and he left, northbound over the trail back to Mile 90. We parted regretfully, but the best of friends.

"Good luck with that Millar girl," he yelled, waving goodbye.

CHAPTER XX

Edson, with a population of approximately 1,200, founded in 1911, was a divisional point on the Grand Trunk Pacific Railway. It boasted a 10-stall roundhouse and a machine shop for servicing the coal-burning locomotives that hauled the long freight trains and passenger cars, passing through Edson. There was a railroad "yard" with many separate tracks, for making up the freight trains and, a car repair shop near the roundhouse. About 15 miles west of Edson, a branch line extended into fantastically productive coal mines. Appropriately, this line was called "The Coal Branch." Administrative offices for the Grand Trunk Pacific Railway were in the upper floor of the Edson Depot, the lower floor being reserved for a cafe or "beanery," the railway express agent's office and "waiting" room.

I mention these facts for the simple reason that, if I were to stay in Edson for more than a few weeks, I would have to find a job and, except for a few clerical jobs in the local stores, the only employment was on the railroad. Two hotels were run by owner-families and a Japanese and Chinese restaurant, employed no whites.

Frank Knowles, Cliff's father, had been keeping up with the war news and in our first serious discussion on the subject, said that he thought his son was not subject to a Canadian Army draft, as long as he kept his job as fireman on the Grand Trunk Pacific.

"They're real short on engine crews," he said, adding, "I'm sure you could get a job like Cliff's."

Cliff Knowles, my recent partner, while we were operating the Athabasca and Baptiste River cable ferries, confirmed his father's conclusions and suggested, "You might talk to Bill Hare — he's janitor for the Division Master Mechanic, down at the roundhouse. Bill sure knows what's going on down there!"

W. R. "Bill' Hare had run the Mile 90 Post on the trail for a few seasons and I knew him and his wife, Ritia, very well.

The Hares were living in the Immigration Hall, not far from the Millar's and I was glad to renew my acquaintance with them. After visiting for some time, recalling Edson Trail experiences, etc., I asked Bill Hare whether he thought there was an opening for more locomotive firemen.

"I'll ask Mahan (his boss), but I'm sure they are short of help in all departments. The war, you know," Bill answered.

Talk about indecision! I had bought some clothes and, after checking with the ticket agent, saw that I had enough cash to support me for a couple weeks and still have the price of the railway fare to my home in central Washington State. My uncertain state of mind, however, was really centered in my confused feelings toward Ruby Millar. One evening, when Cliff was in from a "run" on the Coal Branch, I told him that I was "falling" for Ruby.

"You don't want to marry her?" he responded.

"Well, hardly, since I don't think she feels the way I do. Anyway, we would be taking a chance marrying — with the war like it is. So, why do you ask?"

Cliff shrugged his shoulders, then suddenly blurted, "I don't think Ruby Millar is the girl for you!"

I was to recall Cliff's words a few days later when, unknown to me, he had arranged a date for me with one of Ruby's girl friends, Rhoda Sutherland, to go on a sleigh ride with him and a second girl. I could hardly believe my eyes when the other girl proved to be Ruby Millar!

Ritia Hare, a good friend to both Cliff and me, couldn't resist asking about the sleigh ride, the episode having become known to our immediate friends, overnight.

"Cliff is just trying to get my goat," I told Mrs. Hare.

"Maybe so, Ray, but that's a poor way for a friend to act. Knowles has been hanging around both the Millar and Ruby's sister's home, ever since he moved in from the Athabasca. Bill says Cliff is sweet on either or both of those gals! It's none of our business, but Bill and I think you should watch your step."

Ritia Hare's words puzzled and disturbed me. Her warning did serve a useful purpose, as it caused me to question my own motives where Ruby was concerned. There was only one way I could tell, for sure, whether I really loved that slim, brown-eyed gal, or that I simply was starving for a woman's love. So, I frequented the Millar home, day after day, as soon as Ruby got home from her job at a local store. Twice, Ruby's mother "ordered" me to stay in George's room, because it was so late.

Then, one night, when Ruby and I were alone, I said, "Remember last summer, when I told you I loved you, just as George came up to the porch, with my team and rig?"

"Of course, I remember," Ruby quietly replied.

"Well — I meant what I said then and I still do!"

Impulsively, I raised up from a chair in which I had been sitting and drew Ruby into my arms. She neither resisted nor "melted" into my embrace and her lips were quite unresponsive when I kissed her. Shortly after, I left, more confused than ever, I "cussed" myself, wondering, maybe Ruby was in love with my ex-partner.

An old saying: "Faint heart never won fair lady," came to mind, but instead of pressing my attentions on Ruby, I chose a course in the opposite direction and stayed away from the Millar home for a few days. Then, I met George on the street and followed him into the Jellis General Store, where Ruby worked. She was busy with a customer, so George introduced me to Beatty Harris, William Jellis' sister-in-law. Jellis was often out, leaving the management to Miss Harris, assisted by Ruby. The only other help was a part-time, 14-year-old delivery boy.

In my first visit to the Jellis store, I learned for certain that Ruby Millar was a young human dynamo. Beatty Harris, her boss, was slightly crippled in one foot and Ruby seemed literally to be all over the place.

I had barely spoken to Ruby during the several minutes I was waiting for George and was about to leave, when a customer asked about oranges.

"Another crate's in the storage," Miss Harris answered Ruby's questioning, adding, "Maybe George will bring one up."

But, Ruby's brother was in a hurry, on his way to check the "spare board" or list of switchmen posted at the Railway Depot.

"Give 'em a hand, Ray — maybe you can get on as delivery boy," he chuckled, waving good-bye.

Naturally, I was glad to help. Ruby led the way to a trap-door at the back and I followed her down a steep stairs into the basement storage where Jellis kept vegetables that might otherwise have frozen when the temperature dropped to 40 degrees below zero, as it was well-nigh impossible to keep the main store warm, with only two coal-burning stoves. I packed what produce they needed, up the stairs.

"This is pretty rough work, Ruby," I said rather lamely. 'Can't you get a man to help?"

"Jellis is trying to — but the war has taken our boys and the Railroad is short-handed. I heard that you may tackle a fireman's job, like Cliff did."

"I might, Ruby — if I stay in Canada. Anyway, I'll be glad to help out here, for a few days."

"Beatty would appreciate that," Ruby said, "and if you'd like a ride on our delivery sled, a horse is in a stable in back of the store."

It appeared that their delivery boy, who also had a job as a "call boy" for the Grand Trunk Pacific, couldn't help at the store that particular evening, so Ruby had to take over.

I was a little miffed at Ruby's "Beatty would like that," instead of at least thinking of me, on her own account. But, I found "Jeff," a skittish pony in the stable, harnessed and hitched him to the delivery sled and loaded the orders Beatty and Ruby had made up during the day.

"My brother, Will, owned a hardware in 1911, when we arrived in Edson," Ruby remarked, adding, as we drove north to the outskirts of the pioneer town. "I had dogs and a toboggan for hauling kerosene to Will's customers then. It was fun — I like driving dogs — what did you do with yours? Cliff says you two had some good dogs up on the Athabasca."

Here was a subject we could discuss without any suggestions or implications. "I left my dogs in good hands, at Mile 90 and if this crazy war ends within a year or so, I may go back north. Walters will keep my two best dogs, both lead dogs, for me."

So, we stuck to dog talk on that first trip delivering orders to outlying areas of the town. Then, we stabled Jeff and I walked home with Ruby. She didn't invite me in, but did melt a little with, "Thanks for the help and we could sure use more for the next few days. Mr. Jellis is due back soon!"

Cliff Knowles kidded me when he learned about my helping at the Jellis store. Cliff, a boyhood chum, fishing, hunting and trapping partner, could be sarcastic and inferred that I was "hanging around the store and at the Millar home — just to pass away the time." But that didn't stop me. I made a few deliveries alone and one evening, on returning to the store, I said to Ruby, "That Jeff isn't worked enough — how about a sleigh ride tonight?"

She seemed to hesitate, as if wrestling with a real problem.

"Afraid of me?" I blurted.

"No — should I be?"

I laughed, "Answering a question, with another question?"

It was Ruby's turn to laugh. "We'll drive Jeff home. Fan (her sister living next door) has a cutter sleigh. We can drive a couple of miles out the north trail — some friends I'd like you to meet!"

So, Ruby and I were again on an open, friendly relationship. It was cold, on those few sleigh rides. But, by this time, my emotions had developed to the stage where I simply had to know how Ruby felt about me. Wooing a girl in below-zero temperature, on a sleigh ride, doesn't rate as an ideal situation,

Ruby on horseback, Edson

especially with both boy and girl bundled in heavy mackinaw and woolen clothing. But Dan Cupid is a persistent little cuss.

On one ride in the cutter, Jeff had one of his worst spells of being plain ornery. Ruby said afterwards that she thought Jeff saw or smelled a moose in the woods bordering the trail. Whatever his excuse, Jeff clamped down on the bridle bit, and took off for the Jellis stable. I managed to slow the rascal with a hard, steady pull on the reins, down to a fast trot, as we started down the main street, back in town. But, when I attempted to turn off on a cross street, to leave Ruby at her home, Jeff clamped down on the bit again.

We had passed the turn-off to the Millar home, so I yanked hard on the one rein, hoping to swing Jeff at the next crossing. The rein broke and Jeff veered sharply. The cutter upset and we both were thrown out into an open, ice-covered drainage ditch.

The spill knocked the breath out of us. "You okay?" I gasped, instinctively reaching for the robe-wrapped girl just below me.

"I'm fine," Ruby answered. "You hurt?"

A minute or so later, realizing that neither had suffered from the spill, we started laughing and kept it up until I said good-night to Ruby at her home.

"I told you I'd make you fall for me," I teased.

The delivery pony had broken free of the slightly damaged cutter and I found Jeff at the gate to the small corral back of the Jellis store.

The next day, I borrowed a horse and hauled the damaged cutter to the local blacksmith shop. The shafts and one runner were bent, but Fairfield, the smitty, was a master at repairing wagons, sleds and farm machinery.

The sleigh, or "cutter," belonged to Ruby's sister, Fan (Mrs. J. J. Hodgkinson), whose home was near their mother's, Mrs. Fanny Millar. When returning the sleigh, Mrs. Hodgkinson invited me in to have a cup of tea. I hadn't been in her house more than a few minutes until I knew there was more than a "cup of tea" on her mind. She was, in fact, wondering about my intentions toward her sister. She didn't ask me outright, but her questioning was direct.

"Your partner says you are engaged to a high school girl in your home town. I suppose you'll be heading south soon?"

I thought carefully, before replying. I could have shown Fan my last letter from Isabel, in which she had inferred that we shouldn't even think of marrying, for another five years. I could also have told Fan that Isabel and I had never been engaged and that our mutual friends and a few close relatives, just "figured" that we "would get hitched."

Instead, I told Fan that I cared for Ruby, but that my plans were very uncertain on account of the war. "I don't feel free to ask any girl to marry me," I said defensively.

Fan seemed more or less satisfied with my statement, for, evidently on the spur of the moment, she read portions of a letter just received from her sister-in-law living in Edmonton.

"Will (Fan's and Ruby's brother and a sales representative for an Edmonton firm) says he enjoyed visiting Edson. He said that Ruby has a crush on one, or both, of two American boys. Your mother seems to like both — so we were wondering . . ."

I left the Hodgkinson home, thanking Fan for the loan of the sleigh and for her frank statement of concern for her sister. The letter she had read, from her sister-in-law, also had its effect. I realized, too, that Ruby's mother was naturally wondering about me and her daughter.

Ruby and I went to a few dances. She was much better than I at the most popular form of entertainment in the frontier towns and I quickly discovered that several men liked to dance with her. She was on a "first-name" basis with at least half of the total attendance.

Having Ruby in my arms, even on a public dance floor, had its effect on my emotions. Maybe, I held her too close one evening, for on reaching the gate to the Millar yard, she closed it before I could enter and said good-night.

The very next day, I called on Frank Laycock, a local attorney with whom I had some business formerly in his capacity as the district coroner. In this early meeting, Laycock had asked me to sign a statement, concerning the demise and burial of a Major Thompson (no relative), in the Baptiste River country. Major Thompson, an uncle of Mamie Rapelje's, was a veteran (Confederate Army) of the Civil War. Then in his 80's, he had arrived with the Rapeljes and was living with them in the fall of 1916. The Rapelje ranch was on our already established trapline, so Knowles and I often stopped there. We were hauling in supplies over the Edson Trail, by dog team and on one trip, Gregg Rapelje asked us to bring back some cough medicine for the old veteran.

I'll never forget his last words, when I stopped at the Rapelje cabin. Major Thompson looked very frail, but he managed a smile when I quipped, "You'll be fine come spring — there's some good looking Cree gals further north — Cliff and I will take you with us to Mile 90."

"The spirit is willing, but the flesh is weak," he said, as I held his hand.

Major Thompson never saw that next spring; when Knowles and I returned from Edson, about 120 miles the round trip, we learned that the old soldier had passed on. Gregg Rapelje had to thaw the ground with a log fire, before he could dig a grave. The boards from a wagon box made a rough casket. It was only another lonely grave in the Canadian wilds, but Laycock, the coroner, was glad to have my statement in connection with my knowledge of the sad affair.

Now, two years later, I was anxious to hear what Laycock had learned on his late trip to Edmonton, as I had asked him to contact the U.S. Consul there.

"You've got until June 1st," he informed me. "I advise you to renew your registration with the Consul and, above everything, apply for a passport before that date, if you intend leaving Canada!"

So, that was that!

It was the middle of January. I could try for a job at the roundhouse, work for a couple of months and then decide on future plans.

To become a locomotive fireman, one had first to serve an "apprenticeship as a watchman," under the supervision of a hostler. In this process, the engineer would bring his locomotive in from the main line, on a side track, to the roundhouse. Here, the hostler would take over and "spot" the locomotive on another side track, where the watchmen (usually working in a pair) would dump the ashes from the engine and clean the fire box.

The hostler would then drive onto a turntable, spotted or lined up by one of the watchmen. With the weight of the locomotive centered on the turntable, a platform, supporting a short track for the locomotive, could be moved or rotated in a circle. The turntable was activated by a compressed air pump, so that the turntable track would line up with another track leading into the selected roundhouse stall. Inside, the locomotive straddled a concrete pit, from which the shop men could inspect, and/or make repairs.

When the locomotive was ordered out, for a train being made up in the switch yard, the watchmen had to make a new fire in the fire box and with the hostler's advice, build up the steam pressure to the desired point. Then, the hostler would drive the locomotive out across the turntable, to a side track, where the engineer would take over. It was a cold, miserable job in below-zero weather, 12 hours a day, seven days a week, from 7 A.M. to 7 P.M. and the pay — 25 cents an hour!

CHAPTER XXI

From Knowles' home, where I had roomed and boarded, it was about a mile to the railway roundhouse. In order to report in at 7 A.M., I had to arise at 5 A.M., dress, eat breakfast, make up a lunch, and allow time for the walk. In the evening I never reached my temporary home until at least 7:30 P.M. That left very little time for courting!

It was especially bad on dance nights, usually once a week, as I seemed to barely get to sleep before the alarm went off. I think Ruby's mother felt sorry for me, as she frequently told me on the nights Ruby and I had been to a dance or card party, to stay overnight with George.

After I had been a watchman for several weeks, I was promoted and became fireman on the switch yard engine. The engineer was Fred Haas, a long-time friend of the Millar's. After we had worked together for a few days, Fred stated, "I'll help you get a better job on the Coal Branch run, if you're sure you want to stick to the railroad."

There was an implied question in the engineer's statement, so I told him something of my problems. He surprised me by saying bluntly, "I think you should marry Ruby and let the chips fall afterward!"

I laughed a little, but this was no laughing matter. Maybe my new friend had the right idea and I told him so.

On the way to Ruby's house after work that day, I suddenly decided that I would have a show-down with Ruby. The only way to decide whether I was to remain in Canada was to determine just how she really felt.

Fate has a way of ruling our lives. Ruby's mother was next door at her daughter's house, George was out on a railroad "run," so Ruby and I were alone. It didn't take long for me to have her in my arms and my pent-up emotions took over. She did not resist when I kissed her passionately and said, "I've got to know — do you love me?"

"Of course," she whispered, "I wouldn't let you act this way if I didn't love you."

"You know — you must know that I love you and want you for my wife!"

She stiffened a little and for a moment I thought she was going to resist my further advances, "What about Isabel?"

"What about Eddie Couzens?" I retorted. "Your sister told me he gave you an engagement ring!"

"That was months ago. I didn't want the ring and gave it to Eddie's brother. Now, what about Isabel?" Ruby insisted.

I told Ruby that Isabel and I had decided to call it quits, and so in a few minutes a mutual misunderstanding was cleared up and Dan Cupid had a firm grip on the reins that controlled Ruby's and my immediate future. I was literally dancing on air on leaving Ruby that night. The next day I ordered a diamond from a mail order house in Toronto.

We were married in a simple ceremony at Ruby's sister's home on May 26, 1918. A couple of days later we left for my home town in the State of Washington.

But first, our "honeymoon" was a short journey to Edmonton and return. It was a wonderful and also a never-to-be-forgotten experience. For when Ruby and I arrived at the Edson depot, we discovered that Cliff Knowles, our

Raymond and Ruby
May 26, 1918

"best man" at the wedding, had already gotten a railroad pass to Edmonton and was to be an uninvited guest on our honeymoon!

On the train Cliff made it a point to sit beside Ruby at any opportunity. Whether he was trying deliberately to make me jealous, I never decided, but at one point Cliff had sat beside Ruby until the conductor asked a mutual friend, "Which man is she married to?" I turned on my wife and snapped, "This is no good — *if* you love Cliff more than me, I want to know now!"

Ruby denied ever having any romantic feelings for my ex-partner and boyhood chum, but it was a long time before I could forget that unhappy train ride.

In Edmonton, Ruby and I registered at the Royal George Hotel, as of course Cliff did, too. Then Ruby had a bright idea and called a friend, Isabel Whitlaw, and introduced Cliff. The four of us had a good day exploring the outskirts of Alberta's capital in a Model T. Ford. The outing almost ended in a disaster, when Cliff, driving, rear-ended, of all things, a horse-drawn milk wagon. Fortunately no damage was done and the irate milkman let us off, after threatening to call the police.

I recall that Isabel Whitlaw, a sister of Ruby's brother Will's wife, sensing the conflict between Cliff and me, deliberately flirted with my friend. Anyway the short trip to Edmonton ended with Cliff returning to his job on the railroad, while Ruby and I prepared to leave Canada. We left two days later.

A romanticist, I wanted to show Ruby around Calgary, where we had to change trains on the way south. The Palliser Hotel, owned and operated by the Canadian Pacific Railway, was an imposing structure and I suggested that we stop there overnight.

I told Ruby about my first stay in Calgary with a cousin, Irl Perkins, on my initial expedition to the Canadian Northwest a few years earlier. We had worked about a month on farms and once for a telephone line contractor, digging holes for the long cedar posts.

"We dug spuds for one farmer but he only had eight dollars cash to spare, so that job didn't last."

"I suppose the war has hit the farmers hard — low prices and scarce labor," my wife said.

I mentioned, too, that Irl and I rented a good, clean room in the Dominion Hotel for a dollar a night. So the Palliser Hotel episode went down in our memory of our honeymoon. For a brief period I tried to imagine myself as a successful fur trade tycoon on his honeymoon in some exotic place, with no financial problems and all the time in the world.

We wandered around the streets for an hour or so, but neither of us enjoyed what we saw. A brisk wind was blowing, picking up sand particles from along the shores of Bow River which ran through the heart of the city. I sensed too, that Ruby was already homesick and I felt guilty at taking her from her home and into a strange, new world. Neither of us knew anyone in Calgary.

We returned to the hotel. Somehow, my search for romance in such surroundings had taken wing. I looked around the beautifully furnished room. It was the same — only different now. Even the bed, where I had made love to my bride only an hour ago, now seemed pompous and uninviting.

"Honey, there's a train leaving for Spokane in about an hour — let's take it!"

"I can be ready in fifteen minutes," Ruby replied, unquestionably happy with my suggestion.

A branch line of the Canadian Pacific Railway connected with the Spokane International and during the night we crossed the Canadian-U.S. Border and a couple hours later, reached Spokane, Washington, in my home State.

"Well, Ruby Thompson," I quipped, "You're an American in your new home country now!"

"I've been in the U.S. before," my wife replied, rather indifferently it seemed to me. We had stepped off the train, someone called my name and my younger sister, Blanche, greeted us.

Curiously, in one letter to my sister, I had mentioned a "Scotch-Canadian" girl whom I was courting. For some odd reason, Blanche thought I was about to marry a half-breed, the "Canadian" heritage of the girl, my sister assumed to be that of an Indian!

Blanche later confessed that she was surprised that my wife, though often in Scotland with relatives, was in fact "full-blooded" English, born near Liverpool, England.

Shortly after our arrival in Spokane, we registered at a hotel near the railroad, on which we were to continue on west, to my boyhood home in Almira.

It was while eating lunch that Blanche exploded a bombshell, when she quizzed, "And how do you plan on supporting a wife?"

For a moment, I was unable to think of an answer, but noting Ruby's puzzled look, I snapped, "Running the ranch, of course — unless Uncle Sam drafts me!"

"What ranch? If you're thinking of helping Al on the Del Rio property that mother bought, forget it. Al is head over heels in debt now and is running Roy Rose's ranch in Strahl Canyon. The land that Mama bought may produce a fair crop this fall, but you and Ruby will have to eat — in the meantime!"

I showed Blanche my last letter from our mother. It was full of optimism and hope, with the underlying faith that, if I would return home with my new bride, everything would be okay.

"Poor Mama," Blanche sighed, "She thought it was a good idea — but, Ray, she mortgaged our home to buy that land for our brother-in-law!"

Later, I told Ruby as much as I knew about my mother's purchase of some marginal land, a few miles from a ranch managed by my brother-in-law, Alfred Northrup (the "Al" Blanche had referred to in our conversations). With the U.S. at war in Europe, our farmers were urged to plant crops in every available space and our mother's venture, on the surface, appeared wise.

We took Blanche out to the nearest park and visited other familiar spots in Spokane. But Ruby, I was certain, wished she were back in Canada.

"Things can't be that bad. I can surely get work on a farm. I promise, Ruby, that I'll take you home just as soon as the war's over."

We had said farewell to my sister and were on board the passenger train, when Ruby exclaimed, "But what if you're drafted?"

"You can go back home, of course!"

So now we were embarked on a really uncertain course. Thinking back, I wonder that Ruby didn't insist on me buying a ticket on the Spokane International for her return to Canada, instead of my taking her further away from home.

CHAPTER XXII

It was early evening when we reached Almira, my hometown, about 80 miles west of Spokane. My mother met us and we walked to the house as it was only six blocks from the depot. The local liveryman who always met the train in case there was one or more traveling salesmen with sample cases to be hauled to the hotel, would have taken us and our luggage to mother's home for $1.00. But mother said she had asked a neighbor boy to pick up our one trunk in his homemade cart.

I was overjoyed to see Mama again and my sister, Mary Ely, who was in to spend the night from a farm just west of town, owned by her husband Jack Murbach's folks.

If Ruby cried that night, she never let me hear her. I knew she must have been shaken when informed that Mary Ely's husband, in spite of being a farmer and a married man, had been drafted and was still overseas. My mother tried her best to make Ruby feel at home, but the war news was so discouraging nothing else seemed worthy of discussion.

Alfred Northrup came to town the day following our arrival. He owned a Model T. Ford and drove me to the county seat, where I registered with the local draft board.

Back in Almira mother had news that, to me, sounded encouraging. The local Washington Central Railroad agent was looking for a man and wife to operate a wheat farm and stock ranch. The pay, $85.00 a month, plus any produce the place afforded — vegetables (in season), milk, eggs, and all the smoked hams (at a neighbor's smokehouse) that we could use.

"We could save enough to get back to Edson!" I said.

"I suppose we could," Ruby commented, but her eyes held a far-away look. Suddenly, realizing how difficult this must be for my wife, I decided to leave the next morning, for the nearest recruiting office (in Spokane) to see if I could enlist in the U.S. Marine Corps.

"The way I have it sized up," I told Ruby as soon as we were alone, "I'll be drafted shortly and I'll at least have a choice by enlisting!"

Ruby kept her silence for several moments and I felt like my world had come to an end. Having to face the distinct possibility of service in the armed forces of my country, did not in itself, make me feel downhearted. But Ruby's silence did. If she had only said, with some emotion, that she hated the thought of my leaving — I would have felt that life was still worthwhile.

When my wife finally said, "Whatever you decide is all right with me," I had regained my composure.

"I'll catch the eastbound train in the morning!"

I was due for another and dramatic surprise, when I reached the recruiting office for the U.S.M.C. in Spokane. After a short interview and a physical examination, the sergeant in command handed me a slip of paper with a date on it. "Your classification, according to your draft card, is to be reviewed after harvest, on November 15th. Come back and see us then — that is, if you still want to join the Marines!"

I guess you could have "knocked me down with a feather" at the sergeant's words. I wondered afterward, if that Marine had some crystal ball that told him World War I would be over by the date he had mentioned.

Raymond Thompson, Mother, sisters Ely, Blanche and Grace

The train ride back to Almira, was agonizingly slow. But, when I held Ruby in my arms and felt her tremble, as I told her about my trip, I knew everything was in order again. Fate, so cruel to many of our friends, during those awful war years, had somehow smiled down on us.

E. P. Wilcoxen, the rancher, had a Saxon automobile and he drove Ruby, my mother and me out to his Del Rio ranch. Mother wanted to see what might be expected in the way of crops, from her land and, to see that her son and his bride were "settled" in the ranch job.

"Don't be upset," I cautioned Ruby, "Mother thinks of me as still her little boy!"

To reach the Wilcoxen ranch, we had to cross a canyon, called the "Mouth" of Grand Coulee (near the site where Coulee Dam was to be constructed some 20 years later, although little did we dream of this then!). After crossing the canyon, a pioneer wagon road led up Wallace Canyon, on to a plateau, a thousand feet above the floor of Grand Coulee and approximately another 500 feet elevation, if measured from the Columbia River valley. About 12 miles northwest of the coulee crossing was the Del Rio post office and store and, another two miles to the west, was the Wilcoxen place.

This was in marginal wheat growing country, as it was too rocky. Ages before, when the land had been formed after a period of lava flows, the incredible force of receding ice had carved out the canyons and left huge formations of what we termed "haystack" rocks. There was one of these rocks just behind the house.

When Wilcoxen drove into his yard, Ruby exclaimed, "Look! That rock's as big as the house!"

"Hens lay eggs on top — one side slopes so they can scratch their way up," the rancher said.

I was lucky to have married a girl who knew a great deal about pioneering. Otherwise, she might have insisted on returning to Almira, with Wilcoxen and from there, on back to Canada. But Ruby, a few years before, had done most of the clearing on her mother's homestead, about two miles south of Edson. Uprooting willows, cutting down poplars and pulling the stumps out with a team of horses, had been one of the projects that Ruby, rather than her older brother had worked at.

Another incident that gave me a much-needed mental lift, had occurred on the drive from Almira, when Wilcoxen mentioned that we would have a fine saddle pony. "Good for rounding up the cattle on the range south of the farm." Ruby was one of the best horseback riders I had ever met and I was really elated when she answered our employer with, "Sounds great — I can do the roundup jobs."

When we entered our first home, I was thankful to note that Ruby helped mother set up a three-burner kerosene stove, get water from the well and dust off the scant furniture in the combined living room and kitchen — that comprised the lower floor of the 20 x 24 foot, unpainted, weather-beaten farm house.

Wilcoxen showed me the three-bottom gang plow, the harrows, harnesses, etc., and explained how he wanted me to operate.

"There's an 80 (acres) to plow first — then, you can tackle the 240 just east of the barn. You'll have to run the horses for pasture at night, as there's only enough hay for the noon feed! Call on Tindall, if you get stuck!"

So that was that! The Tindall ranch house was only a half mile to the west. I thanked Wilcoxen and promised that Ruby and I would do the best we could.

"I'll drive out in a week or so and see how you're making out. If your mother is down at Al Northrup's ranch, I'll see if she wants a ride back to Almira," the rancher said on leaving.

Mother had brought a small stock of supplies, including several loaves of bread. Ruby discovered where the hens laid their eggs, but when I had asked Wilcoxen about a milk cow, he answered offhand, "There's over 75 cows out in the south pasture — must be around half of them with calves!" We were to remember that comment!

The house was typical of squatter's and homesteader's prairie homes. There were no logs within hauling distance and rough lumber had to be brought in to the Del Rio country in heavy freight wagons. Most pioneer homes were rarely spacious. The downstairs, in addition to being both a kitchen and living room, had to provide space for a stairs, along one wall. The upstairs was one room and privacy could be had by hanging blankets on a wire stretched across the room. The floors were bare boards and the downstairs one showed signs of having been scrubbed hard, many times. One fairly good rocking chair, a table, some shelves, kitchen chairs, benches, etc., made up the furnishings downstairs. Upstairs there was an iron bedstead, with a sagging set of springs and a straw "tick" mattress.

"Sure some difference from the Palliser Hotel," I remembered adding, "Glad Mama brought that folding couch along!"

Ruby surprised me with, "Oh, it's not that bad. The mattress could stand some new straw — that's for sure!"

Although it was only mid-June, the temperature was nearing the century mark. It was sultry, too, both Ruby and I, coming from a country where it was always cool at night, suffered keenly.

We were never to forget that first night at the Wilcoxen ranch. Mother had insisted on sleeping downstairs on the cot. Upstairs, I opened the two windows, one at each end of the room, but the air had little movement and the heat promised to keep us from sleep. My mother had loaned us some bedding and the clean, fresh, white sheets looked inviting. But, then, I was so enamored of my wife, I scarcely thought of the time and place when she lay beside me. But, that first night, any romantic idea I may have had, like "initiating our new marriage bed," was rudely interrupted. Ruby, following me, sat on the edge of the bed and the tired, old frame collapsed!

"What will Mama think?" Ruby giggled.

"Oh boy!" I laughed. "This takes the cake! Wait 'til I see Wilcoxen — not even a decent bed — we'd better try the hay mow!"

I yelled down to my mother and told her what had happened. Then, we tore the old bedstead apart, decided it was beyond repair, spread the straw mattress on the floor and finally went to sleep.

Rising at 5 A.M., I saddled the pony and rode out to round up the horses I needed for the plow team. They were grazing along the county road right-of-way, fenced on both sides of the road and luckily they had ranged only a mile or so from the ranch house. By the time it took me to drive them into the corral and barn and harness them, an hour and a half had passed.

"We've had hotcakes, ham and eggs ready for over half an hour," Ruby complained. "And how much work can you expect from horses that have to feed all night?"

"That bothers me, too," Mother said. "Too bad Wilcoxen is short on hay!"

"I'll talk to Tindall," I answered. "The horses look in real good shape and, if I can use them on the plow for even six hours a day, we should make out okay."

That evening, I visited George Tindall and found him very concerned. "Wilcoxen is heavy in debt; I've sold him all the hay I can spare. But if I were you, Ray, I'd run the horses in the south pasture for a week or so. They'll be fenced at least. If you run them on the county road allowance, they'll keep moving farther away and you'll be riding after them more hours than on the plow." I told Wilcoxen what I thought — but here our neighbor hesitated, "He's a better railroad man than a rancher!"

Mother, rarely prone to giving advice in matters with which she was not familiar, remarked, "I have known the Tindalls for years — I think you should listen to George."

That was settled; we'd try the south pasture for the work horses. It was more convenient, and Ruby, after I had got bucked off the gang plow when it struck a rock, rounded up the horses for me and even tried to handle the six-horse team on the plow.

Ruby was really in her element! The second day we were at the Wilcoxen place, my wife rounded up two cows with calves, got them into the barn and tried to milk them. But, the cows wouldn't cooperate and, after being slammed against the manger, Ruby decided we would have to settle for canned milk, which we could get at the Del Rio store, in exchange for eggs.

For the entire month spent there, the only income we had was from the eggs traded at the store. Wilcoxen drove out and I asked him for a small advance.

He took out a notebook and read from it, "I paid $27.00 for the stove, which is more than you have coming. Sorry, but I'm short on cash, too!"

I was furious, but held my temper. We had thought the three-burner oil stove was a part of the ranch house kitchen. "It's a wonder he didn't charge us rent for that broken-down bed!" I stormed, when alone with Ruby.

Mother left Wilcoxen and insisted on loaning us a few dollars. "Try and stay with it for a month — Wilcoxen may come to his senses," she said, in parting.

Ruby never did master "the crazy thing" as she called the kerosene stove. There was an oven that sat on the burners, in which mother had managed to cook biscuits and corn bread, but Ruby couldn't seem to get the knack of it, so we made out with hot cakes and soda crackers from the Del Rio store.

As July neared, it became hotter still. The haystack rock next to the house was like a furnace. Ruby and I were both working 14 hours a day, but the plowing, especially in the 240-acre field, didn't go as well as I had hoped.

Then, we had new troubles with the cattle. A spring in the center of the pasture threatened to dry up and Ruby spent hours, day after day, keeping the water flowing. A heavily fenced stand of corn on a ranch bordering

Wilcoxen's, was a prime target for the hungry, thirsty cattle. One maverick, a big, rangey cow, was expert at breaking down, or breaking through the strongest fences we could build with materials at hand. At Tindall's suggestion and with the help of his son, who was good with both horse and rope, we got that ornery critter down and wired her neck with a device that would prevent her from working her way between strands of barbed wire.

That made the red-eyed maverick plenty mad. I had opened the Tindall barnyard gate; the beast made a run for it, but was brought up short when the Tindall boy roped her. Then, she swung around, into the slack of the rope and almost caught me as I got hung up on the barbed wire fence. They all had a good laugh on me, but it could have been serious, as that cow had a set of Texas-type long-horns!

CHAPTER XXIII

Ruby and I had discussed visiting my sister, Grace and her family, who lived in Strahl Canyon, about 10 miles northeast of us. But, we had only the one pony and we doubted whether the frisky cayuse would stand for double riding.

"Tindalls might lend us a saddled horse," Ruby suggested, but, when we asked our neighbor about this, he said, "Okay, if you can go during the week — our kids ride on Sundays!"

This didn't stop my amazing little wife. I was surprised to see someone, horseback, on a mount I did not recognize, approaching across the field I was plowing.

"Ready for a ride to the Northrups?" Ruby quizzed, as she rode up and slid off a gelding, "the smallest in the band," she explained.

Well, that spunky little gal, all on her own, had saddled the lighest work horse she could separate from the range band and, after leading the animal out on a plowed field, had broken the horse to the saddle.

"He didn't act up too much, Ray, and the ground's pretty soft where you plowed!"

Thinking back, I recalled that Fan, Ruby's sister, had told me about Ruby breaking horses to the saddle, for homesteaders around Edson, when she was only sixteen.

"I was afraid you might get hurt, Honey; it's nearly 40 miles to the closest doctor and over one hundred to a hospital!"

The extra mount solved our problem and the very next Sunday, we borrowed a saddle from Tindall and rode across country to Al Northrup's ranch. There were only a few fairly productive wheat farms that we passed around, or through.

In 1908, about 10 years earlier, the last land rush for available homesteads, had seen every quarter section (160 acres) filed on. There was little possibility that one could make a living on 160 acres of land, where an average of only 50 percent of the better acreage would prove tillable and productive. Small pot-holes, most of them drying up by July, rocks, sage brush, rye grass and greasewood, interfered with planted crops and generally, the land that could not be plowed was fenced for pasture. I remember that we opened at least a dozen barbed wire gates on our ride to the Northrup ranch, Tindall having drawn a map for us.

Al and Grace Northrup had three daughters, Marian, Edith and Frances, the youngest. They lived in a well-built roomy ranch house, on one side of a small creek that already was dry, with barns and other outbuildings on the opposite side of the creek. A year-around spring formed a small pool just below the house, affording pure water for the household.

"Sure wish we had a place like this," Ruby commented, as we rode up and, of course, I agreed.

We were in for a disappointment. No one answered, when I knocked on the door. This did disturb a big grey gander, that came hissing at us, beating his wings as if to challenge our presence. I surprised Ruby, when after peering through a window, I started to open the unlocked door at the front of the house.

"How do you know this is your sister's house?" she demanded, staying well behind as I stepped inside.

"Because I recognize some things like the stove, that Mama must have given Grace." A little later, I pointed to a picture of my parents hanging on the wall. Ruby saw that the woman was my mother. But she still thought I was a little nervy, when I raided Grace's kitchen and made us lunch.

"Grace would have thought we were weird — not to help ourselves. Farmers and ranchers around here don't ever lock their doors when on a short visit to some neighbor!"

We were to learn a great deal more about Al Northrup's ranch, a little later on.

As we left Al's place, we noted dozens of hogs moving down toward the barn yard gate, from a fenced range on the slope back of the house. "Must be money in hogs," Ruby said. "Look at that expensive fence — must be a half mile of it!"

"You're right — the army buys a lot of pork. But Tindall told me that Roy Rose and Al Northrup are barely breaking even; they have to fatten hogs with $2.00 wheat!"

We rode back up the canyon and back to Wilcoxen's ranch. "I liked the ride and Strahl Canyon is sure better than this place," Ruby said. But when she added, "I still think we would be better off with you on the railroad!" it brought me sharply up against stark reality. In short, our first month of married life had been a period of hard work and little else.

We were in for yet another surprise. Wilcoxen was waiting for us and the first thing he did was to complain about the amount of plowing I had done. I didn't bother to list all the problems we had had to deal with.

When the rancher was gone I told Ruby that I, too, was fed up with Wilcoxen. "Tindall told me that he'd take over if we decided to pull out. He can do everything, except the plowing. Also, he promised to drive us down to Al Northrup's ranch. Should we take him up on his offer?"

Ruby was elated, "Anything would be better than this oven!"

We walked over to Tindall's and both George and his wife agreed with us, namely, that we would never get ahead at the Wilcoxen ranch. Tindall also again offered to drive us down to the Northrup ranch. But, through another bit of good fortune, we didn't need to ask our neighbor for help.

Just as we were leaving Tindall's, a Velie car approached — its driver was Roy Rose, Al Northrup's brother-in-law and partner in the Strahl Canyon hog business. Rose had driven over from his own wheat farm, about 15 miles northwest of Almira, that very day. It was he who had joined the Northrups in a Sunday visit, earlier in the day. Roy Rose had also read the note I had left at the Northrup home, telling of our visit, etc.

"Your mother told me that you were looking for a better job, Ray, how about working for me?" Rose apparently had recently been in Almira.

Of course, we eagerly accepted his offer. We stopped at the Wilcoxen place, gathered our few belongings and climbed into Roy Rose's fine touring car.

It was past midnight, when we reached the Rose farm. Roy had just started haying and the familiar pungent odor of freshly mowed oat hay was welcome after the dry, burned bunch grass in the Wilcoxen pastures.

Emma, Roy's wife, insisted on coffee and cake for us and we enjoyed a good hour's visit before retiring. Emma was Al Northrup's sister, one of five children of the George Northrup pioneer family. Northrup Canyon was part of the Grand Coulee and the south and east rims of the 1000-ft. deep gorges, were only a few miles from the Rose farm.

"Well, what do you think of the Rose family?" I asked Ruby, when we entered our bedroom, which incidentally, was some different from our "bake oven" and straw tick at the Wilcoxen ranch.

"I love Emma," she said. "She let me take a peek at Lois — only six months old — asleep in her cradle. Roy is nice, too, maybe we can save some for our trip home!"

"You aren't getting any ideas — about babies," I teased, kissing her good-night. "Hardly," Ruby replied. "It takes good wages to support a family. Your sister, Mary Ely, gave me her formula for not having kids and you'd better not get any ideas either!"

I laughed, although actually I didn't feel like laughing. It was apparent to me that Ruby's plan for our future was centered in one solution: we would return to Edson, as soon as the war ended and I would take up where I had left off with the Grand Trunk Pacific and become a fireman on the railroad, with a fair income and "regular passes to Edmonton, for better shopping."

I could easily have started an argument, even at that late hour, by reminding my wife that I had never emigrated to Canada, for employment on any railroad. But I remarked, "Don't worry! You're right — and the war isn't over yet!"

The next day, I shocked the oat hay that Roy had cut with a binder, around the border of a field of wheat he intended harvesting with a combine. It was hard work, but at least one had the satisfaction of surveying the fruits of toil!

A "shock" was simply a number of bundles of hay cut and automatically tied with twine, as the combination reaper-binder machine cut a swath. The worker started by leaning two bundles against each other, with the butts firmly thrust into the stubble and soil, with additional bundles then propped against the first pair. The object of the shocks was two-fold: (a) to prevent spoilage of the hay bundles laying flat on the ground, in case it should rain and (b) to allow the heads to cure better, with improved circulation.

Roy Rose owned a combine (harvester) that cut, threshed and delivered sacked grain, in one continuous operation. His machine, with a 14-foot sickle (or cutter) was hauled by 12 horses. The separator, or thresher unit was powered by a gasoline engine. Earlier combines were totally dependent on horse power, with all the reaping (cutting) and separating of grain from the heads done through chain drives off a "bull wheel." As many as 32 horses were used on combines that cut a 20-ft. swath. The larger mobile thresher required a crew of five men, while the more modern ones, of the period when I worked for Roy Rose, were easily handled by two men. Roy drove the horses and watched to see that the separator was functioning satisfactorily, while I sacked and sewed the bags of grain, as it poured out of the separator.

We worked hard at the Rose's. Ruby helped Emma in the never-ending chores of a farm wife and cared for baby Lois, as if she were her own.

Harvest was over and we were hauling straw to central stacks, when Roy learned that Al Northrup had broken his ankle.

"We can get along here, okay," Roy said, "and the Northrups could sure use your help for a month or so!"

Ruby didn't want to go back to the area that reminded her of the Wilcoxen place. "We've got enough to make it back home," she said, wistfully.

But, again I reminded her that although the war effort seemed rapidly turning in favor of the Allies, the Germans might yet launch another offensive.

"I'm sure we can make it back to Edson by Christmas," I half promised.

We said good-bye to Emma and Roy, after they drove us across the Grand Coulee, over to Strahl Canyon and the Northrup ranch.

CHAPTER XXIV

Al Northrup's broken ankle greatly restricted his ability to do the essential chores on his ranch, such as feeding the stock, milking several cows, keeping the house supplied with wood, etc., to say nothing of feeding over 300 hogs.

As soon as Ruby and I arrived at the ranch, Al (on crutches) showed us around the barn yard, feed lot, etc., and we took over. Ruby was eager to help, in or outside the house, for which Al and his wife (my sister, Grace), were thankful. The two elder girls, Marion, 12, and Edith, 10, were already good cooks and house-keepers. I can't help comparing the average farm girl of that period, with the millions of youngsters of today. Then, both boys and girls, especially on farms, contributed a great deal toward maintaining a stable economy in the home.

Ruby didn't like cattle, especially bulls, the result of a harrowing experience as a child, when she and some young friends were chased by a herd bull, at a relative's ranch in Saskatchewan. Nevertheless, Ruby helped me milk the cows and the girls ran the hand-cranked cream separator. The cream was set out on the road, in a special type milk can, each morning, for pickup by a man who made the route, from the farms to the nearest creamery.

The added cash income from milk and cream, was of considerable importance to the farmer who had only wheat as a marketable crop. There was no local market for pork, so Al and his partner, Roy Rose, had to haul the hogs they had fattened, to the nearest railroad at Coulee City.

Feeding the hogs once a day, in the evening, was quite an experience. In the middle of a hog-wire fenced feed lot was a set of double feed troughs, separated by an alley, or enclosed corridor. The troughs, each 50 feet long, were open on the outside, so that the hogs could feed on the grain poured into the part of the trough extending far enough inside the alley, by a man carrying the sacked wheat. The grunting and squealing of the hogs as they crowded each other for position at the feed trough was something neither Ruby nor I would ever forget.

One day, while I was in the granary, loading a wheelbarrow, one of the girls yelled, "Uncle Ray, that old sow has killed another hen!"

I picked up a board and ran after the sow, but it was too late. The swine, an expert at breaking through, or rooting her way under supposed-to-be-hog-proof fence, had eaten half of a fat Plymouth Rock hen, by the time I could reach it.

A day later, after the same sow had killed two more chickens, Al handed me a .38 Colt revolver, with instructions to shoot the culprit. So, we had fresh pork, dividing it with a couple of neighbors, as we could not spare the time to make "salt pork" in brine, or to cure the hams.

Roy Rose arrived one day unexpectedly, and Ruby and I returned with him to the Hartline farm. Roy had several big hogs for marketing and our job was to haul them over to the Strahl Canyon ranch, to be included in the next shipment to the railroad, with hogs from the Northrup place.

We drove four big farm horses, hitched to a stout wagon, boarded all around to hold the hogs. We had to cross the mouth of the Coulee by what was known as the Almira Grade, about three miles of steep, winding wagon road.

There were two sharp switch-backs on the grade. One, about a quarter mile downhill from the top, ran out onto the bank on the outside of the curve, with little danger of an upset into the gulch, or dry creek bed. But about a mile down the grade, an even sharper switch-back, was located right on the brink of a drop-off of more than a thousand feet down to the Columbia River.

With the wagon brakes set tight and the two wheel horses holding the load back with their harness breeching, we approached the second "hairpin" curve as slowly and carefully as we could.

Then it happened! On the wagon seat, between us, was a can of small stones, where Roy had placed it saying, "Barney (one of the horses in the lead team) may need a little encouragement now and then. He's been eating his head off." Little did Roy dream that, just as we would approach that bad curve, the can of rocks would tumble off the wagon seat, hit the double tree just behind the wheel horses and bounce several pebbles onto the flanks of the horses! The clatter of the stones set off a simultaneous lurch of the lead team and all four plunged down the steep grade. This startled the hogs and their racket was enough in itself, to drive the horses mad.

How we managed that curve without upsetting the wagon, the hogs and us remains well at the top in my "list of life-saving miracles!" Luckily, after making the switchback, the east stretch, though fairly steep, led in a straight line to the floor of the canyon. "Thought we'd never make it!" Ruby cried.

Once again at the Strahl Canyon ranch, normal routine took over. One especially interesting project involved the grinding of our wheat into flour, at a neighbor's small mill. White flour was taboo among most farmers and ranchers and, it was my sister's use of whole wheat flour that made me an advocate of its use for life.

At the Northrup's, Ruby and I had our first serious quarrel. It was on a Sunday. Two of Al's cousins, men in their mid-twenties, had finished working on a cattle drive and had stopped to help us load hogs.

It was raining and we had finished eating one of Grace's sumptuous dinners.

"How about some poker?" Al said, bringing out a deck of cards.

I had discovered the winter before, while with Ted Walters on the Tony River in northern Canada, that I wasn't much of a poker player. But, of course, I sat down with Al and the other two boys. We had played a hand or two and it was my turn to deal. I started to shuffle the pack and suddenly Ruby leaned over and grabbed the cards.

"You (meaning me, of course) aren't playing cards on Sunday," she said and stormed out of the room.

The silence that followed was awkward, to say the least. It took Al Northrup a long time to get over his initial reaction to Ruby's intolerance.

I talked with Grace about the incident and was pleased when she said, "We shouldn't be too hard on Ruby — she's a long ways from home. I remember how lonesome it was for me, in a strange city, the first year of our married life."

That same evening, one of the boys said, "We saw quite a few deer on the cattle drive — several times we spotted them grazing right in with our herd. It would be easy to get one or more bucks, Ray."

But when I asked Ruby what she thought of my joining in a deer hunt, she was strangely opposed to the idea. So, I thanked the man who had suggested the outing and the subject was dropped.

In the meantime, Al had made arrangements with one of the cattlemen to take over my job shortly. The end of World War I was imminent and I told Al that we were going back to Canada.

Then, just as the war did end, we received the sad news that Cliff Knowles, my ex-partner had died with Spanish Influenza. My youngest sister, Blanche, arriving in Strahl Canyon with Roy Rose, brought the word of Cliff's dying at Fort Borden, in Western Washington.

Actually, it was a letter from Ruby's friend, Ivy Reed, that told us of the tragedy. Blanche had only delivered the letter from the Almira Post Office. It was hard to realize that my boyhood chum had passed away so sudenly, only two weeks after being inducted in the U.S. Army. Ruby was badly shaken, too, and coming on the heels of our first quarrel, the bad news was hard to take.

On a frosty November morning, Al Northrup, Roy Rose, my sister Blanche, Ruby and I, left the Strahl Canyon ranch and drove to Almira. Al's ankle had healed enough for him to drive his Model T and Roy had his own car. In Almira, we collected our few belongings and prepared to leave for Canada.

I hated the good-byes to my mother and sisters, but I knew that wheat farming was not for me. I had fallen in love with the Canadian wilderness and was determined to gain more knowledge of the wildlife there and to continue my experiments with methods of capturing furbearers, with as little suffering as possible.

My overall ambition was to become a naturalist and writer and I already had sold a few adventure stories to both Canadian and U.S. magazines. This career had been temporarily disrupted by our leaving Canada.

Reaching Spokane, via the Washington Central Railway, we found it necessary to stay overnight, as the train for Canada left early in the morning. Looking out of our hotel window, we could see people having a good time in a public dance hall, only a block away.

"Let's go, Ray!" Ruby said excitedly, "It's been a long time!"

"Sounds great, honey! I guess it's safe enough!"

The ban on public gatherings, during that awful flu epidemic had just been lifted, so taking a chance, health-wise, we went to dance.

"Not much like Edson," Ruby said, after we had finished a waltz.

I nodded agreement and was about to sit down, when I noticed a man, several inches taller than my six-foot height, walking toward us.

"Bob Ray!" I exclaimed.

"Ray Thompson!" the man said and I introduced Ruby to an old friend, who had worked for Al Northrup, some years before.

We stayed a while longer and Ruby danced with Bob. Then, we went to a nearby lunch counter, had coffee and doughnuts and then parted.

"Bob Ray, driving a four-up hitched to a heavy wagon load of fruit box lumber, went off the Scheibner grade in Northrup Canyon, late at night. My mother and sister, Blanche (about 2 years old then), were with Bob. It was a miracle — one horse was so badly broken up, it had to be shot. Mother and Blanche narrowly escaped, when the wagon and its load bounced right over them on a steep, rocky slope!" I related to Ruby.

Ruby shook her head. "That's too much like our near spill with the hogs!"

It was late when we finally got to bed. The next morning, on arriving at the Spokane International Railroad depot, we were in for another surprise. Frank Knowles, Cliff's father, was also returning to Edson, after attending his son's funeral. Although we were glad to see each other again, it was difficult for each of us. Frank Knowles and his son, Cliff, had been very close and the father was surely grief stricken. "There's a lot of the flu in Alberta, too," he remarked.

We got on the train and suddenly, I became violently ill. At Calgary, where we had to change trains again, Frank and Ruby had to help me the short journey between depots.

Another 200 miles north to Edmonton and we had to call a cab to take Ruby and me to the Royal George Hotel. There, the desk clerk became suspicious and shipped me off to an emergency hospital, full of Spanish Influenza patients.

Ruby went to her brother Will's house, but a few days later, she, too, arrived at the emergency and was placed in a room, up on the floor above me. I was in the "Home" hospital for two weeks and barely made it. Ruby wasn't quite so bad and was allowed to walk around and, incidentally, to visit me the day before I was released.

That was a sad experience, but Ruby and I were among the lucky ones. I can still hear the screams of one man, just across the hall from me, as he fought a nurse and plunged to his death from a window overlooking a deep ravine.

When we both recovered, we continued on to Edson, arriving there with only $20.00, but thankful to be alive. Ruby's sister, Fan, and her mother met us at the station. They, too, had been lucky, suffering moderate attacks of the flu. Several of Ruby's best friends had died, during the worst of the epidemic.

Ivy Reed, visiting us one day, cut me to the quick, when she turned to Ruby and said, "You married the wrong partner. Just think — if you had got hitched to Cliff, you'd be $10,000 richer. That's the U.S. Army insurance his dad is getting!" Ivy didn't mean to upset Ruby and me, but she did just that.

We stayed with Ruby's mother for a few days and then, after I had landed a job as clerk in the roundhouse foreman's office, we decided to move into Mrs. Millar's homestead cabin, south of Edson.

"That two-mile hike, twice a day, is just the ticket," I told Ruby, adding, "Lots of coyotes out that way, too, for one to work on!"

"Trapping!" Ruby exclaimed, "Can't you get that out of your system? Next thing, you'll want to go back up the Edson Trail!"

I didn't reply — possibly afraid she may have read my mind.

CHAPTER XXV

The first winter of our married life was a period of adjustment for Ruby and me. In other words, we had the normal conflicts and problems that invariably confront newlyweds. To complicate matters, my health started to deteriorate and Doctor Proctor thought it was a sort of hangover from Spanish Influenza.

I was employed as a Clerk (the occupational term for most beginners in railroad office work) and, in succession, handled inventory in the car foreman's office, was payroll clerk in the roundhouse offices, did accounting for the (district) department and in the B & B (Bridge and Building) office for the Edson district of the Grand Trunk Pacific Railway. The G.T.P. was in serious financial difficulties and was being taken over by the federal government under the name of the Canadian National Railway.

Ruby and her Edson relatives were apparently satisfied that I had "settled down," with an assured income from my railroad office employment. The District Master Mechanic, A. H. Mahan, had evidently taken a liking for me, as he told my brother-in-law, J. J. (Jack) Hodgkinson, who was a car inspector on the railroad crew, that I could expect swift promotion if I worked at it.

But, instead of being pleased with all this, I was very disturbed. I wanted to be a writer, specializing in outdoor (wilderness) adventures, and to accomplish this objective, I firmly intended to do more hunting, trapping, and wildlife photography.

I was really handicapped for lack of funds, as our income was modest. But, I did manage to buy film for a cheap, borrowed camera and purchase a few steel traps, along with some wire to continue experimenting with a "humane" snare trap for taking furbearing animals.

Ruby didn't object to this, as she often hiked on snowshoes with me, while covering my short traplines. I also made a toboggan and harnesses for a small dog team.

My wife knew most of the country around Edson. She had traveled horseback over homestead wagon roads and the abandoned railroad camp and Indian trails, during the several years she had lived in Edson, prior to our marriage.

A few miles southeast of Edson, an abandoned homestead wagon road extended on into the McLeod River valley. On weekends, we made trips with our dog team and I even ran this short trapline a few times on moonlit nights.

The snowshoe rabbit (Varying Hare) was receding population wise, into a low cycle and there was very little "fur" in that area, except big coyotes, called locally "Brush Wolves."

Ruby showed me a frozen pond on the river bench land. "I once borrowed a .22 rifle from Will's hardware and started shooting at the rats here," she said. "We had just arrived from England and I didn't know the difference between muskrats and any other rats. Of course, I know better, now."

We were almost always happiest when together, hunting, fishing, or just exploring. Although it was concerning my trapline that first winter, that Ruby and I had a rather serious quarrel.

On Christmas Day, 1918, we had dinner with the Hodgkinson's. Jack, Ruby's brother-in-law, had to report for his job as car inspector, so we had

The Hodkinsons with R. T. dog team.

Buster and Laddie - with R. T. near Mile 27

dinner early. About one o'clock I thanked Fan for the "turkey and trimmings" dinner and excused myself, saying, "I've got a few coyote traps set on a deserted homestead, that need checking. I'll be gone a couple hours!"

"You wouldn't!" Ruby's sister exploded and Ruby quickly asserted, "He's not going, of course! This *is* Christmas!"

That was too much for me. "A coyote or fox caught in a trap doesn't have a calendar," I snapped back and, without further comment, put on an extra pair of moosehide moccasins, slipped into a mackinaw coat, a pair of mittens and left the Hodgkinson home.

Ruby shouted something, but I kept on going. Just as I reached a trail branching off from the wagon road leading out of town, she caught up with me.

The snow was well packed and we had not bothered to wear snowshoes on the two-mile hike into town, from the Millar homestead. Neither of us spoke for at least an hour. Then, on the deserted homestead, we came to a set where a coyote had stepped directly over the trap pan, without springing the trap.

"Jaws frozen down?" Ruby quizzed.

"That's right! It's hard to keep steel traps from freezing down in this kind of weather. That's why I keep experimenting with wire snares. They hang above the snow and won't freeze down."

I don't remember which one of us was the first to say, "I'm sorry," but by the time we got back to Ruby's sister's home, everything was squared away. And Fan, evidently pleased to see us happy again, insisted on driving us home with her horse and cutter, or one-seated sleigh. Ruby asked me if I remembered the time, a few months before our marriage, when we had a "runaway" experience with that same cutter, when it was hauled by Jellis' delivery pony, "Jeff".

"How could I ever forget," I teased and pinching her leg, added, "not only the upset, but what happened out on the trail, just before we turned back and headed for town!"

"Don't get fresh, mister," Ruby shot back, "or I'll tell Fan on you!"

Our social life that winter wasn't worth writing home about. A few public dances; card parties; church "socials"; etc., was the extent of our entertainment.

I worked hard and kept pecking away on my typewriter, selling most of my short articles written around my experiences north of Edson, along the abandoned wagon road to the Peace River country, much of which has already been covered in previous chapters. The extra income from my writing was welcome and I commenced thinking that, with trapping, writing and a possibility of getting back into the fur trade business, I might still pursue some of the goals that World War I had forced me to abandon.

I don't remember that I deliberately planned any strategy on how to win Ruby over to my way of thinking. She loved the outdoors, especially the trout fishing, as spring appeared.

North of Edson, there were a few homesteads still occupied. One of these was a small hay farm and stock ranch owned by Bob and Ed Couzens. A small stream, the Muskeg River, ran through their farm and it was well stocked (by

Mother Nature) with brook trout, Dolly Varden (called Bull Trout) and grayling.

Ruby had been engaged to Eddie Couzens before I came into the picture and the two Couzens boys had remained good friends with the Millars, after Eddie returned from the war. I was a little jealous when Ruby suggested a fishing trip out on her ex-boy friend's farm. But, I agreed to the trip and, as events later proved, it all worked to my advantage.

We were fishing an abandoned beaver dam (pond) only a few yards apart, when Ruby whispered, "Ray — a big bull trout — my hook's too small!" I edged up behind her, just as she hooked a small trout and was lifting it from the water. A bull trout grabbed the smaller fish, then let go and dropped back into the beaver dam.

"Just a second, Honey," I said, and quickly tying a larger hook on to my own line, baited it with a piece of pine squirrel and handed it to Ruby.

Only seconds later, my wife exclaimed, "Isn't it a beauty?" holding up a Dolly Varden, weighing at least five pounds.

"Sure is a dandy," I agreed. Then, seizing on an opportunity to promote an outing that I hoped would work to my advantage, I added, "Lots of bull trout bigger than this one in creeks running into the Athabasca. Let's take a trip up that way — I can get a week off!"

Ruby didn't exactly shout with enthusiasm over my suggestion at first, but on the way back to town, she asked several questions about the Edson Trail beyond Mile 20.

"Of course, you know that the Rapeljes have moved from the Baptiste River to the old Hindmarsh place on the south bank of the Athabasca. I'm sure they would welcome a visit from us," I argued. I remembered, too, that Ruby had met Gregg and Mamie Rapelje, Gregg's blind sister, Sarah, and Mamie's uncle, Major Will Thompson (a Civil War veteran), when they arrived in Edson, from Manitoba, in the spring of 1916.

"Yes, I know about their move," Ruby answered, "and I would like to see them again. Cliff told me that Gregg had built a fine new log home, Red River style, near the old Jim Hindmarsh place. But," here Ruby seemed to read my thoughts, "if we do take this trip, it won't change my mind about your going up north to run a trapline, next winter."

"It's only June — a long way from trapping season," I hastily replied. "Anyway, I couldn't take time off my job for more than a week."

We discussed the situation a little more in detail and finally just before Ruby kissed me good-night, she made me real happy with, "See about the vacation — soon as we know for sure, I'll make up a list of what we need for the trip."

CHAPTER XXVI

The trip over the Edson Trail to the Athabasca River Crossing, at Mile 53, was uneventful. Driving a team of Jack Hodgkinson's horses hitched to a light buggy, we reached Mile 35, easily the first day and the Athabasca home of the Rapeljes in mid-afternoon of the following day.

Beyond Mile 20, where we had stopped to visit briefly with John Hackett and his young son, only deserted road houses, called "stopping places," broke the monotony and silence. This wilderness road only a few years before, had been literally alive with pioneers and their outfits, headed north to seek homesteads in the Peace River country.

Ruby had known these pioneer families much better than I, as her family had arrived in Edson in 1911, and her brother Will, who owned a hardware, had helped to outfit many of the homeseekers. This was four years ahead of my appearance there.

Ruby also knew that Cliff Knowles and I had dissolved our partnership at the Athabasca and Baptiste River Crossings, because Knowles had decided against continuing efforts to build a trading post and small stock ranch business.

"I think Cliff thought there was no future in it," Ruby said, when from an elevation in the trail, I pointed to a series of fine meadows crossed by a stream that as we saw a little later, was alive with native trout.

"Maybe he was right," I retorted, "and maybe he wasn't willing to give it a good try."

"We'll nver know what Cliff might have done," Ruby said and I changed the subject, for, although my ex-partner had been dead for almost a year, it seemed as if every time his name was mentioned, a curtain of controversy dropped between Ruby and me.

We spent three days with the Rapeljes. Ruby and the women folk had a wonderful visit and, when my wife inadvertently said that I was lonesome for my old trapline trails, Sarah, the blind 70-year-old spinster, remarked, "Raymond could become a famous writer, especially if he had more experience in this new land. You know, Ruby, this is North Canada's last frontier."

Ruby told me what Sarah Rapelje had said and then commented, "It's all right for people like the Rapeljes — out here. Gregg sold his Manitoba ranch and Mamie told my mother that they had plenty of capital to start a big stock ranch here. With us — what would we live on while we got a start?"

I could have cited many examples where homesteaders, in my own country, had arrived there with a "little of nothing," to later become well-to-do farmers, ranchers and stockmen. But, I wisely chose to agree with, "It would be taking a chance."

The two trips to a stream emptying into the Athabasca, about three miles upriver, opened Ruby's eyes as to trout fishing like, in her own words, "I never dreamed of." And to cap the climax, she caught a huge bull trout, lurking in the shadows of an overhanging cliff, where the creek, at the foot of a sandstone cliff, had scooped out a deep hole.

Rapelje had built a small smoke house for curing or drying, grayling and we must have added at least 10 pounds of trout, for smoking, in addition to all we could eat for several meals.

"Raymond used to keep us in moose meat," the irrepressible Sarah commented, while we were at the table.

Later, my wife remarked, "That Sarah thinks you're just about the greatest! Isn't her brother a hunter?"

"He shoots grouse now and then, but I've never known that he killed any big game. Knowles and I always shared moose and bear with them."

I recall that Ruby was as reluctant as I, to leave the Rapeljes. The old Civil War veteran, Major Thompson, had died the winter of 1916-17 and, since the provincial government had abandoned the Edson Trail, including the operation of cable river ferries at the larger stream crossings, visitors at the Rapelje place were few and far between.

On our way back to Edson, Ruby summarized her feelings about wilderness living with, "Sure is beautiful, but except for a few trappers and the Rapeljes, we'd never see anyone for at least six months!"

There was no arguing with her assessment, so we returned home with only memories of a short wilderness adventure.

CHAPTER XXVII

Home again from our trip to the Athabasca, our life settled to a monotonous routine, for me at least. I kept my job at the railway roundhouse office, hiking across abandoned homestead lands, to and from work, between the Millar place and Edson.

For some strange reason, my health suddenly deteriorated, with loss of appetite and nausea at mealtime. Then, Ruby had a dental problem and, since there was no dentist in Edson, she took the train into Edmonton. She was gone for a few days, staying with her brother, Will.

On the third morning of Ruby's absence, I was eating breakfast at the homestead cabin, seated at a small table near the wood-burning stove. Suddenly, without the slightest warning, I passed out, falling against the stove. The impact collapsed one leg of the stove, spilling a pot of coffee down the side of my face and onto my neck and one shoulder. Luckily, the door to the fuel box on the stove, remained closed and none of the hot coals fell out.

How long I was "out," I couldn't know, but when I regained consciousness, the pain was excruciating. It was torture getting to my feet and propping the stove up before the live coals could set fire to the cabin floor. Then, not daring to even try to put on a jacket, I stumbled outside and started on the muddy, rutted wagon road toward town.

It had been raining for hours and I could barely keep going. There was about a mile on a stretch of road due north to a cross road pointing west, on into Edson. By cutting across two abandoned homestead lands, I could save a half mile or more. So, I took the shortcut, part of which involved crossing a muskeg. Every step was a torture. Once, I stumbled over a root and fell, face down, onto the spongy, swamp-like surface. For several minutes, I lay there, half conscious. Then, realizing that it would take several days for a search party to locate me, I got to my feet and kept going until I reached the Millar home. The sight of me, muddy, wet, and burned on my face and neck, must have shocked Ruby's mother.

But she quickly bandaged my shoulder, face and neck and I went on down town to the local doctor's office. Fortunately, my burns were not too severe and in a week or so, I was able to work part time.

In the meantime, Ruby had returned from her trip to the dentist. I met her at the depot and she was visibly shaken when she saw me wearing bandages on my face and neck. I told her not to worry and that I was not badly burned.

Doctors in those frontier towns operated with the most meager equipment. The Edson physician at the time, was a Captain Proctor. He had served in the Medical Corps of the Canadian Army, during World War I and was a very competent family doctor.

On my final visit, while removing my bandages, the doctor said, "You'll be all right, Ray, but I'd suggest you get out of that railway office."

I told Ruby about Dr. Proctor's remarks and she suggested "Maybe you could get on as a fireman, in the yard or on the Coal Branch run."

"Maybe so, Honey, but Fred Haas told me he had been demoted from engineer down to fireman, on account of "bumping" by war veterans and, in short, that I was lucky to have *any* railroad job! But, I'll try again — my office job sure isn't so hot!"

My search for outside work was in vain. It was like my old friend, the demoted engineer had said — soldiers returning from the war had preference, and my health wasn't improving in the meantime.

Harold Parnall, one of three trappers who had bought Gregg Rapelje's interest or "squatter's rights" on a small ranch a few miles upstream from my former location on the Baptiste River, stopped by one day.

"Ray," Parnall said, "this next season should be real good for marten, on some of your old trapline. Fur buyers in Edmonton told me that good pelts will average $50.00 each. Too bad you can't take over Ole Aasen's old line, on Wolverine Mountain — it's good marten country."

It was a real pleasure to visit with a trapper from the wilderness area where I had operated during the three years preceding my marriage, and naturally I didn't hesitate to tell Ruby about my conversation with Parnall. My wife knew the Parnalls, as they had homesteaded near the Millar place.

Looking back, I can appreciate Ruby's attitude toward trapping as a profession. While working in her brother's hardware, and later in a "general" store owned by the Jellis Trading Company, she had come to know a number of trappers, several of whom had wives and families.

"I don't know a single trapper who isn't broke at least six months out of the year," she countered once, when I was defending a mutual friend who, periodically, left his wife to fend for herself, while he went away in search of employment. I had defended Crawford Mason who, in spite of his aversion to a steady job, was anything but lazy, and I could sympathze with him as he wanted to become a known western artist. Mason had more natural talent for painting wilderness scenes, including wild animals and birds, than anyone I had ever known. He also was a very good trapper, horse wrangler, and all around woodsman.

"But Crawford can't get more than a few dollars for a painting he might work on for days," Ruby had said.

"I suppose you think the small checks I get from outdoor magazines aren't much either," I had retorted, adding, "Let's forget it, I'll hang onto the railroad job!"

But that was before Harold Parnall's visit. His remark about the high price for marten pelts was especially intriguing, as I had been corresponding with a fur farmer who was interested in live-trapped marten, for his experiments in ranching that valuable furbearer. Lew Aumock, the Pine Woods Fur Farm owner, had offered me $200.00 each for live marten, as the marten in northern Canada were superior in color and fur coats to those in northern Idaho, where he was located.

Fate works in mysterious ways. Will Millar, Ruby's brother, had sold his Edson Hardware store and had moved to Edmonton, where he became a department head for Revillon Wholesale, a rival of the giant Hudson's Bay Company. Now, while he was on a business trip to Edson, we visited at the Millar home. Will Millar frequently outfitted trappers and fur traders bound from the vast territory north of Edmonton. And, although Revillons didn't buy raw furs, the department heads of the company kept in touch with the fur market, worldwide, because of their business with fur traders.

Will was interested in my writing, and in my experimenting with animal snares. Also, he openly championed my resolve to get away from railroad work. "Maybe we've got another Zane Grey or Robert Service in the family,"

Noble and Parnall on the Athabasca

he remarked when Mrs. Millar suggested that my desire to become a well-known writer was a worthy, but precarious (money-wise) ambition.

My brother-in-law also verified Harold Parnall's report on the raw fur market. "Marten fur is very popular in Europe," he said. Will also thought I might do very well with my writing, and suggested that I buy a good camera and photograph old cabins, river ferries and river crossing buildings on the abandoned Edson-Grande Prairie Trail. "There'll be a need for that sort of thing, for historians," he prophesied.

I never knew exactly what Will said to his sister, when I wasn't around, but a day after he had left Edson, Ruby surprised me when she wanted to know just how I would work a trapline, and from what point on the old trail. It didn't take me long to find paper and pencil and draw a rough map.

"We could borrow Rapelje's team and snake out logs for a cabin. We'd build right near Rapeljes and you'd have Mamie and Sarah for company, while I was out on the trapline. I wouldn't be gone over a night or two on any one trip, and as soon as we could get a dog team together, you could come along, too."

The trails I marked on the map really intrigued my wife. She loved the outdoors and asked questions like, "Any streams or muskeg to cross? Any grizzlies? And what about cabins on Ole Aasen's old 'line?"

I assured Ruby that bears weren't bad that time of year and showed her two different locations of trapline cabins, one at the mouth of Lynx Creek, where it emptied into the Athabasca River, and the other several miles up the creek valley not far from the source of the stream, on the north slope of Wolverine Mountain.

"Looks scary — 'way off there in that wild country,' " she said. "Don't know if I'd be very happy worrying about you alone up there in the hills."

But, the more we talked, the easier it became for me to win Ruby over and we set a date for early in September, for our wilderness adventure. With a light rig called a "democrat" drawn by a team of horses, we made the 53-mile trip in three days.

CHAPTER XXVIII

Gregg and Mamie Rapelje and Gregg's blind sister, Sarah, welcomed us warmly. Gregg had just started cutting wild hay in meadows about a mile from their home at Mile 53, the Athabasca River crossing, on the Edson Trail. Ruby and I worked with Rapelje and the Baptiste River boys, whom he had already hired and, in a few days we had the wild peavine and vetch hay cut and stacked. Then, Ruby and I went over and helped the Baptiste River trappers, Lingrell, Parnall, and Henderson, cut and stack their own wild hay. These boys used horses on their traplines until the snow got too deep.

Backtracking, I recall a most pleasant surprise that happened during the first week of our arrival at Mile 53. An Indian girl named Fawn, was staying with the Rapeljes, waiting for her man to arrive on a river scow loaded with trade goods. The element of surprise developed when I learned that the expected trader was none other than my former partner, Ted Walters, from Mile 90, or Tony River, on the Edson Trail.

Walters and I had parted in late December, 1917. This was when I had decided to quit the wilderness and remain in Edson. Walters had returned to Mile 90, and a few months later was married to Fawn, a young daughter of Isaac Abraham, the Iosegun Lakes band chief. I, of course, remembered "Old Ike" from my earlier partnership with Walters.

"Sure wish you and your wife could visit us, Ray. I've got a pretty good trade at Mile 90," Walters said. "Maybe," I answered. "We'll see how things shape up here."

That intrepid woodsman had built a scow at a point near the railroad crossing over the Athabasca River, a hundred miles upstream. Then, loading the scow with trade goods shipped by railway, Walters had "run the river" all by himself, through treacherous waters that included a stretch called "Goose Neck Rapids."

This "bad water" was a part of the river course about 20 miles upstream from one of my trapline cabins. I knew from experience in running rafts through the "Goose Neck," just how dangerous the rapids were.

"Wish I had known — I could have managed to help," I told Walters, while we were transferring his trade goods from the scow to an abandoned log cabin that had belonged to the original owner of Mile 53 stopping place. From here, Walters would haul his supplies and trade goods, with horses hitched to a wagon, over the trail to his trading post at Mile 90.

"It was a rough run," my ex-partner admitted. "The river is low for this time of year and some of the rocks stuck out of the water, as big as barns!"

We talked about mutual acquaintances, among them the LaRocques, old Natoka Gomma, the Cree "moccasin and snowshoe mender," Dan MacMillar, and others. Walters said that as far as he knew, my young friend, Petite Jean (Little John) Fortier, and Marie LaRocque, were still in Lac Ste. Anne and that Vic LaRocque and Big Ike, the troublemaker, were with the Iosegun Lakes band of Cree Indians.

I asked about Hugh McKinnon, the trader who had mysteriously disappeared from Crooked Lake.

"No one ever heard of him," Walters answered. "I still think that Vic LaRocque had something to do with McKinnon's being scared and chased out at Crooked Lake."

Walters and his wife, Fawn, left with a wagon load of trade goods the same day Ruby and I rode over to the Baptiste River to help out in the hay harvest. The Mile 90 trader later returned to the Athabasca Crossing for the last of his supplies, while Ruby and I were at the Baptiste ranch, so we missed Walters and I never saw him again. We did correspond for a few years and then my letters were returned, marked "unclaimed." I heard conflicting stories about his success as a trader. Charley Lingrell, one of the Baptiste River trappers, had heard that Walters' Indian wife, Fawn, had died giving birth to a child, and that Walters had re-married, the second time, to a white woman.

In reminiscing, Ruby told me of a conversation with Walters' first wife, while we were at Rapeljes'. "We were picking wild gooseberries where the trail crosses Canyon Creek, when Fawn asked, 'Why you not want *oskawasis*?' I was really surprised, but not amused."

Ruby and the Cree girl had learned to communicate quite well during the few days they were together. Fawn could speak some French and English and my wife, in turn, had Fawn teach her some basic Cree words.

Oskawasis meant "baby" in English and Ruby quickly answered the inquisitive, but serious girl, with a question of her own. "What makes you ask? Ray and I would like a baby. Down south where he was raised, the Indian word for baby is 'papoose.' We didn't want a child when Ray might be called into the army. Now things are different."

In recalling her conversation with Walters' wife, Ruby said, "Fawn was curious, apparently because Walters definitely didn't want any *oskawasis* in his home. While we were picking berries, Fawn pointed to a bush the branches of which were loaded with white berries. I always thought them not fit to eat, but Fawn gulped down a small handful and said, 'Eat Wapisu Menisu and not have what you call papoose. Walters say me do that."

Ruby learned that Indian women dried the white berries and brewed them, along with bark from the bushes, to make a contraceptive, for 'year around use'.

When my wife told the Indian girl that she was taking nothing to prevent pregnancy, the girl brightened and with her dark eyes flashing, said, "You have strong baby for hunter like Ray, you make bed on grizzly bear hide. You good *iskwao*, too, and *okistutoo* — want sure to help!"

Although the incident had a slightly amusing angle, Ruby didn't laugh when telling me about it. "Fawn wanted a baby more than anything in this world. She paid me a real compliment too, when she said I was a good *iskwao* and could have a strong son."

We were at the Baptiste River ranch for two weeks. Then, we rode horses north to Jackfish Lake, camping in one of my old trapline cabins. I was making a sort of survey of furbearer populations and had to admit that signs of fox, lynx, and brush wolves were not promising. Snowshoe rabbits were scarce and, as the Varying Hare was the main meal ticket for the above-mentioned animals, the prospect for a good fur catch looked anything but promising.

"I'll concentrate on trapping marten, further south," I told Ruby, so we rode back down the trail to the Athabasca.

There, we finished the cabin near Rapelje's and I was free to lay in supplies at the mouth of Lynx Creek, about 12 trail miles southwest of Rapelje's.

Returning from one of my trips, Ruby greeted me with, "Guess what, honey — we're pregnant!"

I remember sitting in a chair that Mamie Rapelje had given us and holding my wife in my arms and saying, for lack of any well-chosen words, "Are you sure?"

Ruby smiled, "Well, Mamie says I must be! So now what, Mr. Trapper?"

We talked far into that night and finally agreed that we would stay at the Athabasca cabin, where Ruby was only a hundred yards or so from the Rapelje's when I would be away. I would stock my cabin on Ole Aasen's trapline and before the mountain trail became impassable between the Athabasca and Edson, Ruby would move back to town and stay with her mother. I dared not think of how I would miss Ruby, and tried instead to concentrate on blaming myself for trying to make an *iskwao* (Indian squaw) out of my wife.

Anyway, early and heavy snow storms threatened to block Mile 35 Pass, and as Gregg Rapelje wanted to make one more trip into Edson for supplies, Ruby decided she had better go along. Rapelje had a team of exceptionally strong horses, so he hitched them to the front bobs of a sled, loaded the box with hay, grub and blankets and with Ruby perched on top of the hay, made the trip into Edson.

After establishing my Wolverine Mountain trapline, I blazed a trail over the divide to connect with the Edson Trail at Mile 27. This proved of considerable advantage. I collected enough dogs for a team and started running my traplines from Mile 27, with a toboggan and five sled dogs. I was then able to spend some time with Ruby, as my dogs could make the extra 27 miles into town, in a few hours.

I did fairly well with marten trapping, which ended in March. Then, in late April, with John Wells for a partner, we waited in one of my Lynx Creek cabins for the spring to break, hoping then to make a good beaver catch.

Snowbound in the high country and then flooded out by early warm rains, Wells and I failed in our expected harvesting of beaver pelts. We managed to get back to Edson only a few weeks before Ruby gave birth to our first child. We named her "Frances Alberta."

Ruby kidded me one day, while I was holding Frances. "Fawn was right about the bear rug — remember our baby must have happened when we were haying at the Baptiste and sleeping on a grizzly bear hide. But, I'm glad our first wasn't a boy — I couldn't stand having two men off in the hills like this last six weeks!"

Having a family did cause me to change my plans. For one thing, I gave up my idea of a horse ranch and trading post on any location along the northern streams I knew so well. Maybe, at a later date, when airplanes opened new transportation routes, it might have been feasible and little did I dream then, that vast coal, oil and natural gas discoveries would dramatically change the life style of Indian and non-Indian alike, in the very country I had roamed so freely.

George Hackett, Harold Parnall with R. T. dog team at Mile 27.

Lynx Creek cabin

CHAPTER XXIX

Broke, and still in debt after paying a few bills, I started looking for work as soon as John Wells and I reached Edson, after our disastrous spring hunt.

Jack Hodgkinson wanted to finish an attic in their Edson home, for use as bedrooms and offered me a job. A man named Holman rented another small house owned by Jack and Fan Hodgkinson and, while I was carpentering on the attic, visited me.

"You're pretty good with a saw and hammer, young fellow," Holman observed, adding, "I've lined up a job building a house for a railroad man — how about us working together?"

I was flattered and, of course, interested, so I went into partnership with Holman, thinking that because of his being much older than I, was probably an experienced builder. I was wrong. We had worked only a day or two, when the railroad man for whom we were building, fired Holman and said I could finish the job!

Holman, it seemed, hadn't the slightest knowledge of how to use a carpenter's steel square, as an example. He had simply used me, hoping I would carry the mechanic's load in any building project. While I was mulling over my problem with Holman, he suddenly left Edson and I felt free to finish the job we had started. Fortunately, shortly after the Holman episode, I met and worked with Jack Tran, an experienced cabinet maker and all around mechanic, with wood working tools.

For the next two years, I worked at carpentering during the summer and trapping in the winter. And I also kept experimenting with so-called humane traps and snares, and kept sending out more and more articles on my north country experiences.

The winter of 1921-22, we spent on the McLeod River, with our good friends, Tom and Gertie Murphy. The Murphys, whom I have mentioned frequently in earlier chapters, had leased a homestead ranch, near the "Big Eddy" on a bend of the McLeod River, about 10 miles west of Edson. There, they ran a small dairy and Ruby and I went out to help in that operation. I could also run a trapline and keep my typewriter working — in between the dairy chores.

In February, 1922, we moved back into Edson, to add on to a log cabin we had purchased earlier. I borrowed Jack Hodgkinson's work horses and hauled in logs from an abandoned homestead a few miles north of Edson.

With very little help, and in spite of her condition, Ruby and I added the sizeable room in which our second child, Anna Rhoda, was born on March 18, 1922.

Dr. McCordic had said on his visit a day earlier, that Ruby had plenty of time before being taken to the local Lawrence Nursing Home. Around noon on the 17th, Ruby started having labor pains. Alarmed, I went for a nurse who lived closer than the Lawrence Home. This nurse insisted that I get hold of Dr. McCordic at once. I located the physician and we were soon all set for a night of ordeal.

It was still dark, in the early morning, when Ruby finally won her battle. I'll never forget that experience, as I held a kerosene lamp for the doctor and nurse. Within an hour, both mother and babe didn't seem "any the worse for wear," but Nurse Mackenzie came down with the flu and we had to move

Raymond - 1922

Frances - Edson Cabin - 1922

Ruby and our baby to the Lawrence Nursing Home, bundling them up in a cutter (small sleigh) hauled by one horse.

We paid Mrs. Lawrence with proceeds from a writer's check I had received only a few days before Anna was born. Our second child was named for my mother, Anna, and for one of Ruby's girl friends, Rhoda Sutherland.

Now, with still more responsibilities as a family man, I looked up my good friend, Jack Tran and we both landed a job remodeling railway box cars into construction type bunk houses; cook cars; mess cars, etc., for the Canadian National Railway's B & B (Bridge and Building) department.

I suspect that Ruby and her mother breathed sighs of relief when I got a steady job with a regular pay check. Within a few months, aided by fairly frequent checks from magazines and newspapers, we were in pretty good shape, financially.

The railroad job proved seasonal and we decided to spend the winter on a homestead farm leased by Frank and Florence Tucker. Frank had been my partner for a few months, running our traplines from the old Mile 27, Edson Trail roadhouse or stopping place. While Frank and I were out on the traplines, Florence stayed with Ruby, so now with the situation reversed, we were thrilled with the prospect of wintering with our good friends.

The Tom Attrill homestead was about 15 miles west of Edson and could be reached by a narrow, but passable, wagon road. Attrill, a bachelor, had cleared, plowed and sowed for a hay crop about half of the 160-acre homestead.

"No wonder he gave up," Ruby commented on first viewing the Attrill place, "And look at that big log house and barn — Tom sure must be a hard worker."

Ruby was so right and, after Frank showed me around, I wondered how he hoped to wrest a living from that hostile land. The Tuckers had taken over Attrill's livestock, consisting of a few head of cattle, including two milk cows, four good work horses, some pigs and poultry.

"I guess a man and wife could exist on a place like this," Ruby said, late that evening.

I had to agree with her rather pessimistic attitude, but replied in defense of the Tuckers, "I don't blame them for leaving the city and looking for something more satisfying. You know, Honey, I was raised in a farm and ranching country and, believe me, horses, cows and even pigs, are easier to get along with than some people!"

Ruby laughed, then admitted, "I'm really happy. It will be great being with Frank and Florence again and you can write that book now." She referred to an idea I had for writing about my experiences and Ruby thought that the title, "Wilderness Trapper" was a good one.

Above the kitchen there was a small space near the stovepipe, extending on through the kitchen ceiling, into the attic. A stairs led from the kitchen to the upper floor, so I set up shop and wrote "Wilderness Trapper," with my typewriter atop an upended orange crate.

I typed for an average of four hours each day and on the 18th day, I had completed my first book, 175 pages in all. I'll never forget the warmth from that friendly stovepipe, only a few feet from where I sat while I typed, nor the odor of food simmering on the cookstove in the kitchen below. Florence prepared the meals and Ruby washed the dishes. But often our cook was exasperatingly slow! Florence would sit and play solitaire for hours at a stretch. She was a wonderful vocalist and pianist and I realized she must have missed her piano and music very much.

While working on my book, I also helped Frank with the chores and ran a short trapline every few days. I never felt better in my life.

The Tuckers had harvested a fair crop of potatoes, cabbages and rutabagas, but Frank had killed neither deer nor moose and we were all pretty well "fed up" on hotcakes, cornmeal, rice, beans, etc.

"Guess it's time to butcher a steer," Frank said one morning.

I had heard Frank and his wife talking about finances and knew that they, like Ruby and me, weren't too well fixed for ready cash. I knew that Frank had figured on selling any beef from butchering the steer, in Edson, for cash with which to buy sugar, flour, lard, tea, coffee, etc.

"Hold off for a few days, Frank, I've seen some moose tracks not too far from here."

"Okay, Ray," he answered with a grin, and quipped, "Good luck, but you said yourself that moose tracks make poor soup!"

Ruby was a little miffed when I didn't invite her on the special moose hunt, but she admitted afterward that she knew a lone hunter is a sure hunter.

Moose feed early in the morning and just before dusk, except during the mating season in late August on through September. It was December now and both sexes of moose ranged over considerable territory, separately. A cow moose might allow yearling calves to stay with her, while bulls often traveled in small groups. Moose calves, beyond the suckling stage, must forage for themselves and, even when near a cow moose, are most vulnerable to attack by wolves.

I hunted for two days without success, as far as big game was concerned. But I did trap two brush wolves whose pelts would buy a fair supply of groceries. Frank still wanted to butcher the steer, saying, "We could sure stand some steaks, roasts and soup bones."

On the third day, I was snowshoeing parallel to a low, long ridge of land we called a "hog back." It extended in a general east and west direction and I was passing through a sparse growth of poplar on the north side of the ridge. Just as I neared the west end of the "hogback," a bull moose broke from cover, headed for the south side of the ridge.

The bull was in my view for only a few seconds, but I managed a shot just as he disappeared behind the ridge, on the side opposite from me.

Kicking off my snowshoes, I plowed through the snow, retracing my steps. If I could reach the east end of the hogback, I might get another shot at the bull, as he must be running in that direction, with only the narrow strip of land between us.

Sure enough, as I reached the east end, a bull moose hove in sight and I felled him with one shot from my high powered rifle.

Imagine my surprise when, on rounding the end of the hogback, I discovered two bull moose down, within a few rods of each other. One had a set of antlers with 5 points on each side and the other, 6 points. I had not missed the first shot and the brief glimpse of moose number 1, wasn't enough for me to bother counting points on antlers.

Luckily, too, I had downed the two moose in sparsely timbered woods so

Frank Tucker - "Special" moose catch.

Frank and I had no trouble in making a trail for a team and the front bobs of a sled, with which to haul out that veritable windfall!

We had a lot more meat than we could use, so Frank took most of it into Edson and gave it to our special friends and relatives.

That was one big game hunt I didn't brag about. An unwritten law in that frontier recognized that homesteaders, trappers, and miners, were allowed considerable leeway for subsistence. But, two moose in one day! Well, that story remained best untold.

On the trip into Edson, Ruby and Anna accompanied Frank. Anna had developed a cough and we thought it advisable to have our little daughter examined by a doctor. Fortunately, she had only a temporary cold.

We remained with the Tuckers until the trapping season ended, then moved back to Edson. During this period, I had received several letters from Lew Aumock, the Pine Woods Fur Farmer in northern Idaho. Lew was still anxious to have me live-trap marten for his experiments in ranching that furbearer. My previous attempts had failed and now Aumock suggested that I try again, in an area of northeastern Washington, near the Canadian border.

"Sounds interesting," I told Ruby, after discussing the fur farmer's proposal.

Another interesting aspect was that the area Lew Aumock had suggested, was only 50 miles northeast of my home town. "It's been five years since we visited my folks," I remarked.

"Well, okay if we can manage. You'd better get some of these plans worked on before our girls reach school age!" Ruby said.

Shortly afterward, I received a substantial check from my publisher, along with a friendly note stating that they would start working on the *Wilderness Trapper*, within a few weeks.

That was our big moment, as from then on, my wife accepted my writing career as an asset and not a liability or excuse for my shying away from steady employment.

In the early spring of 1923, we left Edson, by train and a couple days later arrived in my home town, Almira, Lincoln County, Washington.

CHAPTER XXX

It was wonderful once more visiting my widowed mother, two sisters and friends I had known since childhood. My younger sister, Blanche, had left Spokane and was now an assistant to the Almira postmaster, Will Connors. Mother had moved back into our Almira home and, as she and Blanche needed only three rooms, mother had renters in most of the house. My elder sister, Mary Ely, was married to Jack Murbach and they farmed only two miles west of town.

My girl friend of high school days, Isabel Stevens, still lived with her parents, just across the street from my old home. She was the local telephone operator.

Isabel was visiting Blanche one evening while Ruby and I were away at the Murbach farm. Returning to mother's home, we found Isabel still there and, one thing leading to another, Ruby, Blanche, Isabel and I got into a card game.

Suddenly, it was midnight and Blanche said, "You'd better walk Isabel home, Ray. She has to either cross through the barnyard, or go the long way around. There's a herd bull in the barnyard."

Ruby looked at me. It was an awkward moment. "You want to stretch your legs, too?" I said, facing her.

"Go ahead — you know I'm afraid of bulls," Ruby said, a little nervously, I thought.

Isabel and I passed by the small herd, through a gate on the street side between the two homes, without incident. I said good night to Isabel at the opposite side of the barnyard, opening another and smaller gate, just a few rods from the Stevens' back porch.

I wondered about Isabel's thoughts and whether she remembered our school days and the hours we had spent together, mostly in and around her Almira home. It all seemed so long ago, and the many events that had taken place when we lived so near each other, now were only vague memories. But for my wanderlust and my emigrating to Canada, I most likely would have married Isabel and have become a farmer, like my father before me.

I was little bit annoyed when Blanche asked me to see that Isabel got home safely. But, on the way back, I felt grateful toward my sister. The few minutes I was alone with Isabel were enough to make me realize, more and more, just how deeply I loved Ruby. Before we went to bed, I looked at our two precious tots, asleep on a small cot, and said to myself, "You're a lucky man, Ray Thompson!"

My writing was producing a slim but far from adequate income, so I looked around for odd jobs. A former high school friend was a painter and paper hanger and had more work than he could handle. I mentioned it to Ruby and she was all for taking on the job of papering several rooms in the local printer's home.

"I'm sure we can do it, remember I helped Edith paper her house," my game little wife argued, when I told her that I wasn't too enthused over my friend's offer.

The "Edith" she referred to was a sister-in-law of our old Edson (Alberta) friend, Tom Murphy. Tom was an expert paper hanger and had taught Ruby and Edith the fundamentals of the trade, so, after Will Evans, the Almira friend, said he had extra brushes, pasting board, etc., we tackled the job.

Fred Pier's home had 10-ft. ceilings and I suspected that Evans was glad to sublet that papering job. But, with Ruby's knowledge and indomitable spirit and my skill as a carpenter, we did such a good job that Fred Pier got us another for a neighbor.

Then, a local carpenter told me that he had a seasonal job repairing company-owned buildings in northern Idaho and was sure he could help me land a carpentering and/or painting job with the Potlatch Lumber Mills. It sounded great, as $1.00 an hour was good wages. But, we had no transportation and very little cash to invest, even on a down payment plan for an automobile. There were no cheap used cars in the two Almira garages. "You might try Coulee City," Abe Nichols, the carpenter suggested.

Coulee City was about 16 miles west of Almira and, guess who offered to drive us there! My ex-girl friend, Isabel, whose father had just bought a Model T. Ford.

Well, we located a 1917 Dodge touring car in Coulee City. The car dealer wanted $200.00 for it and offered to take $50.00 down and $25.00 a month. This, we could handle, so we started back toward Almira about dusk.

I could write a book about that 1917 Dodge! It would run fairly well for about five minutes and then, like a tired old mule, stop for a rest. Isabel would drive her Ford ahead of us, then when she saw we weren't close behind, would turn around and see what was wrong.

We finally reached Almira and, for ten days that Dodge baffled every "expert" in town. We even borrowed a carburetor and a vacuum tank from a kind old lady who had a similar model Dodge resting idly in her barn.

"I think we should haul it out to the nuisance ground!" Ruby suggested.

"We call it 'dump grounds'," I answered wearily. "But, I've got one more idea — I'm going to drain the gas tank."

There was the trouble and the solution. Sediment in the gas tank was sucked up through a line of copper tubing into the engine carburetor by suction from a vacuum tank system but, as soon as the motor developed a modest power, the sediment being sucked up along with gasoline from the tank, clogged and completely shut off the fuel. What was so baffling was that, after the motor was idle for several minutes, the sediment clogging the flow would settle back into the tank. Cleaning the fuel line and tank resulted in fair transportation in that badly abused old Dodge.

After two months carpentering at the lumber mills in Potlatch, Idaho, we returned to Almira. On the way, we stopped in Spokane, Washington and traded the Dodge in on a new car. My earnings as a carpenter, plus some very welcome checks from outdoor and juvenile publications, made the purchase possible. But for several weeks, our elder daughter, Frances, only three years old, wanted to know what had happened to "Ours Car," meaning the old Dodge. No wonder that she was attached to it, for I had hinged the front seat so that it would lay back to make a bed. Frances and her 15-month-old sister, Anna, had slept in the Dodge, while we were camped in a pine woods on the outskirts of Potlatch. We had built a floor and wood frame for a small tent where Ruby and I slept and where meals were prepared during the few times it rained. Mostly, Ruby cooked on an open fire outside.

On our return to Almira, a letter from Lew Aumock, the fur farmer, awaited us. He was still anxous to have me try to live-trap marten and, after we met later, Ruby became quite enthused. "Okay, but remember your promise for next year!" She was reminding me that she had the previous spring, agreed only to one year's absence from Canada on a re-visit to my home country.

Late in September, 1924, we prepared to spend the winter with Harry Crounse, an old miner who had two cabins in a remote and unsettled part of Ferry County, Washington, about 30 miles south of the British Columbia border.

The decision to make this move developed after a search of several areas where heavy woods, pine, spruce, and tamarack, provided cover for several species of furbearers, hopefully among them, the pine marten. The areas were drained by tributaries of the mighty Columbia River. Among these tributaries, the West Fork of the San Poil River heads a few miles north of Aeneas in east central Okanogan County, then flows southeast into Ferry County and on to join the San Poil River.

Gold Creek, a tributary of the West Fork, also flows east to join the larger stream. Deerhorn Creek, fed by rain and melting snow from Strawberry Butte, joins Gold Creek. That area was a favorite for gold and silver prospectors as recently as the late 1920's.

In the summer of 1923, I met Charley Shoemaker, while driving from Strahl Canyon "across the Coulee," to Almira. I told Shoemaker that I was interested in a fur ranching venture promoted by Lew Aumock, owner of Pine Woods Fur Farm, near Rathdrum, northern Idaho, and I reiterated that Lew raised pine marten, a valuable furbearer closely related to the Russian Siberian Sable, and he wanted me to trap, alive, some marten for his fur farm.

Charley Shoemaker thought there might be pine marten in the mountains back of his homestead at the foot of Strawberry Butte. Later, Ruby and I visited the homesteader, but found no signs that indicated the furbearers I sought, frequented that area.

Shoemaker then suggested that we explore the Sherman or San Poil Mountain range some 30 miles to the east, in Ferry County. This range, forms a divide between the San Poil and Columbia rivers.

He also suggested that we visit Harry Crounse, a retired miner and prospector, living on Lime Creek, a tributary of the West Fork of the San Poil. "Crounse knows every creek, valley and mountain in that area," he said.

So, Ruby and I drove back down the valley to the West Fork, and up to Lime Creek. We found Harry Crounse at home and when we told him that Charley Shoemaker had given us his name, the prospector literally welcomed us with open arms. He lived alone, appeared around 60 years of age and was handicapped with a crippled leg. He had two snug log cabins, two horses and a miscellany of tools and equipment, all of which he said we were welcome to use.

"I'm no trapper," Crounse said, "so don't know about marten, but there's lots of deer in the hills, plenty of firewood handy and a fair road, even in winter, to Republic. It gets kinda lonesome here — glad to have you spend the winter. And, if you care to lend a hand, I've got a prospect hole to clean up, that should net a few ounces of gold."

Our two girls, Frances and Anna, were 3½ and 1½ years old and, of course, under school age. Ruby and I had planned on returning to Canada that fall, but Harry Crounse's offer made us change our plans for the winter of 1923-24.

I was doing fairly well with my free lance writing and had an offer from a Canadian magazine for a series of articles that would pretty well grubstake us for the winter.

We agreed with Crounse that in exchange for the sharing of his cabins, the use of his saddle horse and miscellaneous equipment, we would buy food and incidental supplies and pay a nominal rent, as our contribution to the arrangement.

Then, a curious twist developed. A Model T. Ford "touring car," with the top and windshield sheared off, but with the body hardly scratched, had been in Crounse's back yard for several months.

"I towed it in from Gold Creek where it had been wrecked," Crounse said. "I've billed a Spokane man several times, for towing, etc., and the sheriff says now I can claim possession and sell it."

It happened that I had worked for the Ford dealer in Almira, a short time earlier that year, so I knew what it would cost to repair the damaged Model T. This was after we had returned from Potlatch, Idaho. The Ford would need a new top; windshield; front spring and carburetor.

"I'll take $75.00 for it," Crounse said, so Ruby and I returned to Almira, where I bought a front spring and a new carburetor, all that was necessary to get the Model T on the road again. Back to Lime Creek, I fixed the Ford so it would navigate under its own power, gave Harry Crounse a check for $75.00 and Ruby followed me, driving our own car, back to Almira. About ten days later, a farmer paid us $250.00 for the Model T!

The curious side of this incident developed when we learned later that the Model T had been abandoned by bootleggers, after it was wrecked on a whiskey smuggling run from Canada. Remember, this was in 1923, at the very peak of "rum running" during Prohibition.

Settled for the winter in Harry Crounse's cabins, we were often regaled with the old prospector's tales of his adventures. He had mined and prospected up and down the West Coast, from Mexico to British Columbia, and north to the Yukon country.

Curiously, Harry Crounse swore that he had never been a hard drinker, although he admitted that the intrepid "mountain men" and fur traders, along with the miners and prospectors who followed them, lived rough and often lonely lives and were notoriously hard drinkers. The frontier saloon was common in most settlements and whiskey peddlers thrived in remote and isolated spots, such as small mining camps.

When "Prohibition" became the law of the land in 1919, illicit whiskey smuggling from Canada became big business overnight. Little did Ruby or I dream that the road down the San Poil was frequently used by rumrunners bringing booze in from British Columbia, until our return to Lime Creek, in September, 1923.

While driving up the San Poil Valley, we came across a big touring car that had plunged off the road, down a steep slope, to slam against a pine tree. There, the "Case" automobile had caught fire, or had been set afire by its occupants, and it was still smoldering when we stopped. There was a small caliber rifle in the car, the wooden parts burned away. No sign of a cargo remained.

At the West Fork road house, further up the valley, we got our first real "ear-full" about whiskey smuggling from Canada (later confirmed by Harry Crounse). The road house or way station people weren't at all surprised at our report. Apparently, "the law" and the rumrunners were involved in a bizarre, but very real war. Every possible and sometimes impossible route was being used by the rumrunners, in their attempts to elude the sheriff or his deputies.

We heard that one liquor smuggler had been shot and stabbed to death a short time before, in a cabin a few miles below West Fork. There, a white man with an Indian wife, was supposed to maintain a sort of haven for whiskey smugglers. The manslaughter, or murder, resulted in a fight over the Indian woman.

A few weeks later, after we had moved in with Harry Crounse for the winter, Ruby was driving down to West Fork to pick up any mail left there. At the fork in the West Fork and Republic-Wilbur roads, Ruby was confronted by a road block. The sheriff and his men let my wife pass and explained they were trying to trap a man suspected of using the Gold Creek road in transporting liquor by that route, and across the Columbia River by cable ferry, a few miles above Nespelem.

Surely, some of the older old-timers must recall those hectic prohibition era incidents. Harry Crounse must have known some of the rumrunners, but he certainly had no contact with any of them while we stayed there on Lime Creek.

The next summer, Julius Johnson, an Almira banker, and a long-time friend of ours, told me that the Okanogan County Sheriff had phoned him "about a young couple wintering with Harry Crounse." I guessed we were temporarily "suspect" because we were driving a new car and the sheriff had no knowledge of any visible means of support to our credit.

The repeal of the Volstead Act, some years later, changed life on the San Poil back to normal.

During our stay with the old miner, Ruby became good friends with a woman, who with her husband, ran the West Fork road house, near the junction of West Fork Creek and the San Poil River. On some of my hunting trips in the higher ranges, Ruby and our girls stayed at the West Fork. But, often, on shorter trips, we would run my traplines, horseback along the valley trails.

On one longer trip, I rode Crounse's little mare, named Mary Jane, up an icy dangerous trail to a miner's vacant cabin, at the head of 17-Mile Creek. There I stabled the horse and, early the next morning, climbed the mountain wearing snowshoes.

While camped for a short break on the brink of a precipice, I had reached by a mile-long detour, I accidentally lost one of my snowshoes by thrusting it into the snowbank, too near the cliff's edge. Exasperated, I tossed the other snowshoe over the rocky ledge, figuring I would pick the pair up on the way back down the mountain.

Frances Alberta Thompson by Crouse home, Summer of 1923

That mishap almost cost me my life! High on a bare slope, about mid-afternoon, a chinook wind cut into the snow crust and I was soon floundering up to my waist. I managed to reach a clump of mountain willows and found enough of them to build a fire.

It was a night to remember! At daybreak, I made some crude snowshoe frames of the willow, using some cord and strips of leather from my packsack for the snowshoe webbing and escaped back down the mountain to my discarded snowshoes and on to the miner's cabin.

Mary Jane, the sturdy little mare, whinnied a welcome when she heard my voice. She had spent a bad night, too, for there were fresh cougar tracks at the spring, only a few rods from the stable!

The almost tragic expedition on 17-Mile Mountain, was my last effort toward trying to locate pine marten for Lew Aumock's Pine Woods Fur Farm. Ruby had worried because of my unexpectedly long absence and was naturally relieved when I said, "Let's go back to Almira — I've had enough!"

We had been corresponding with George Stevens, the Almira farmer, and he had offered me a job starting with spring seeding and on through harvest.

My game little wife, although disappointed that we couldn't return to Edson sooner, agreed that I had better work on a farm and finish paying for our car.

"We'll be back north by September, for sure," I promised her.

So we said good-bye to Harry Crounse and our friends at West Fork and drove on down the valley, across the Columbia River on a ferry and on to Almira.

George Stevens had a small house in an orchard a short distance from the farm house, barn, and machine sheds. This was to be our home until September, 1924. In May of that year, Raymond, Jr., was born in my old home just across the street from the Stevens' farm.

Just before we left for Canada that fall, I completed a book-length manuscript for *Forest & Stream* and things seemed to be going well for us, as we headed north for new adventures.

CHAPTER XXXI

A few weeks before we left Almira, on our way back north, a young farmer named Bill Burke, came in town to see me.

"I heard you were looking for a trapping partner — Ray Johnson told me. I'm no trapper, but I'd sure like to spend a winter in a real big game country," Bill said. He had learned from our mutual friend, Ray Johnson, some of my plans as Ray and I had discussed them on several occasions, when he had thought of joining in the venture.

Bill Burke's wife, Beryl, was also enthused and, since they had no children, there was no difficult problem concerning housing for the coming winter, as Beryl would stay with Ruby while Bill and I were on the trapline. It didn't take long for us to agree on partnership terms and in mid-September, we all left for Edson, Alberta, Bill and Beryl in a big touring car, a Westcott, and the Thompsons in our Dort touring car.

Leaving Washington State, we angled across southeastern British Columbia, over several hundred miles of new road, graveled, but often steep and always rough.

Nearing Cranbrook, B.C., we had the misfortune of breaking the main leaf in the rear spring of the Dort. The nearest possible supply for a new leaf was in Spokane, Washington, about 200 miles back over the road we had just traveled. A local Ford dealer said, "I can telegraph an order, but I'd say it would take at least two days — if the dealer who handles your make of car has a leaf in stock."

The Burkes were ahead of us, but we had agreed to meet at Canal Flats, a point about 100 miles north of Cranbrook.

Ruby and I were worried, too, as our baby, Raymond, Jr., was quite ill. We were three or four days' hard travel from Edmonton, where Ruby's brother, Will, lived.

"We'd better look for a campsite and take Ray to a doctor," I concluded.

Ruby agreed. "Leave me and the baby at the doctor's while you ask about camping," she said.

I drove slowly on account of the broken spring and was about to pass a small shop that advertised "Auto Repairs" and, on the spur of the moment, stopped at the not very imposing "garage."

It proved to be a blacksmith shop and when I asked the man working on a forge in the rear of the establishment, about a campsite, he mopped the sweat from his brow with a grimy rag and came outside in front of his shop.

"You can set up your tent on an empty lot just around the corner," he said, pointing out the direction I should follow.

Then, "Couple of cute kids you have — kinda rough for a man, alone with kids," he suggested, half apologetically.

I laughed and told him about my wife and our four-months-old son, at the doctor's.

That blacksmith turned amateur auto repair mechanic, was an angel in disguise. For, while I was speaking, he suddenly noticed the sag in our car on the side of the broken spring.

"That's why we have to camp and wait for repairs from Spokane," I explained.

"H-m-m! Too bad! Mind if I take a look?"

Bill Burke and R. T.'s pack dog, Buster, 1924

Of course, I didn't object and a short time later was thrilled when the blacksmith said, "I can weld that spring — as good as new — take about two hours."

I didn't even ask what the job would cost. "Go ahead, the girls and I will walk back to the doc's and see what the verdict is."

Lady Luck was really smiling on us that day. The doctor said that our infant son was suffering from malnutrition and that Ruby would have to quit breast feeding Ray, Jr. and try Borden's condensed milk as a substitute. Also, Ruby got a scolding when she told the doctor how much corn-on-the-cob and watermelon she had been eating!

Anyway, that one day was the only one when real trouble stared us in the face, on the entire journey of some 1,200 miles. How times have changed! The Cranbrook blacksmith charged us $8.00 for the spring welding job and the doctor, only $2.00 for his advice, which incidentally, proved the answer to our problem with our baby son.

We caught up with the Burkes at Canal Flats, camped there and traveled together from that point, on to Edmonton. The Banff-Windermere road through B.C., passed through a ruggedly beautiful mountain country. It was also big game country and we passed several small bands of Big Horn or Rocky Mountain sheep.

We stopped at a forest ranger station and met a ranger's wife, alone and "scared to death," in her own words. Only an hour before, a big black bear had pushed open a screen door of the ranger's cabin, lumbered on into the kitchen, feasting on a wild-berry pie, making his exit by breaking through another screen door in the rear of the station.

"See there," the frightened young woman said, pointing to the broken screen.

"Maybe we'd better offer to stay until the ranger gets home," Ruby whispered.

I agreed and made the offer. "Oh, thanks so much, but Jack should be in shortly. Anyway, it was my fault. I won't trust a screen door to hold out a bear, from now on, especially when I'm baking blueberry pies," she said with a nervous chuckle. then, as we were leaving, she took a pie from the oven and insisted on us taking it.

We corresponded with the ranger's wife and in one letter, she mentioned that Jack, her husband, had bought a pair of huge wolfhounds for her protection as "those pesky bears keep coming around, maybe hoping I'll bake pies just for them." Ruby and I were to remember that incident particularly, as we both had already experienced encounters with wild bears, even including the unpredictable grizzly.

Continuing our journey, we reached Edmonton a few days later. We stayed overnight with the Will Millar family and then on west another 120 miles, to Edson, Alberta.

It was good to be back with our old friends, but it had been hard for me to say good-bye to my mother and sisters, when we left the town where I had lived most of my life.

In Edson, we rented a small house near the Hodgkinson's. Ruby's mother's home was next door to her sister's home. The Hodgkinsons had an extra "light housekeeping" room that suited Bill and Beryl Burke, so with our families settled, Bill and I shipped our outfit west, about a hundred miles on the Canadian National Railway.

At a water-tank stop, a place called Bliss, our grubstake, tent, traps, camp utensils, etc., were unloaded. We hired a packer, Jack Wilson, to take us into the wilderness, on a trail that led to an abandoned trapper's cabin, on a small stream that emptied into the West Fork of the McLeod River.

There we wintered, while I again tried to capture marten in live traps, with the idea of sending breeding stock down to Lew Aumock's Pine Woods Fur Farm in northern Idaho.

That phase of the venture failed. I made some traps out of wire netting, that proved successful in taking the valuable furbearers alive, but, it turned bitterly cold and the marten froze to death. Even though I had made warm pens for the animals and kept them inside our tent, they worked their way out of the nest boxes, to die from the 40-below zero exposure. Although the marten trapping was a failure, I did benefit from continued experimenting in snaring fox and wolves.

In January, 1925, we pulled out of the "High Divide" country, back to Edson. Bill and Beryl Burke sold their car in Edson and returned via railway, back home to Almira.

There were many brush wolves along the McLeod River, so I renewed my experiments with wire snares, finally discovering a certain grade of steel wire cable that would hold a wolf most of the time.

Then, one night, I woke Ruby with, "I've got the answer — a lock to keep the snare noose from opening, once it's closed around a wolf's neck!" Ruby, from the very start, had confidence in my "invention," especially when she saw a model snare using a crude but effective lock.

I hired a patent attorney, Sterling P. Buck, to file a patent application in Washington, D.C. After a couple weeks of "selling" my invention, I collected a few hundred dollars and boarded a train, eastbound, for New York, with the naive notion that any manufacturer would seize the opportunity so apparent to me, in promoting a self-locking steel snare.

CHAPTER XXXII

I reached New York City in early March, 1925, stopping in Ottawa, Ontario, to make application for a Canadian patent on my invention of a self-locking animal snare trap. In New York, I visited the editorial offices of *Forest and Stream, Fur News* and *Outdoor World, Fur Age Weekly* and others, several of whom had published my adventure stories of the Canadian North.

Fur Age Weekly published a sizable article on my invention. Shortly after this, I received a phone call from David C. Mills, Managing Director of the National Association of Fur Industry.

"I'd like to know more about your self-locking snare," Mills said. I, of course, was thrilled that such a prestigious organization was interested in my invention, so I gladly accepted an invitation to meet with the fur industry representative.

David Mills was immediately impressed and, a few days after the interview, phoned that some friends of his, the Doran Brothers of Danbury, Connecticut, were interested in manufacturing my snare. "If you like, I'll go with you. Danbury isn't too far." Naturally I "liked," so Mills and I took a train trip to see what the Doran Brothers, James and John, thought of my invention.

The Dorans, especially Jim, thought I had something very much worth while and shortly an agreement, on a 50-50 basis, resulted. Doran Brothers would manufacture the snares and I would see to the distribution and sales of the finished product.

There followed over four months of delay on the Dorans' part, with hedging on a revised patent application, with Dorans' insistence that the patent be applied for in a "disinterested party's name." Also, there would be the stipulation that the patent, when issued, would be re-assigned, 50% each to Doran Brothers and 50% to Raymond Thompson.

On my questioning for more details on the Doran proposal, I learned that the "disinterested party" to whom the patent would be issued, was none other than the Doran draftsman! When I objected to this plan, the Dorans agreed to a patent application in my name, with an assignment of 50% interest in the patent to Doran Brothers of Danbury, Connecticut.

The Dorans had a fine manufacturing plant and several hundred employees and, as the summer months slipped by, with no progress in the manufacture of my animal trapping device, I became suspicious of Dorans' motive and was very depressed.

This period was most trying and unhappy for Ruby, too. She was expecting our fourth child in early August. The climax came, when she accused me of stalling by keeping on writing that I couldn't set a firm date for my return. I showed her letter to the Dorans' secretary and she, knowing the situation, talked to James Doran. James wrote my wife (as I learned later) explaining the situation as they viewed it, and that he would personally see that several thousand snares, already in process of manufacture, would be completed shortly and that I could now return home.

James Doran's word was good. We signed the patent application forms, revised to name me as the inventor, and I left Danbury early in August. I reached home only a few days before our son, Norman, was born.

In retrospect, I envision that period as very trying and even dramatic. I was

FOUKE FUR CO.

DIRECT BUYERS OF RAW FURS

ST. LOUIS, MO. U.S.A.

April 14, 1925.

Mr. Raymond Thompson,
c/o Fur Vogue Publishing Co., Inc.,
47 West 34th St.,
New York City, N. Y.

Dear Sir:

We are very much interested in the Snare you have invented, as described in an article on the first page of the Fur Age Weekly of April 13th.

We issue a catalog each season quoting all kinds of traps and trappers' supplies. These catalogs are mailed direct to more than a half a million trappers in the United States, Canada and Alaska.

As soon as you have completed your plans for manufacturing these Snares, we wish you would send us a sample, quoting us your very lowest prices delivered St. Louis.

Yours very truly,

FOUKE FUR CO.

SSM/CB

S S Marks

desperately lonely for my wife and three youngsters and very worried over Ruby's distrust. I could not blame her as she couldn't understand the situation in which I was trapped. But my wife had a lot of stamina and, soon after Norman was born, was as strong and active as ever.

We rented a fine log home about 10 miles west of Edson on the McLeod River, and here I proceeded to test the snares that Dorans had manufactured. There were some minor flaws in the lock design, but, fundamentally, my new snare trap was an instant success. I snared a number of wolves, never losing one, after it entered the wire noose with locks on both ends of the snare wire.

My enthusiasm over the possibilities in my invention, shortly suffered a setback. On reporting to Dorans that the snare was a success and that I had a request for a firm price of 20,000 snares from a fur trader in Edmonton, I was informed, by telegram, that before they would proceed with additional manufacture, I would have to change my percentage of assignment interest to Dorans in my patent, to 51%.

Ruby was disappointed, along with me and said, "Maybe you can get back with Jimmy Knox." Knox was a Bridge and Building (B & B) foreman on the Canadian National Railway, under whom I had worked the previous summer.

"Let's wait and see what our furs are worth," I answered, trying to hide my depressed feelings. Had I wasted five months in trying to promote my snare manufacturing venture?

Then, out of nowhere, came the solution! First, I received notice that a Canadian patent for my snare was being granted *in my name* and, secondly, a local machinist was very much interested in manufacturing the locks for my snares. We could buy the wire in eastern Canada, cut it to the desired length and assemble the snares in a small shop, or even (as we actually did for a while) in our own home. Jack Anderson bought a small interest in our invention and set up a punch press in his own shop, stamping out our snare locks with dies made in the railway shop and we were back in business.

Moving to Edmonton was our next stage. Here, we could contact distributors who could sell our snares all over northern Canada. We had the wire shipped to us from eastern mills and when cut in lengths, assembled the locks in Edmonton and thus were able to keep in the snare business. In a few months, we had a small but growing mail order business to augment our sales through jobbers who distributed a wide range of supplies to fur traders.

Even before our move to Edmonton, I had made contact with R. A. Godson and Charley Young, owners of the Metropolitan Press in that city. They published *Good Roads Magazine*, the official organ of the Alberta Motor Association. My interview with Godson and Young was very much of an advantage to me. They agreed to include an "Outdoor Recreation" department in *Good Roads Magazine*, with Raymond Thompson as editor. Through this connection, I became acquainted with several prominent and influential business executives in Edmonton and, after our move to that city, the capitol of Alberta Province, I met some government officials who later helped me in my various activities.

One person in particular, proved especially helpful. This was Ben J. Lawton, Alberta Game Commissioner and, through him, I contacted A. C. MacFayden, a former assistant to the Game Commissioner. "Mac" had resigned his government post and had gone into muskrat ranching. Mac-

Fayden asked me to edit a booklet on Muskrat Ranching, which I was, of course, glad to do.

Mac's headquarters was in a downtown Edmonton office building and, on my first visit, I was introduced to R. H. Trouth, an architect and building contractor. Trouth also was interested in muskrat ranching and had invested a small fortune in buying land and fencing a large portion of an area enclosing a sizable lake and marsh. MacFayden, who had persuaded Trouth to establish the fur farm, estimated that the initial population of 200 muskrats could be quadrupled in two years.

The Trouth property and Elk Island Game Preserve were separated by a heavy wire fence, designed to hold within its confines, a sizable herd of buffalo. The fame fence, at one point, crossed a small lake inhabited by a few hundred muskrats. Part of the lake was on Trouth land and, because of the type of "buffalo" fencing, muskrats swam freely in and out of the game preserve. Ralph Trouth wanted to trap, alive of course, the muskrats in the lake just mentioned.

"Could you do that?" he asked, on our very first meeting.

I had trapped hundreds of muskrats for their pelts, but to take the furbearer alive and unharmed, was another matter. It was a challenge.

"I'll have to look over the setup first," I told Trouth.

In the winter the ice on small lakes in that part of the north, could easily be two or more feet in thickness. But, with the spring breakup of ice only days away, I set up my tent camp on the Trouth place, near his caretaker's cabin and proceeded to make some floating "live traps" out of wire netting. When the lake opened up, we set out my floating traps and in a few days, had captured over 200 muskrats from the "outside" lake, releasing them unharmed inside Trouth's fenced, muskrat farm.

Trouth was so elated over our success in the live-trapping and transplanting project that he offered me a partnership in his Elk Island Fur Farm, plus a job as assistant manager in his office. I was working part time as a bookkeeper and editor of *Good Roads Magazine.* I talked to Charley Young, one of the partners in the Metropolitan Printing Company. Charley had no children and, from our first association, had treated me like a son.

"We'd hate to lose you, Ray, but you'd be foolish to pass up Trouth's offer."

For over two years, my business mail had come to the Metropolitan Printing Company office and Charley Young knew of the slow but steady growth in my snare business and the increasing sales in my writing. He knew, too, that R. H. Trouth Company, Ltd., was the maintenance and construction agent for the Hudson's Bay Company. Also, Trouth had just recently been awarded a contract for renovating and, in some cases, replacing Hudson's Bay Company posts in Canada's North West Territory.

"That Bay contract could mean a lot to you," Charley said, "Think of the material for your adventure stories — Trouth is sure to send you on regular river trips."

A few months previous to my talk with Charley Young, we had established, or incorporated, Raymond Thompson Company, Ltd., with myself as President; Charley Young, Vice-President and Ruby Thompson, Secretary-Treasurer. Our objective, in addition to the manufacture of animal traps, was to publish "methods" books dealing with trapping and fur farming and adventure books with juvenile appeal. The Metropolitan press had already printed my first book, *The Steel Snare* and, both Charley Young and his partner, Reggie Godson, were enthusiastic over the possibilities in additional publishing of my stories and articles.

Charley Young's unselfish attitude, plus my wife's whole-hearted support, led me to accept Ralph Trouth's offer. Trouth was a fine architect, but he hated office work and I soon discovered, on taking charge of his books, that he hardly knew from day to day, whether he was about to make a fortune, or go broke over too many "irons in the fire." My experience in the railroad offices, especially in the payroll, accounting and supply departments, proved invaluable.

Trouth was already employing about a hundred men, in constructing a new warehouse for the Hudson's Bay Company and in the maintenance and repair of many other buildings owned by that company. I made friends with the Trouth Construction superintendent, a man named Alex Henderson. I found him thoroughly competent, honest, hard working and *worried*!

"Ray," he said, only a few weeks after our initial get together, "I think Ralph is being cheated on lumber from B.C. He showed me a lumber bill the other day and I didn't like what I saw!"

One of my jobs while working for the Bridge and Building department of the Canadian National Railroad in Edson, was to help Jimmy Knox, a B & B foreman, while he checked several carloads of lumber, principally to check on both quantity and grading of lumber.

"How about us going over some of the bills, together," I suggested.

Henderson quickly agreed. "There'll be several carloads of lumber in the yards (railroad) next week. We can't do much inspecting, in sealed cars, but maybe Trouth can get an order to change that. Otherwise, I bet he'll want you to be in Waterways when the lumber is loaded on a river barge!"

Henderson and I approached our employer with our proposal and he agreed to see what he could do about getting a permit to break the car seals, so that we could inspect the lumber. First, Trouth wired the supplier in Prince George, British Columbia. The answer was very evasive, stating in effect, that a representative of theirs would have to be on hand when the car seals were broken and that R. H. Trouth, Ltd., would have to assume the cost of travel and expenses for the supply house agent.

"Guess we'd better skip that," Trouth said and, turning to me, "You'd better plan on a trip to Waterways, in about two weeks. That's the date the cars will reach there."

This seemed to settle the matter. I told Ruby about the situation and she was visibly disturbed. "I think Trouth will have you in the Arctic until the rivers freeze over next fall," she said.

Selfishly, I had been thinking too much of my own projects rather than my home life. But, when I knew how concerned Ruby was, no doubt remembering my "few weeks" trip to the East, that lasted nearly five months, I told her that I would quit the Trouth Company before becoming involved too deeply.

"I hope you won't have to do that. I think Trouth needs you more in his office here, anyway."

Then, out of a clear sky, came the answer. Ruby phoned me the very next day with some astonishing news.

"I've a letter from my father, enclosing a check for $100.00, saying he'd be in Edmonton in a very few days!"

That was news! Walter George Trench, an explosives expert and chemical engineer, had been estranged from Ruby and her brother, George, Jr., for 20 years. Ruby's mother had divorced Trench, when their two children were very young. Mrs. Trench, in order to avoid continued harassment from her ex-husband, had moved to northern Alberta in 1911, assuming her first married name, "Millar," after a sea captain who had died a few years before she married Trench.

Sure enough, Walter G. Trench arrived in Edmonton, and registered at the city's best hotel, the McDonald. Apparently, he was a very successful business man, with a well-established clientele of steel mills who purchased large quantities of chemicals from his firm. Trench, in his 60's, was a man of medium height, clean shaven, balding and impeccably attired.

He arranged for a small banquet and invited not only Ruby's close friends, along with her half-brother, Will Millar's family, but his ex-wife as well. Then came his proposal: He would guarantee a substantial salary if I would join his firm and would set us up, housing wise, in either Windsor, Ontario, or across the river, in Detroit.

Ruby objected to our acceptance of her father's offer right from the start.

"He only wants to get even with mother, by taking us away from here!"

A real crisis developed and at one point, I said, "This is our real opportunity and I'll never forgive you if you won't go along with your Dad's offer!"

Curiously, I had written the Chamber of Commerce, Windsor, Ontario, only a few months earlier, requesting information about housing, steel and wire supply houses, and transportation links between that Canadian city and Detroit, U.S.A. There were both ferryboat services and a bridge spanning the Detroit River, between the two cities. We could locate in either and carry on our business without duty or customs restrictions by supplying Canadian customers from Windsor and the U.S. buyers from Detroit.

When I explained over and over, the advantages in such a move, Ruby reluctantly agreed. It was most difficult to say good-bye once again, to our relatives and friends in Canada. My employer, Ralph Trouth, was very disappointed, but after talking to my father-in-law, he said I would be foolish, indeed, to decide against the move.

And, once more, my writing had been a factor in our sudden departure from Canada. Ruby's father had apparently tried for years to locate his son and daughter. But even his own sister, who had corresponded with Ruby's mother, had kept the secret of their whereabouts. The sister did tell Trench that she had heard that Ruby had married a writer, and that his first name was Raymond and that he wrote adventure stories of the Far North. With this meager information, Walter George Trench did some inquiry in the New York City Library. There, he learned that a Raymond Thompson had written a book, *The Wilderness Trapper*, and that it was published in Columbus, Ohio.

The publishers of my book also published *Hunter-Trader-Trapper*, a magazine that frequently carried my stories. By simply writing the Columbus, Ohio publisher, Ruby's father got our address.

The wheel of fortune had spun once again, stopping with our name as the target! What was in store for Ruby, me and our four kids, in a strange world two thousand miles away?

CHAPTER XXXIII

Arriving in Windsor, Ontario, early in June, 1929, we rented a furnished house on Oak Street and phoned Ruby's father, in Detroit. He wished to see us at once, so Ruby and I, with the children, settled in our temporary home, took a bus ride across the river and on to the Tuller Hotel, where Walter George Trench had his Detroit office.

Imagine Ruby's mixed emotions when, on our arrival at the hotel, her half-brother, Allan, was there with their father. Ruby had last seen him when he was an infant. Born out of wedlock to Trench and a girl housekeeper, Allan had been the innocent party to a triangle in which Ruby's mother, her husband and the girl, Molly, were involved. After Ruby's mother had divorced Trench, he had married Allan's mother and Molly had borne two more sons and a daughter.

Allan was a handsome, warm-hearted and intelligent young man and both Ruby and I liked him from the start. He was working as an apprentice in the engineering department of the Great Lakes Steel Corporation, incidentally one of W. G. Trench's customers.

Ruby's father was on his best behavior and a perfect host, ordering a fine meal delivered to his hotel suite. One "fly in the ointment" that kept bothering me was Trench's deliberate avoidance of anything to do with the real reason Ruby and I had agreed to move to Detroit. He and Allan talked in such glowing terms about the steel business and Allan's plans for entering law school, that, as Ruby commented on our way back to Windsor, "He acted like we were just here on a visit."

I had to agree with my wife for, when I mentioned that we should locate a small shop for snare manufacturing, Trench said, "All in good time. I want the Thompsons to meet the rest of my family, in Short Beach, Connecticut. Allan will loan you his car and he'll look after your house in Windsor, while we make the trip!"

There it was — the hateful, domineering side of Walter George Trench! Apparently, as both Ruby and her mother had prophesied, he had never changed in those 20 years since his marriage to the widowed Fanny Millar had broken up.

But there was no good reason for us to refuse her father's invitation, so Ruby, our four youngsters and I, crowded into Allan's small Chevrolet coach, and following Trench in his Lincoln, drove nearly a thousand miles to Short Beach, Connecticut.

At the Trench home there, we met Molly, his wife, whom of course, Ruby remembered, and their other three Trench children, Bae, a really beautiful 17-year-old girl, and two younger children, Erick and Jack.

It was a miserable visit, although we did enjoy the fine beach only a few blocks from the house. Trench and his wife quarreled frequently.

"I think your Dad wants to divorce Molly and is trying to provoke her into some rash act that he can use as evidence against her, if he does file for a divorce."

"You're right," Ruby said. "I certainly remember how mean he was to my mother! That's why she took George and me out west."

Nothing really serious happened however, and after a few days' visit, we headed back to Windsor. We took a different route and thus avoided traveling with Ruby's father.

A week later, learning that Trench was back in Detroit, I met him and demanded an explanation for the delay in attending to the snare business. Trench had previously intimated that he would be glad to buy a share in Raymond Thompson Company. Now, he was hedging and when we went to his bank to open an account in that name, he filled out the information sheet, showing Raymond Thompson as sole owner and, therefore, wholly responsible for any dealings, financial and other, in the operation of the manufacturing and publishing business that I expected to establish. In short, Walter George Trench, was literally "washing his hands" of any responsibility connected with the goals we had set when deciding to leave Canada.

Ruby was worried, but not surprised, when I told her what had, or rather had not, happened in my showdown with her father. We still had a little money left, and realizing we had made a mistake in renting the Windsor house, we moved to Dearborn, a Detroit suburb, in the U.S.

Allan was really disturbed over their father's actions and told Ruby so and that we could borrow his car again, while looking for a house to rent. We drove mile after mile in the suburbs of Detroit, without success, until our daughter, Frances, spotted a sign tacked on a telephone pole. "Look Daddy, it says house for rent!"

Sure enough, two blocks off the main road through Fordson, we came to a fine-appearing, fairly new house.

A woman answered the door with, "Boy, it sure pays to advertise! I tacked that note on the post about 15 minutes ago!"

She looked us over. "Fine bunch of kids. You can move in tomorrow — rent $45.00."

After searching for two days and being turned down a few times by rental agents, because of our family of youngsters, this was welcome news. Curiously, we had taken possession only two days when men would come knocking, asking if girls of a certain name, were busy. Of course, Ruby advised that there was "no Irene; no Flossie; no Cissy, here!"

We were lucky, as on either side of us were decent, hard-working men and their families. Lou Compeau worked for a Detroit paper and our other neighbor, Joe Moroco, was employed in the Ford factory at Dearborn. It was Lou Compeau who told me that the last renters of the house we had just moved into, ran a bootlegging business in the basement and that Irene, Flossie, and Cissy were whores. The operation had apparently ended with a police raid a few days before we arrived there.

The owner, from whom we had rented, did not appear to be a person who would operate an illicit business. But, we were never to know for sure, as a week after we had moved in, a young couple came to tell us that they had just bought the house. After talking with Ruby, the new owners said we could keep the house, at least until fall, when they might like to occupy it themselves. We arranged for schooling for Frances, Anna and Ray, Jr., in case we were there in the fall.

I rented a small office space in the Transportation Building, in Detroit; sent in ads to outdoor magazines and ordered wire and locks for our snares and Raymond Thompson Company was in business in the U.S.A.

The fur trade is a "tricky" business. So fickle is fashion and fashions in fur so dependent on economics, raw fur supply, etc., that anyone engaged in any facet of the business is a gambler!

There was an uneasiness in the air, during the summer months of 1929, preceding the disaster, when the stock market crashed in October. We sensed that something, very serious in nature, was about to happen.

I talked to several houses who traded extensively in raw furs. "Both domestic and foreign buyers are suspicious of Wall Street," one dealer told me.

I tried to keep the bad news from Ruby, but she, of course, knew that orders from our several established dealers in Canada, were coming in reduced quantities, or not at all. As an example, the Shubert Fur Company of Winnipeg, Manitoba, had ordered only 1,000 self-locking snares, for their early fall supply, instead of the 5,000 or more in previous seasons.

I was getting small checks regularly, from my writing, but it was not enough. We all needed new clothes, especially our kids about to start in school. A part-time job in the Sporting Goods department of a huge Sears store, helped.

Somehow, we got through the winter. I'll never forget October 29, 1929. I had moved my office from the Transportation Building to 714 Lafayette Building, nearer the center of Detroit. Someone, passing my office door, yelled, "Stock market busted!" and I, of course, went out into Cadillac Square to see what it was all about. The streets, and the square, were so jammed with people emptying the many surrounding office buildings, the mounted police were helpless in trying to control the mob. It was two hours before buses could operate in and out of the congested area. That financial disaster is history now, as I write this, the market crash happened 49 years ago.

In retrospect, I am humbled by the memory of my wife's behavior in that crisis. Not once did she complain or accuse me of getting us into such a mess through my insistence on making the move to Detroit.

"We'll make it, Honey — we always have!" she said.

To cap the climax, Ruby's brother, George and his wife, arrived from Canada "dead broke"! George also had been promised a job in his father's business, but the senior Trench now refused to help his son in any way. So, we had two more mouths to feed, which made a total of eight. My part time job at Sears, small checks from Detroit newspapers, juvenile, and "outdoor" publications, provided less than a subsistence income.

Detroit, having experienced a real boom through most of the 1920's, was undoubtedly hit harder by the depression than any other city in the United States. Auto sales dropped dramatically, with resultant lay-offs totaling tens of thousands in Ford, Chrysler, and General Motors plants. Ford had raised the starting wage for unskilled labor to $6.00 an 8-hour shift and lines of unemployed, as high as 5,000 at a time, stormed the Ford employment office.

I registered at the Dearborn, Wayne County, employment office. A woman, probably in her late thirties, proved sympathetic, when I confessed that I had left a good job in Canada, hoping to improve manufacturing and distributing facilities in our little business.

"We were assembling our animal snares on the kitchen floor just before we left Edmonton. Guess I was too ambitious," I told my interviewer.

She smiled and said, "Don't be too hard on yourself — Henry Ford started in a small garage."

I thanked the employment office gal and kept on fighting the mob of job seekers that often crowded the walk outside the courthouse, in four rows wide, over a half block in length.

I landed two job tickets, the first delivering coal, in small lots, to houses scattered over Dearborn and Fordson. This was a temporary job, but the few dollars netted was a help. The second job was in breaking up a concrete sidewalk outside a bank. One man broke up the concrete, often in slabs much too large for a wheelbarrow, and the rest of us had to use heavy steel mauls to finish the job.

It was hard work, but I never thought of complaining. Some of my fellow workers did. "I'm mad enough to throw a chunk of sidewalk through the window," a big, burly Swede said. "I come from Minnesota, to make cars — not bust concrete for no damned banker!" That was a mild outburst compared to the helpless, hopeless rantings of the unemployed during those "Dark Days in Detroit."

On the last day I was on the sidewalk repair job, I was surprised to look up to see a familiar smile.

"Hard work, I bet! We'll try for a better job — soon!" It was the gal from the employment office. She chatted with me and the big Swede for a minute or so, then drove off with a man, in a county sheriff's car. There were already many radicals who quickly turned against government authority, whether federal, state, or local and who posed a real threat of mob violence.

The bank job paid $26.50, most of which went for groceries. Then came a real break! One morning, I was in line at the employment office. and had barely gotten inside the building, when I heard a man call out two names. One was A. R. Thompson, so I followed the announcer into the office. Out of over a thousand men in the lineup that morning, myself and one other, were offered employment in the Ford Motor Company factory at Dearborn. I was overwhelmed at my good fortune. We two men were taken by auto to the Ford plant, where I was assigned a job in the sheet metal, car body shop. My badge number was L-1112, a figure I'll never forget!

CHAPTER XXXIV

For a short time it seemed that our fortunes had changed. I landed a job in Ford's Model A body shop on the day shift. Starting at 7 A.M. I rode a street car to and from the huge plant and, $6.00 a day seemed like a fortune.

Then disaster, in new form, overtook the Thompsons. When I changed to night shift, my health suddenly deteriorated. I simply could not sleep during the day, even though Ruby had a bed set up in the comparatively cool basement for me. My nervous system, no doubt aggravated by the exposure to the noise of the huge sheet metal stamping presses at Ford's, just couldn't take it. I became really ill, with loss of appetite and stomach trouble.

W. G. Trench showed up one day, in a Lincoln car driven by a woman chauffeur.

"I've got a small farm, about eighty miles north of here," Ruby's father said, "I'm gone most of the time and need someone to look after the place. Good garden, corn, potatoes, and fruit from the orchard plus fifty dollars a month, Ray, if you and Ruby are interested. Also, there's a small lake on the farm and quite a few muskrats, in case you want to build some live traps — like you used in Canada."

Without any hesitation, and in spite of the small cash wages, we accepted my father-in-law's offer. We had some furniture which we sold to the new owner of the house we were renting, and then moved out to Trench's farm at Lake Nippissing, near Lapeer, Michigan, about two hours drive from Detroit. Maybe — just maybe — I could regain my health and by trying to increase my income through free-lance writing we could start building a more solid future.

In retrospect, I was to realize years later, that the nervous breakdown while working the night shift at Ford Motor Co., was the early stages of multiple sclerosis, a crippling disease that would literally "floor me" from my early forties through "old age."

The Great Depression, starting with the stock market crash in October, 1929, affected many people in many ways. W. G. Trench traveled by motor car with his chauffeur, Bea Taylor, from Detroit east to Massachusetts. Gas was cheap, as low as 10 gallons for $1.00, but my father-in-law's big Lincoln was a gas guzzler and his travel expenses were high.

We had moved to W. G.'s "gentleman's farm" in good faith but soon found that Trench, too, was often short of cash. While sorting apples and selecting the best for winter use, I overhead Trench and Bea Taylor quarreling over her "allowance." "Damn it, Bea, here's my bank statement for last month! My commission checks are smaller, and some accounts are two and three months in arrears!"

Ruby and I had begun to wonder about her father's finances, and now I, an innocent eavesdropper, had learned the truth while working in a cellar immediately below the kitchen where Trench and Bea were at that moment. Just another proof that the depression was widespread.

The Trench farmhouse was large, with several bedrooms on the second floor. Bea Taylor's room was just across the hall from her employer's, so Ruby and I suspected that only one of the bedrooms was in use when Trench and his chauffeur stopped at his farm while he was working the Detroit area, selling chemicals to several steel mills such as those operated by the Great Lakes Steel Corporation.

Early in our stay at the Trench farm, Ruby's father had an unexpected, and unwelcome, visit from his wife, Molly, who lived in Short Beach, Connecticut. Molly, apparently anxious for a showdown with Trench, was seeking a divorce with some reasonable settlement. But in a hearing before the nearest federal judge, Molly lost out but was lucky enough to force Trench to pay transportation costs for herself and two children back to Connecticut.

In the court hearing, it was brought out by Trench's attorney, that Molly had become pregnant while working for Trench as a housekeeper when she was only eighteen.

Ruby was furious and remembered when she and her brother, George, had been literally kidnapped by her father after he had taken them from their home in Glasgow, Scotland to Regand, Quebec where he was living with Molly. She told me that she was indeed "through with any father-daughter relationship with Walter George Trench." We broke with Trench shortly after his wife left, but learned later that he had been granted a divorce from Molly and, soon after, married Bea Taylor.

We rented a cottage at a summer resort called Piper's Landing, on nearby Nippissing Lake. I had regained my health and would now set to work to try and regain some literary markets. I specialized in juvenile stories, both fact and fiction, slanted toward the average teen-ager's love for outdoor adventure. Writing for boys' and girls' publications and on newspaper features, I began to sell my stories and articles quite regularly.

Ruby and our four youngsters helped by collecting hazel nuts and wild berries and, in late October, 1930, it seemed we might make the trip west by car to Idaho where my mother then lived. We hoped to begin again to build a future for our family. But, hard luck plagued us. Our Oldsmobile broke down, and our "nest egg" of cash suffered. By the time we had put in a new transmission, and repaired the universal joint on the car, we were in a bad financial state. Then, to cap the climax, the Olds' transmission broke again. It seemed we had purchased repair parts from the wrong auto supply house!

Ruby took all this in stride with her usual indomitable spirit. "We'll make it next spring, Honey," she said. Three of our kids had to hike about two miles to the nearest school, now that we were temporarily without transportation, and when the weather got too rough, a neighbor, Hank Andrews, took them to school in the morning and a nearby farmer brought them home.

So, we wintered in Doc Tinker's cabin. I trapped muskrats, raccoon, and weasel, in the woods and along a stream that flowed through farms into Lake Nippissing. There was good fishing through the ice on the lake and Ruby learned how to spear pickerel, too, when Hank Andrews showed her how to operate in his small fishing shack. The little house was set over a hole cut in the ice, and one used a small, live fish as bait lowered through the hole. The trick was to lure a pickerel close enough to the spearsman so that a thrust from the pronged shaft would impale and hold the intended victim.

I was working on a story for a Detroit newspaper one morning, when Ruby burst excitedly into the cabin.

"Look — isn't it a beauty!" she gloated, unwrapping a whopping big fish, "Perch — I guess!"

"My gosh, kid, that's a bass — a strictly illegal catch this time of year," I exploded, "Anybody see you with it?"

Ruby was, of course, taken aback, especially when she realized that she

Ruby Trench, age 8, Glasgow, Scotland

had walked right by the game warden, with the illegal bass wrapped in a newspaper. Luck was with us. The game warden had not questioned Ruby, and he soon after left for Lapeer. During the evening meal, Frances, our eldest, remarked, "This tastes better than roast coon, Mom. Sure is a nice piece of fish!"

"Sure is," I agreed. "Your mother can throw a good spear — guess I'd better take some lessons!" I didn't dare to look at Ruby at that moment, for fear of saying something that could result in more comments from our kids. So the episode was merely noted in my diary, "Ruby had good luck today, spearing fish!"

The winter passed quickly. Fur prices had dropped, but I still found it profitable to trap muskrat and raccoon; the "rats" bringing an average of $1.00 each, and raccoon from two to three dollars. I showed our son, Ray, Jr., how to make a cubby house set for weasel, and I'll never forget the thrill Ray showed at his first catch!

Our fuel cost nothing except labor. There was a patch of maple close by and Dave Wilson told us to help ourselves, avoiding the cutting of certain live maples, which he pointed out. Kenny, the farmer's 16-year-old, even helped by lending us a "cross cut" saw, and a good axe. Our own two boys, Ray Jr. and Norman, were too young to be of much help with the actual cutting, but Frances and Anna were regular little work horses. "Daddy," Anna said while we were loading a crude sledge I had made for hauling in the wood, "Sure wish we had some dogs like Buster and Laddie!" Which only reminded Ruby and me of the wonderful days we had spent together, often using our dogs hitched to toboggans, in carrying heavy loads in Northern Alberta.

The mail carrier, leaving our mail in a box about a half mile distance, continued delivering small checks from editors but the aggregate wasn't enough to enable us to buy another car. Also, as spring rolled around, we had to purchase a larger tent for summer occupancy to save rent, plus a strong, two-wheeled trailer to carry our worldly goods if we possibly were able to head back west, that summer of 1931.

The kids helped Joe Komell's gardener and general handyman. Anna remembers picking dandelions, 5¢ a bushel basket to be used in making wine! I did some carpenter work to pay for camping space. Ruby assisted Cora Komell, wife of Piper's Landing Resort owner, when sizable groups of business people held parties at the resort. There was never any cash exchanged for this except an occasional tip a visitor insisted on Ruby taking.

We were really happy the summer of 1931. Frances had completely recovered from a burn suffered the previous winter when she spilled a cup of scalding hot chocolate into her lap. We used a sizable wall tent for a general "living room" during the day, and as a bedroom for our youngsters. Ruby and I had an umbrella tent, in which we slept and where I used my portable typewriter. The tents were about ten feet apart and an open front kitchen was arranged in the space made of heavy canvas.

There were several families who spent the summer at Piper's Landing, in tents of various types. A bad wind storm one night leveled every tent except ours. Fortunately, warned by radio of the impending "big blow," we campers sought shelter in Komell's Inn or in well built cottages surrounding the Inn. No one was injured, nor were any tents badly damaged.

The summer wore on and, not unexpectedly, a slump in the market for free

Thompsons, 1931

lancing articles and stories developed. An incident occurred, in the shape of a visit from a Canadian friend that, while heart warming, proved embarrassing when we had very little cash to spare.

"I'll arrive in Windsor a week before your birthday, Ruby. If you can't meet me, let me know how to get to Lapeer," Jessie wrote.

We had managed to get the Olds running again but, on counting our cash, decided that Ruby had better drive in alone to Detroit, and on across the river into Canada, to meet our friend. "If I go along, we wouldn't have enough cash to stop in Detroit even for a show," I said. Ruby was of course disappointed, but left early on the appointed day. There was a trace of anxiety in her voice when she said good-bye, and Frances asked me why I didn't accompany her mother. I made some lame excuse about Joe Komell needing help and said, "Jessie Wannop is almost like a sister to Mom — they'll have a great visit on the way back."

How helpless we are to stem the tide of events! I was really low that day — that is, until the kids, all four of them, hiked out to the main road and returned with the mail.

"Hope this is good news, Daddy," Frances said while handing me a long, white envelope. It did contain good news — a check from *Detroit News*, for $85.00. The check was payment for a front page feature article in the magazine section of Detroit's largest newspaper.

Ruby was, of course, overjoyed when she arrived safely with our guest. And, although we could hardly afford it, we showed Jessie a good time during the week she spent with us. She was employed as secretary to one of the top regional officials of the Canadian National Railway, in Edmonton, Alberta. Anyone with a fair salary and steady employment during the depression of the 1930's was indeed fortunate. Jessie Wannop was a real friend and we had a great visit. This was in late August, 1931, almost two years after the stock market crash. The three industrial giants, Ford, General Motors, and Chrysler, had reduced their work force by over 50%. Ford had a hit in their Model A, but sales had plummeted for all auto manufacturers.

With another winter coming on, Ruby and I once again bowed to the inevitable, and decided we must stay another winter at Lake Nippissing. Joe Komell let us have a furnished, snug little cabin, for $15.00 a month.

We settled down for the winter with several things in our favor, including cheap rent, and a good supply of vegetables in Komell's root cellar. We had some income from my writing and, starting in November, some revenue from our muskrat trapline, plus all the fuel we needed, courtesy of farmer Wilson, who owned some timbered land just south of Piper's Landing. Our greatest asset, by far, was our good health and the incredible spirit that prevailed in our family. If any of our kids had problems, it was a well kept secret.

We played cards a lot and listened to each other, uninterrupted by radio (we couldn't have afforded one anyway), and, of course, T.V. was unheard of. I was Santa Claus at our county school Christmas program, and Ruby visited frequently with the neighbors. Some of our friends must have worried about us. Early on Thanksgiving morning, we heard someone knocking at our door. When I answered, no one was in sight, but there was a large basket filled with roast turkey and all the trimmings, for a Thanksgiving dinner Ruby and I especially will never forget. We never learned who had left us that reminder of compassion and good will, but we suspected that more than one of our neighbors were involved.

CHAPTER XXXV

Lapeer, about eight miles from Lake Nippissing, was a typical farm community town. The local Chamber of Commerce invited me to give a talk on my northern Canada adventures. I did so, and was pleasantly surprised when the secretary handed me the entire contents of their donation (collection) plate. It was a little less than ten dollars. Then the owner of the one movie theater in Lapeer allowed me to show a silent movie of wild animals and mountain scenery that I had obtained from the Canadian National Parks. The pay was small, but welcome.

I also had a small library of glass slides and a projector, and I showed these in churches and schools. There was never any set fee, only an understanding that I was to receive half of the donations from the audience. In no instance was *any* share withheld by the sponsor; in every case, the manager in charge insisted on giving me 100% of the contributions. It gave me a warm feeling, and I was most fortunate to live in such a community.

But Ruby and I could not forget our goal — to move back west, as soon as school was out. We were determined to skimp and save every dime possible.

One day Ruby had been visiting Doc Tinker's wife. "I landed a little job for us, Ray. The Tinkers own a little house, just off the highway near Lapeer. Helen says there are two rooms to paper, and she said "Doc" is too drunk most of the time to do some carpenter work. I've seen the place, the ceiling area won't be too difficult. You need a change from pounding that typewriter and I told Helen I was sure we could do the job!" Of course I agreed and, in a few days we had finished the paperhanging, and I had repaired a kitchen cupboard.

Helen Tinker was well-pleased with our work. "I wish Doc and I made a team like you and Ruby," she declared. Then as if by afterthought, added, "The plumbing under the kitchen sink keeps leaking. I think Hank Andrews has some pipe wrenches, Ray. Care to tackle the job?"

"Sure thing," I said, "I'll take a look and see what's wrong."

There was a small trap door in the Tinker cabin kitchen, and I lowered myself into a space only about three feet in depth — between the floor joists and the ground. But I easily located the leak, and climbing back out of the hole, reported my findings.

"Short piece of pipe needs replacing — we could have it cut and threaded in town. It will take two good pipe wrenches."

And that's how I happened to find myself in a most peculiar situation, with a very attractive, and almost drunk, woman "plumber's helper." For when I attempted to disjoint the pipes, so as to replace the leaky section, I found it extremely difficult to handle two pipe wrenches at once. Helen Tinker, waiting in the kitchen above, decided I needed help, and before I realized what was happening, there she was wearing an expensive "street" suit and wriggling through the sand and dirt until she reached me. She saw the trouble I was experiencing and though slightly groggy, took one of the wrenches and grasped it, without the slightest consideration for either the clothes she wore or the awkward position she had to assume, lying there flat on her back!

Anyway, it required only a few minutes to complete the repairs, but when I started toward the trapdoor, Helen Tinker just lay there. "Let me rest a minute, Ray. Besides, what's the hurry? I'm drunk, but not too drunk! There's a bottle in the kitchen cupboard — we can celebrate."

Here was a predicament, for as I have already mentioned, Helen Tinker, probably in her mid-thirties, was a fine looking, and really sexy, female. But, I was very much in love with my wife, and I realized that my companion in those tight quarters was actually drunk.

Luckily, Ruby showed up to see how we were getting along and to take me on home if I was finished with the plumbing job. We persuaded Helen to let us take her back to the Tinker home on Lake Nippissing, rather than let her wait for her hubby, who was seeing to some business in Lapeer.

"Doc" and Helen Tinker had a fine home on Lake Nippissing, and we had rented one of their cabins just across the street from them, the first winter we had spent at the Lake. It was a half mile or so from Tinker's to Piper's Landing.

We had heard that Doc and Helen derived their main income (they seemed always to have plenty of money) from sources other than boat and cabin rentals. We did know that while we were living across the street from them the winter before, they frequently held some pretty wild parties. One episode was really disturbing, when Doc and two of his guests, or customers, did some target practice with high powered rifles, shooting at targets almost in front of our cabin. Prohibition was still in force and we wondered if by chance, the Tinkers might be involved in handling illicit booze.

But the plumbing job had paid well, for those times, and slowly our cash capitol increased to the point where we decided to trade in the Olds for a newer model car.

Along in April, 1932, we traded our Olds for a "Light Six" Willys sedan. It was a late model and apparently in excellent mechanical condition, and we thought it would haul us back west, and drag our limited possessions in a two-wheeled trailer along without any trouble. We had paid $10.00 for a trailer, and now we had only to wait for school vacation.

Another curious turn of fate worked in our favor. A trapper living near the Canadian border, down the Red River from Fargo, North Dakota, wanted us to buy a Model A Ford and deliver it to him at Fargo on our way west. I looked at several used cars in Detroit, and wrote Carl Sanders that I could buy a Ford for him and charge only for gas, oil and any minor incidentals, if he would send a check for $250.00. Sanders responded immediately with a check and we bought a Model A that looked almost new for $125.00. A widow, unable to drive the car, had warehoused it.

One good friend we hated to leave, was an eye specialist named Dr. Yeoman. He practiced in Flint, Michigan, about 20 miles from Piper's Landing. His wife and young daughter spent every week-end, during the summer, at a campsite close to our own.

Shortly after we became acquainted, Dr. Yeoman showed a keen interest in our daughter Anna's eye condition. Then ten years old, our daughter's sight in one eye seemed to be deteriorating. Dr. Yeoman was especially critical of an "eye specialist's" operation (about which we of course told him) in Edmonton, when Anna was only 6 years old.

"A steady exercise of the injured eye muscles might help," Dr. Yeoman said, "and if you can bring Anna in once a week it won't cost a dime! I have never seen a case so baffling, but I think it's worth a try."

Unfortunately, Dr. Yeoman's generous offer came too late, for as soon as the kids were out of school, we loaded our belongings on the trailer and said good-bye to our friends at Piper's Landing. I drove the Willys, to which the trailer was hitched, while Ruby drove the Model A Ford.

We studied road maps carefully, and decided that Ruby should keep in the lead. In that way, she could more readily turn back to see what happened to my car or trailer if there was trouble.

We were making fair time, around 40 miles per hour, until mid-afternoon, when Ruby pulled off the shoulder of the road.

"Something's wrong — listen to that knock in the motor," she said, obviously worried.

I listened to the Model A motor and shook my head. "Real bad — sounds like bearing trouble. Let's look at the map."

The kids were concerned, too. Anna, very observant for a ten-year-old, remarked, "There's a roadside camp we passed not long ago."

I thanked our daughter with, "We'll check the map first — lots of garages along this highway!"

The map showed no towns within 20 miles but there was a crossroads where two highways intersected.

"Drive real slow, Honey," I admonished my wife. So we kept on, heading west.

In recalling that trip back to my home country, I am fascinated by one factor, which was the fortunate turn of events, when on several occasions we were confronted with real problems. The Model A engine problem was a shining example.

There was a roadside garage at the intersection, in fact, it was called "The Crossroads Garage."

The owner diagnosed the engine trouble at once, "The main front bearing is shot."

This sounded like bad news, indeed. "Can you fix it?" I dared to ask.

'No, but I'm going into Lansing tomorrow and I know some experts there who'll fix that engine in short order. You can help me pull the motor, if you like."

I hardly knew what to say, but since the Crossroads Garage owner seemed to have a good "listening ear," I decided to tell him the whole story, of how we happened to be driving two cars.

"I came from Montana," he said, "and sure can't blame you for wanting to leave that bad mess in Detroit." Then, as if he considered the matter settled, while pointing to a sizeable building just across the highway, "School's closed, of course, but you can pitch your tent anywhere on the play field."

Talk about a good Samaritan! I helped remove the disabled engine block and "Good Mister Crossroads," as one of the kids named our benefactor, returned from Lansing the next afternoon with the engine "good as new."

Cars in those days were simple in design, compared to today's mechanical monstrosities, but even so, the thirty dollars charged flabbergasted me. "Seems more than fair," I said, "but I do feel that I should pay more."

"I see lots of people headed west. Some are dead beats — one fellow stole a battery right under my nose. It was a pleasure to meet you and your fine family," were the parting words of the Crossroads Garage man.

"Too bad there aren't more like him," Ruby remarked as we again took up our journey. I think we were both a little scared, having suffered a near calamity in the first 100 miles of a 2,500-mile trip!

CHAPTER XXXVI

Our route was, of course, generally west, but we had to make a wide loop to the south, around Lake Michigan, crossing through northern Indiana and Illinois.

"Looks like we'll have to drive through a lot of Chicago," Ruby said. "Hope we don't get separated in the heavy traffic."

I was concerned too, but pointed to a spot on the South Chicago route where we would meet, in case we did get separated. We had one bad experience. I was ahead of Ruby, in real heavy traffic, when she, trying to keep up, ran a traffic light. "Daddy!" Ray, Jr. shouted, "A cop is stopping Mom!"

I pulled into the first open space, and ran back to where Ruby was about to be handed a traffic ticket. Our three other kids riding with her were out of the car wondering what to do.

"Mom didn't see the red light," Frances was saying to the officer. "She was afraid Daddy would get out of sight!"

Again, Lady Luck was with us. That traffic cop must have been a family man. "Take it easy for another mile, then turn north at the next light, and you'll be on a good highway through Wisconsin." What a relief! I dared not ask the patrol officer what a traffic ticket would have cost, but both Ruby and I realized that we were indeed fortunate.

I had planned on visiting the editor of *American Field*, a news magazine devoted to hunting dogs. The editorial office was located in downtown Chicago.

"They have quite a bit of my stuff," I told the family while we were gassing up at the highway intersection the friendly cop had told us about. "I'm going to ask if there's a bus or trolley car line near. The editor might give me an advance."

The gas station manager said there was a street car line, only a block away, that would take me close to the *American Field* office and that we could park our two cars and the trailer on his lot.

"It's worth a try," Ruby agreed. So, kissing my loved ones good-bye, with "Shouldn't take me over an hour," I hiked to the street car line.

I noticed a number of small business establishments along the trolley line with windows boarded up and "closed" signs on doors. I also saw dozens of men on benches and milling around the empty building, evidently unemployed. "Maybe the *American Field* has suspended publication," I morosely said to myself.

But my street car journey paid off. The editor with whom I had been dealing, was not in but his assistant discovered that galley proofs on one of my stories had been set up for the printer. He measured the column inches and handed me a check for $20.00!

I was away a little longer than I expected to be, and we were all overjoyed to be together again. We drove on into a camp site near Elgin, Illinois and stopped there for the night. One of my better juvenile story markets was the David C. Cook Publishing Company, which was located in Elgin. I had sold stories to the Cook editors of three of their papers. They always paid on acceptance and this time, I thought it might enhance our relationship, if I stopped to meet one or more of the editors.

The next morning, Ruby and the kids strolled through the spacious grounds of the Cook Publishing Co. while I enjoyed an interesting visit with Margaret Chase, editor of *The Girl's Companion* and *The Boy's World.* My stories had appeared in both papers. I left with an assignment for several camping articles. "Let me know when you reach your mother's home in Idaho," Mrs. Chase said. She had followed me out to the car and I sensed that she was somewhat perturbed at what she saw. In fact, she wrote me some weeks later that "you surely have a spunky wife — I was really anxious for the Thompsons."

It took two days to cross Wisconsin. A strong wind prevailed both days, and our car, bucking the cross winds, burned gas at an alarming rate. Thankfully, the Model A behaved beautifully but Ruby said one heavy blast "almost blew us off the road."

Camping at night, we were all tired and bone weary, but we managed to visit a little, usually talking about events of the day, number of cars passed, etc. Auto camp sites were few and far between, through Wisconsin and Minnesota. Luckily, we had no rain and generally got by with pitching one tent and sleeping on the ground, some of us in, and the others outside of the tent. Ray, Jr. and Norman usually slept in one of the cars.

We drove through alternating sections of farm land and wooded slopes. Frances said something about the early history of that area. "You're right, Sis, this was a great fur producing country — up until the 1850's. Many streams, and hundreds of lakes, for beaver, mink, and muskrat."

"Times sure have changed," Ruby observed, "A hundred years ago, there must have been a lot of buffalo here too."

On mid-afternoon of our fifth day on the road, we crossed the Red River, leaving Minnesota and entering North Dakota. Here we were to meet Carl Sanders and deliver his Model A Ford. We had arranged by correspondence before we left Piper's Landing that whoever reached Fargo first, would leave a message at a service station, on the North Dakota side of the Red River. Sanders had not arrived at the service station, so we left a note and, following the gas station operator's directions, found a good camp ground on the banks of the Red River. One of the kids dubbed it "Squealing Hog Camp," as we could hear swine on a farm just across the Red River, back in Minnesota.

Remembering tales of the pioneers who traveled on north into Canada, with heavily loaded two-wheeled vehicles that came to be known as "Red River Carts," I told Ruby and our youngsters some of the history of the region known as Louisiana Territory.

Carl Sanders didn't arrive in Fargo until the second day after we reached there, and we were beginning to worry over this extra delay. It cost nothing for our campground on the banks of the Red River, but we had to eat, and our cash was dwindling at an alarming rate. When Sanders did arrive, he was real pleased with the Ford, and said he was more than happy to pay for the engine repairs. "I'll mail you a check just as soon as I get home. It should reach your Coeur d'Alene address ahead of you," he assured us.

I thanked the North Dakotan, who farmed and ran a trapline in season along the Red River further north, near the Canadian border. Then, I told him flatly that we were hard pressed for cash, and that we would appreciate any money that he could spare. "We've got a bad tire on the trailer, too," I added.

Carl Sanders was young, single, and apparently fairly well established in the Red River Valley, a real fertile part of North Dakota. But, he wanted to expand his trapping and to eventually go into fur farming. I had written Sanders about my friend, Lew Aumock, who owned the Pine Woods Fur Farm in northern Idaho. So, I was not too surprised when he said, "You may see me in Coeur d'Alene, this fall. Right now, let's see about getting some cash for you. I know a banker in Fargo."

So we visited the banker and Sanders cashed a counter check, reimbursed us for the repair bill, and we Thompsons once more resumed our journey.

U.S. 10, the federal highway running east and west through central North Dakota, was a good gravelled road in 1932. It had rained heavily a few days before we left Fargo. Luckily, there were very few hills, otherwise our "Light Six" Willys would never have hauled the heavily-loaded trailer. The car itself was well loaded too as, after delivering Carl Sanders' Ford, we of course had only the one car.

Toward evening of the day we left Fargo, we crossed the North Dakota-Montana border, and commenced to look for a campsite.

"There's a farm house," Ruby pointed out. "We need some eggs and milk. Maybe they'll let us camp."

"We'll find out," I agreed. "I'll check the trailer tire again — so why don't you and the kids hike down the road into the farm and see." They left and I turned to the trailer and saw that the one tire was losing air. It was a high pressure, 32" x 4" tire, in an outdated size, and repairing the inner tube, remounting the tire, and pumping enough air to build up 70 lbs. pressure was no little chore.

I was wrestling with the tire mount when Ruby returned from the quarter-mile hike. "Sure fine people — they insisted on the kids having supper with their two girls. And we can camp right in their yard, if we want, too!"

I pointed to the trailer tire. "I've got to get this job done. A sandwich is all I need, Hon." Ruby fried a couple eggs on our little gasoline-burning campstove and we ate a lunch, finished the tire job, then we walked to the farmhouse.

The Stoners were typical marginal type farmers trying to make a go of it through the Depression. "We're luckier than some of our neighbors," Stoner said. He was a big, raw-boned man with a leathery face tanned by Montana's harsh winds. "We've got some cattle and enough feed to carry them through the winter. Had a fair crop of spuds, and other vegetables, but we're too far to a market. Our nearest neighbor just pulled out. He's going to try for a job in Butte. I thought Lewis was making a big mistake — he was actually better fixed than we Stoners are."

When the farmer learned that I had been raised in wheat farming country, and that Ruby and I had "pioneered" in northern Alberta, we had a hard time getting away from the Stoners.

"Be over to help you break camp, Thompson," he said, as we finally said good-night.

"Bet they miss their neighbors," Ruby commented. "Looks like a bleak country to live in."

True to his promise, Jim Stoner showed up at sunrise. Then, while we were lashing the wall tent back on top of our trailer load, the Montanan almost "floored me" with a farm lease proposition.

"Elsie and I had a good talk after you left last night," Stoner commenced. "We decided it would do no harm to see if you'd be interested. We leased the Lewis place for three years, figuring on getting a family like you Thompsons to run it. There's $100.00 a month, plus a share of the crop this fall in it. Also, if your kids would help, a lot of spuds, cabbage, and rutabagas, free for some hard work." Stoner was really worked up over his proposal.

Ruby was listening too, and she was as surprised as I, at Stoner's offer, which we had to pass up. But, when I explained to Stoner our peculiar situation, he agreed that the "middle of nowhere," like the bleak, open Montana range, was no place for us to start rebuilding our snare business. If we did settle in Coeur d'Alene, Idaho, it would be less than an hour's drive to Spokane, Washington, where we could obtain steel and wire used in the manufacture of Thompson self-locking snares.

Ruby said, after we had left, that Elsie Stoner, who had come from the farm to wish us God's blessing, actually had tears in her eyes.

"It was like ships passing in the night," I remarked.

Our journey through Montana was rough. We had to stop twice to repair the trailer tire and, about noon of the second day, it gave up its "tired" ghost, right alongside a huge sign that read, "Welcome to Butte, the Mining Capitol of Montana."

Jim Stoner had given us some short pieces of lumber for use in jacking up our trailer. We took the trailer wheel and useless tire, and headed for Butte, leaving the trailer and all our possessions, unguarded, by the side of the road.

Anna, who watched our mileage, said, "It's 12 miles," just as we entered the city.

"Like hunting for a needle in a haystack," I admitted, after we had visited all the tire shops in downtown Butte. The answer was always the same, "32 x 4's (tires) mighty scarce since balloons (low pressure) are on most cars."

Then we, in modern slang, "lucked out." A tire shop had one 32 x 4 tire, plus a fair-looking inner tube, at an unbelievable cost of only $2.50! Thankful for our good fortune, we left town again. Our trailer, vulnerable to any dishonest party who may have driven by, was waiting patiently, unmolested!

On the afternoon of the third day in Montana, as we approached Lookout Pass, on the border with Idaho, hard luck once more caught up with us. A detour around some road work, led to a climb "as steep as a cow's face," and the valiant little Willys simply gave up! Here was a real dilemma. We had stalled on a narrow, steep detour with passage room barely wide enough for two cars. We had no idea of how far it was to the summit of the locally termed Camel's Hump and I suspected that our car would have difficulty in negotiating the grade even with a part of the load. And would there be a turn around spot at or near the top where we could unload and drive back for a second, or even third load?

A few cars passed us but none would stop! "We'll have to unload," I said, rather grimly. Ruby and the kids were, of course, worried, too. Then, just as I unloosened one end of the rope over our load cover, a rancher, in a heavy touring car, pulled alongside.

"Looks like you got trouble! Maybe I can help — it's only a mile to the top." Another small miracle!

The rancher had a long, heavy rope in his empty car. He drove in front of our Willys, made a short hookup with the rope, and yelled, "Let's give it a try!"

But although the rancher's big Hudson had lots of power, the rear wheels spun in the gravel.

"Hm-m," he said. "We'll fix that! You kids help pile some rocks in here," pointing to the opened car door. "We'll get some traction!"

And traction he did get! At the summit he 'uncoupled' our cars and, waving a hand, cautioned, "Take it easy in low gear — it's all downhill now!"

I yelled back — "Thanks a million — we didn't even get your name!"

"Does it matter?" he shouted, looking back, and was soon out of sight.

"What a difference between people you meet when you're in trouble," Ruby said.

"Yes, and who would have thought of using rocks!" added Frances, as the children helped empty the car.

Entering Idaho, we still had some mountain roads to slow us down, but nothing like the Camel's Hump at Lookout Pass. The last range of hills, part of the Coeur d'Alene mountains, was conquered by Fourth of July Canyon pass. Here, Captain John Mullan, a U.S. military engineer, had camped on Independence Day, in 1854, while building a bridge on the Mullan Road to Fort Walla Walla, in Washington Territory.

"The Mullan Road was widely used by miners, homeseekers and, of course, the U.S. Army," I told the kids. "Also, in the 1880's, your own grandfather, Henry Thompson, operated a wagon freighting line out of Spokane and several times hauled freight to the Coeur d'Alene miles, over this very road!"

"I wish we'd known Grandpa Thompson," Anna observed. "I bet he had trips that would have made ours look like a picnic!"

Late that afternoon, we reached Coeur d'Alene, Idaho, the largest city, population wise, in northern Idaho. Entering from the east, via Sherman Avenue, we turned off onto 14th Street. Realizing that we may have gone too far north, in looking for an uncle's home, I started to stop, only to discover that my car brakes had failed!

"God must have had an angel on board with us," I soberly reflected. The Willys had a mechanical system on its four-wheel brakes. A steel pin had fallen out of a rod connection and one of the kids found it, laying on the ground, not far back from where the car and trailer had rolled to a stop, on level ground. Had we "lost" the brakes on any one of a dozen high grades we had encountered, we could easily have all been killed!

I connected the brake rod and we went on to my uncle's home, on North 15th Street,and later, to my Mother's place, only a short drive from P. P. Johnson's. We warned the kids not to tell their Grandma about our narrow escapes. We set up our tents in Mother's yard and, for the first time in 10 days, felt secure and so very thankful that our 2,500-mile journey was finally over.

None of us had really suffered physically. Anna had stepped on a bee; Ray, Jr., had tangled with some desert cactus and I had barely caught up in time with Norman, while he was chasing a short, but deadly, prairie rattler!

"It was a great experience, but I wouldn't want to do it over," Ruby concluded.

I agreed heartily and, remembering we had reached Coeur d'Alene with only ten dollars as our capital, vowed that I'd never again subject my family to such an ordeal.

CHAPTER XXXVII

Coeur d'Alene is the county seat of Kootenai County, Idaho, with a population in 1932, of about 10,000. Dependent on the logging industry, it had been hard hit by the Depression, with hundreds of men laid off, or working short hours, in the Rutledge, Blackwell and Winton sawmills.

Congress had passed in June, 1932, President Hoover's bill creating the Reconstruction Finance Corporation. Under R.F.C., the federal government would finance private enterprise, through guaranteeing loans from banks, to get industry off dead center. It was too slow, too bound up in red tape, in creating jobs. Labor unrest was getting harder to handle. JOBS NOW, was the nation's wide cry, from the unemployed! In any event, R.F.C. failed to provide relief, and the opposition, backing Franklin Delano Roosevelt in the upcoming presidential election, naturally seized on the R.F.C. failure to strengthen their cries for a New Deal, under Democrat Roosevelt. November, 1932, saw the dramatic results, but as Franklin D. Roosevelt would not take charge as president until January, 1933, hard times prevailed.

My mother had re-married some years after my father died, Daniel Miller, a retired carpenter and builder. Their little home, on a few acres of wonderfully fertile soil, was located in the eastern part of the city. The Millers had a small orchard and a fine garden, plus a chicken house and pens, with lots of chickens.

We pitched our two tents in mother's yard, the umbrella tent for Ruby and me and, the 10 x 12 wall tent for the kids. It was warm at nights, so the boys spread blankets and canvas sheets on their Grandma Miller's lawn, close to our tent.

About the second night in our new "camp ground," Ray, Jr., yelled, "Dad, a big cat just killed one of Grandma's chickens!"

It was bright as day, almost, from a full moon. Ruby and I went outside our tent and listened while our excited 8-year-old son continued, "He climbed out of the pen, up a post and dragged the chicken right across the lawn. Sure is a big one!"

Mother had heard the commotion and joined us. "That'll be Hagen's tomcat; Daniel wants to shoot it. Problem is, the Hagens are very good friends and regular buyers of eggs and chickens. Their cat has been killing my chickens on the average of twice a week. Anyway, don't let it worry you."

Mother went back inside and, for the moment, the killer cat incident was forgotten. But, a day later, talking to my cousin, Vennoy Johnson, who raised rabbits for part of his living, offered a suggestion.

"I've got a BB gun that's fairly good at close range. I use it to keep stray dogs away from my rabbit pens. Why don't you try it on that Hagen tomcat?"

I followed my cousin's suggestion, borrowed his air gun and set up an ambush by raising slightly, a corner of the girls' tent. It was a perfect set-up, only a few yards from the wire netting fence post the tomcat used to climb in and out of the chicken coop.

The second night of my ambush, I caught the big cat just as he paused on top of the post, a perfect target against the moonlit sky. The BB air gun didn't make much noise compared to the tomcat's yowl! Anyway, Hagen's cat never stole another of the Miller chickens. We learned later, from another neighbor, that someone had blinded Hagen's cat! It was an episode our kids didn't forget. But if Hagens ever learned the truth, it never showed in their dealings or friendship with the Millers.

My uncle, Preston Johnson and his wife, Lucille, owned a small orchard and a plant and shrubbery nursery on some acreage about a half mile north of the Miller's. Uncle Press, as we called him, was also a realtor and he showed us around. One of our first stops was at a small farm about two miles north of town.

"You'll enjoy these people," my uncle said, as we drove into the yard.

Jim "Muley" Craig drove mules and horses working for Dad in wagon freighting business in the 1880's. A small, wiry man, Muley had settled just north of Coeur d'Alene, Idaho, on a small ranch. He and his wife had a dairy and sold milk, which his wife delivered in a Model A Ford to customers in Coeur d'Alene. A year-around spring was their milk cooler.

Ruby and I visited the Craigs and wished we had such a place to raise our family. A fine garden, small orchard and lots of pine wood for heat. It wasn't exactly our "modern" living, but it was only two miles to Coeur d'Alene, where there were several schools, including a high school, which Frances and Anna later attended. The Craig place was for sale, but we Thompsons were hard pressed for cash.

"Seems like it wasn't meant for us," Ruby said a little wistfully.

Seattle, our ultimate destination, seemed a long way off. Our snare business gave some promise in Alaska trade, but we needed to get to a city on the West Coast, where wire, steel and other supplies could be purchased. Seattle was the desirable location for our snare business, now at a low ebb on account of the Depression.

One real benefit came from our friendship with Muley Craig, as he told me more about my own father's wagon freight business than even my own mother had told me.

"We hauled freight from Sprague and Spokane, the heavy stuff in winter, on bobsleds. The summer roads were bad, especially when it rained. Your dad lost a lot of money when a load of freight went off the grade into a lake," Muley reminisced.

Just as we were drinking some cold mountain spring water from Muley's milk cooler, the rancher grabbed a shotgun leaning against the stone wall of the milk cooling shed, whirled and fired at a chicken hawk flying over a nearby feeding pen for several hens and a cocky old rooster that had sounded a warning.

"Danged chicken stealer," Muley grunted, "That's the fourth time I've missed that devil on wings!"

The weathered old, single-barreled shotgun didn't look in very good shape, I noted.

As we were leaving, Muley drew a map for me, in the loose soil. "You'll find coyotes in the hills near any of the small ranches, a few mink and some muskrats on Fernan Lake and the Creek. The ranchers will welcome you and you can use my name, if you like. They all know me," Muley concluded, as we finally left.

Other ranchers and fruit growers Uncle Preston helped us to meet, while I searched for employment, were all friendly, but none had money for hiring extra help. I did exchange carpenter work for several fine, big rabbits with a man who was trying to defeat the Depression on a small orchard, a few miles north of Coeur d'Alene.

Our car was still luckily in fair shape as we were paid in potatoes — 26 hundred-pound bags — for harvesting a black man's spud crop.

"Maybe we can trade some for other vegetables," Ruby suggested, as we were loading our "pay" on our two-wheel trailer.

"Well, one thing for sure — we won't run short of spuds for a while."

Curiously, the black man who had hired us, confessed that we didn't look like "spud diggers" and he thought of saying no when I asked about work.

"Then I saw the Michigan license tag and figured anyone trying to get away from that Detroit mess deserved help!"

We had rented an unfurnished 6-unit row of tourist cabins for the winter, only a few blocks from the Miller home. One of the units boasted a small cellar and we stored our 26 sacks of potatoes in the dry, sandy dugout. Incidentally, the monthly rental for that row of cabins was only $6.00 a month.

As winter approached, I decided on writing Bill Strohmeyer, a Kansas motel owner, who wanted to learn how to snare coyotes. "I can't promise too much, but come on out."

He arrived within a week or so!

We were fairly successful trapping mink and muskrat on Fernan Lake and the creek that ran into it. I snared a few coyotes and we trapped a couple of beavers, under permit from district Game Warden, Ray Quarles. Bill also shot a deer, which helped our meager food supply.

CHAPTER XXXVII

February, 1933, marked the low ebb in our resources. Bill Strohmeyer went back to Kansas and I quit trapping for lack of transportation. We were behind in our $16 per month payments on the Willys and reluctantly turned the car over to a local dealer. He would pay off the $80 we owed a Detroit finance company, "make minor repairs, sell the Willys and settle with you for any profit," the dealer said.

You, my reader, guessed it — there was no profit — at least for us! Anyway, we could not have traveled the back roads in a car, the snow was too deep.

Ray Quarles, my game warden friend, who also owned a sporting goods store, offered me an opportunity to "cash in" on a few small colonies of beaver the National Forest people wanted removed, on the North Fork of the Coeur d'Alene River.

"They're planning on new roads come spring," Quarles said, "and beaver would be a real problem. If you take the job, you'd have to use snowshoes and go over Honeysuckle Pass. We'll supply traps and snowshoes and the forestry has a man at Honeysuckle Ranger Station, on the river, and he'll give you any supplies he has in the warehouse."

I thanked the game warden and, after talking things over with Ruby, decided to prepare for the "expedition."

First, I wrote Archie Jacobsen, a logger and trapper who had a homestead some 20 miles downstream from where I was to trap the beaver. "You know that country and that we'll have to work fast, just ahead of spring breakup. Want to join me?" Jacobsen answered my letter promptly. He'd be glad to meet me at Honeysuckle Ranger Station on any specified date.

I built a little sled, with fairly narrow runners that would dig into the slope of crushed snow, on the summit of Honeysuckle Pass. I was fortunate in having most of the gear I needed furnished by the National Forest Division.

Luckily, I received a check for a boy's adventure type story, for $28, just before I left and that would tide my family over the two weeks I would be gone. We had got down to the point where I "swallowed my pride" and had worked on relief projects, two days a week for "pie tickets" or orders on a local store amounting to less than $3.00 per day. The tickets were good for groceries only and since I neither smoked cigarettes nor drank beer, that stipulation was no problem. I recall one incident when, now out of firewood, I bought only $1.00 worth of cordwood, from a neighbor, who cut and sold firewood for $4.00 a cord, delivered.

Ruby and the kids weathered all this in stride. My wife joined a few other wives of unemployed men and organized the "Calico Club." The Veterans Hall was donated, a few musicians charged $5.00 a night, for the "band" and the Calico Club was in business. They held card games and dances, combined, once a week. Admission was 16 cents, which included a cup of coffee and a doughnut.

Christmas, 1932, was made a little brighter for children of financially distressed families, by a group of carpenters and painters. Local lumber and supply houses donated lumber, paint, etc., and the Coeur d'Alene High School allowed us to use their shop. Many really nice toys were the result and I even made some for our own kids.

Our daughter Anna, reminiscing, as she helped me by proofreading my manuscript said, now almost 47 years later, "Dad, I remember very well the little table and chairs you made for me. I stored them in a neighbor's attic when we left Coeur d'Alene and often wished I could have gone back for them." Anna remembered, too, that I had made a desk for Frances; a wooden rifle for Ray, Jr. and a tiny barn for Norman, our seven-year-old and youngest of our four children.

And so, on to April, 1933. Archie Jacobsen and I met, as planned, on the North Fork of the Coeur d'Alene River and we trapped beaver for two weeks, with fair success. A sudden change in the weather, with warm winds and steady rain, forced us to literally "run for our lives" down a pack horse trail, along the river. Crossing the now raging mountain stream on a cable suspension foot bridge, I would never have made it except for my partner. He grabbed my bulky pack of beaver hides when I was stalled in midstream on the swaying bridge, took my load on to shore and then returned to help me across.

Archie Jacobsen was a big man, over 200 pounds of bone and muscle, and I had been most fortunate in securing his help. Incidentally, we were both members of the American Trappers Association and I was about to be appointed regional director — my duties were to revive the flagging interest in the Trappers Association (on account of the Depression) in several northwestern states.

Anyway, we made it over the pack trail downstream about 20 miles to Jacobsen's homestead. He lived near a spur line of the main railroad and borrowed a railway hand car to take us and our two packs of beaver hides, down to the highway. There, we said good-bye, my short-time trapper-partner returning home and I going to a bus stop near a gas station.

I had some time to wait for the west bound bus, but Lady Luck was with me. A big, black sedan stopped alongside and the driver, alone in his fine Nash car, greeted me with, "You're Thompson, I'm George Natwick — want a lift?"

Most thankful, I put my packs in the car and climbed aboard.

George Natwick, owner of a truck line in Coeur d'Alene, was also chairman of the welfare board for Kootenai County and head of the Republican Party.

On the drive homeward, Natwick and I became acquainted. He had seen my slides of the North Country and had heard me talk about my Canadian wilderness experiences at the Sports and Recreation show, in Coeur d'Alene, the summer of 1932. But Natwick seemed particularly interested in my accounting and office management experience in Canada, in the railroad office and while employed by a large construction firm in Edmonton, Alberta.

"I'll be seeing you in a few days," George Natwick said, as he unloaded me and my packs.

I didn't dream of what my new-found friend had in mind and actually thought his remark was nothing more than a pleasantry.

I left the beaver hides with the game warden and he, in turn, sent them down to Boise, to be marketed in the next fur auction.

"It'll take about six weeks," Quarles said, "You've done a good cleanup job on those North Fork beaver."

I knew, of course, that I would have to wait for returns from the fur auction, so I applied for more work relief. About 20 of us were working on a country road project, north of Coeur d'Alene. It was hard, "pick and shovel" work and I was really tired when I got to mother's place. I knew Ruby would also be doing all she could helping mother in planting her large garden. Anna also loved to help her grandma. She made delicious bread. Kneading the dough in a huge dishpan, an almost impossible task for a 10-year-old.

On the street in front of the Miller home, was a familiar sight, George Natwick in his big Nash Eight car. With him was C.C. "Cask" Robinson, Kootenai County Commissioner. They had come to offer me the job of managing the newly set-up county-state welfare program. The pay, at first, would be small, but Roosevelt's New Deal program was about to "bust wide open" and I would have a fair salary within a short time. Of course, I was astonished and wondered if I were dreaming.

But the offer was genuine and I shortly entered a field in which I had no experience, that of battling the Depression with a simple objective, to provide work for the unemployed, with a check for pay.

So, by a curious incident, my meeting with George Natwick at the bus stop, I started a career in the Idaho welfare program that was to last 11 years into World War Two!

CHAPTER XXXIX

My first office was in a stuffy room in the basement of the Coeur d'Alene City Hall. Paul Braun had been issuing "pie tickets" in the period waiting for the New Deal program to get started, but shortly after my joining him, Braun took over the Coeur d'Alene office of the U.S.E.S. (United States Employment Service) and I was left on my own as Kootenai County manager of the welfare program.

The work was simple with, as yet, a limited amount of forms. A carload of salt pork, to be distributed to families on relief, was an unexpected addition to my work load. I wrote orders on this "surplus commodity" product until I, in fact, had writer's cramp.

I recall one incident when a disgruntled man started unloading his tirade to me. Then, abruptly pausing, he said, "Hell, I'm wasting my breath — you never had the rain run down your neck."

I smiled and, after he calmed down, gave him a copy of my book, *The Wilderness Trapper*. A few days later, he returned the book. "I was sure wrong," he said.

The work load got so heavy that I couldn't keep up, so I asked the welfare board for permission to hire a high school girl to become my file clerk. Permission granted, I could ease up a little.

Ruby was worried about my health, as I came home each day completely exhausted, mentally and physically. The strain of dealing with an army of worried out-of-work men, many with families like myself, was taking its toll. On top of this, the increasing list of unemployed, created a real problem with the county welfare board. Henry Caraway, one County Commissioner, was especially critical. "Why don't you investigate some of these people, they still drive cars," he said.

"A few have part time work and need cars," I answered, "and besides, I have little time from the office and no transportation of my own."

Caraway grudgingly agreed that I could use a county owned car, if I would pay for the gasoline I used, in some trial investigating trips. C. C. "Cask" Robinson winked at me and later said, "Caraway is a die hard. I've told the sheriff to give you all the gas you need." "Cask" spoke with authority as he was Chairman of the Board, Kootenai County Commissioners and head of the county welfare board.

A deputy sheriff stopped me on a farm road, noting that the car I drove, carried no license. I told him about the situation and he grinned, "Some people in the courthouse sure have their nerve, but if the sheriff says it's okay, I have no reason to interfere."

I didn't do much field work. Shortly after the episode with my "no license" car, I managed to buy an old Pontiac for $100.00, but Commissioner Caraway was opposed to allowing me any expense money for field work and, the county sheriff suddenly was "short on gasoline" for his department.

A field representative from the Idaho Emergency Relief Administration called at my office to inform me that the C.W.A. (Civil Works Administration), a sort of trial balloon for the permanent I.E.R.A. work projects, was folding and that the Kootenai County office would be setup within a few weeks, with a complete set up of manager, accounting clerk and social service workers who would "investigate" each case before the relief applicant could be eligible for a $44.00 per month job. There would be women's work projects too, such as sewing, nursing and canning programs. It all sounded exciting, but I had no assurance that my county managerial position would continue.

Early in September, 1933, state officials arrived in Coeur d'Alene. They were E. P. Horsfall, State Administrator for I.E.R.A. and field representatives, Orville Peet and Peter H. Cohn. I was to learn later that Pete Cohn was actually a personal field man for C. Ben Ross, Governor of Idaho.

George Natwick, Cash Robinson and I, met with the state I.E.R.A. in a large office space, newly rented. Pete Cohn did most of the talking. George Natwick was to be District Administrator; I, Kootenai County Manager and two college trained social service workers would be arriving soon to help me select several "case workers," each of the latter to be assigned separate sections of the county. These workers would keep records of each man or woman applying for relief and report on the eligibility of each "case."

We had barely got organized in the county office when Pete Cohn arrived again. He, Natwick and I, drove south to St. Maries, at the southern tip of Coeur d'Alene Lake, to see what the trouble was with 350 angry men on strike because of a shut down of a flood control project under C.W.A. It was an ugly situation. A hundred or more men outside the office of retiring manager, Donavan, threatened to "tear the place apart" unless the flood control projects were resumed.

Pete Cohn talked to the Boise office and then phoned Governor Ross. Pete Cohn was not very big, physically, but he had guts and as I later learned, the backing of the Idaho Governor, C. Ben Ross. He confronted the angry men with the news that the flood control projects, repairing the damage from the raging St. Joe and St. Maries Rivers, would resume immediately. "You men can get work tickets right now. Ray Thompson will be in charge here and I'm sure things will get moving again."

Thus, by quick action on Pete Cohn's part, going over the head of the state administrator, when he could not get results, to the governor himself, an ugly situation was changed to a working relationship between the relief workers and the management.

We worked late, assigning men to different foremen and the next day the most critical of the flood control projects was operating.

I was at St. Maries, in Benewah County, for six weeks, driving to Coeur d'Alene twice a week, to see that things were okay in my own county. The former Beneway County manager had simply let a few "radicals" tell him how to run his own office. For instance, I found that a local gasoline distributor had bought several trucks and rented them to the C.W.A. for use in flood control. This man was making money, hand over fist, through his truck rentals and a virtual monopoly in gasoline sales. Then, prompted by this same truck dealer, the non-relief truck drivers demanded $1.00 per hour or "we'll tie up the (flood control) project." I phoned Boise and was told, "You know the situation, Ray, use your own judgment." Being given the authority, I was able to avert a disaster. Shortly thereafter, in going through former manager Donavan's file, I discovered that he had hired a steam shovel and operator for $100.00 per day and Boise refused to honor a bill that now totaled $4,000, or 40 days' work.

In talking to foremen who had knowledge of the steam shovel operation, I was told that one of the most important dikes would have "busted wide open if the steam shovel hadn't been brought in," so I phoned the state administrator in Boise, explained the situation and was told to okay a requisition for full payment to the steam shovel man.

"Tell him a check will be issued promptly on receipt of your voucher, Ray."

I learned a lot in my "trouble shooting" job in neighboring Benewah County, but was glad when Boise approved my recommendation for a new manager there, and I was able to return to Coeur d'Alene. In the meantime, the radicals were headed by Joe Lewis, top-ranking Communist in northern Idaho. Lewis was ably assisted by Darrell Houk, a well educated, professional rabble rouser and Clarence Emheiser, whose job was to spread Communist propaganda among the workers in several projects he managed to get assigned to.

George Natwick was worried and told me that a crisis was developing. "Boise advises we're about to shut down several projects. They've run out of money from I.E.R.A. and won't get more until the first of the month. Joe Lewis has organized a march on our office, probably for tomorrow."

That was bad news for my "homecoming," but I had to face the Communist leader and his radicals. They would be attacking me, as well as George Natwick, my immediate supervisor, in the I.E.R.A. setup.

I was alerted when I reached home and Ruby told me that a sizeable load of wood, in long lengths, had been delivered in our own back yard, just the day before I returned from St. Maries. Luckily, Ruby had not touched the wood, which had come from a tree-thinning project on Tubbs Hill, not far from our home. I called the foreman of the project and ordred him to "get that wood off my place, right now, or I'll call the county sheriff."

The long poles were removed pronto, the foreman's excuse, "I thought you'd appreciate a little firewood!"

"I don't know your motive, but you surely realize how the Joe Lewis gang would play this up!" I retaliated.

Previously, Darrell Houk, in a show of friendship, had urged me privately, to "Join us (the Communists) while you have the chance. The fellows like you and we think you could go a long way in our cause!"

I remembered that incident and told Natwick about it.

"They're pretty slick and I'll bet that wood dumping in your yard was promoted by them," Natwick said.

The confrontation with Lewis and Houk occurred two days after my taking over again at the Coeur d'Alene office. Over fifty men and a few women gathered on the street, in front of our office, shortly after noon. Then, after a brief statement from Joe Lewis, who stood on a coke bottle case, a dozen or so marched into the office. One of the office girls had a box of chocolates on her desk, a gift from her fellow workers.

"Hmm, pretty high living for relief clerks," one of the intruders commented, sampling the chocolates and then passing the box on to the others of his group.

"It's her birthday," I said, trying to remain calm.

In my office, Joe Lewis made known their demands. "Open up this list of projects tomorrow, or we'll tear this place apart!"

I looked at the list and retorted, "Some will be operating in about 10 days. Here's a telegram from Boise, read it!"

The Communist leader read the list but didn't seem impressed.

"Thompson, you call your state office right now. Tell them we've taken over and we'll stay here until we have our demands met!"

"Sure, I'll call Boise and you can listen in," I said and immediately put in the call. I got our state finance director on the phone and he confirmed what I had told Lewis. "We're waiting for funds from Washington. Tell your people to be patient. We're doing the best we can," our finance director responded.

Joe Lewis knew he was licked. "Okay, now, maybe you can talk to the mob outside!"

A further deterioration in the threatened "mob reaction" was averted when I went outside, kicked Joe Lewis' coke box into the street, and told the "mob" everything I knew about various projects.

Within minutes, the crowd dispersed. One man told me, "I'm ashamed for listening to Joe Lewis and for joining the radicals. You have a lot of friends, Ray Thompson. We know you have a tough job!"

It was a big undertaking, getting work projects operating and the engineering and financing were, of course, major factors. Many errors were the natural result, but, thankfully, we in northern Idaho had very little violence to contend with. The Communists early became more of an undercover operation, trying to get their men in minor political offices.

In September, 1933, several C.C.C. (Civilian Conservation Corps) camps were opened in northern Idaho. Curiously, one 60-man camp was located on the North Fork of the Coeur d'Alene River, in the valley that Archie Jacobsen and I had trapped beaver, only a few months before. Many young men from other states were assigned to the Idaho C.C.C. camps. I visited one and showed some of my north country slides. The response was heart-warming.

One of the very first local boys I assigned to a C.C.C. camp was L. J. Carlin. Larry and his wife, Marie, friends and neighbors, commenced working for us in our snare business (part time) in 1936. You would find their names on the Raymond Thompson Company payroll today — in September, 1979. Larry is 76 now, the senior worker in our snare making shops. Marie, only 69, is our lead assembly gal! She also works in our printing shop, part time, binding books that we print and publish.

During the fall of 1933, the Social Service function of the I.E.R.A., was activated. Anita Tidball was the State Director. Two workers, Helen Wiswall and Edith Loveless were assigned to Kootenai. They were to review all the case records of our clients and help families on relief to budget their $44.00 a month income. It was wasted effort, and, we County Managers received many complaints about being told how to budget such a low income. The Social Service reports did have some benefit on the welfare program as a whole.

Voluntarily, feeling the need to keep Boise informed on matters not covered in regular reports, such as total case load, etc., I wrote some rather lengthy papers on the situation, as I saw it. Pete Cohn, still a field representative for I.E.R.A., arrived in Coeur d'Alene one day and asked George Natwick to accompany him on a routine business trip. On the spur of the moment, I took some of my special reports and handed one to Pete Cohn, as George Natwick was driving his own car.

On our way back to Coeur d'Alene, Cohn exploded a bombshell. "Ray," he said, "I've talked to George about this. He says that Art Dingler can handle your office here. We need you down at headquarters; can you make the move, say early in January?"

I really had no excuse, other than that we had made many friends in northern Idaho and that our four kids would have their schooling disrupted. I told Pete Cohn that I would let him know very shortly and, after talking with Ruby, wrote Pete that I'd report to his office in Boise most any time he desired.

"We want you to edit a little news bulletin and to write progress reports from figures and other data provided by the Washington office. We have a good mimeograph set up in Boise. You provide the copy and we'll send the news items to every paper in the state," Pete Cohn had explained.

The kids were a little upset, but with the resiliency of youth, made the mid-term change in schools without any sign of loss in their grade standings.

One disturbing change had taken place in Boise, just before I made the move. E. P. Horsfall, State Administrator, had been demoted to State Projects Director. Pearl Meredith was now I.E.R.A. boss and A. J. Jacomini was his assistant. Governor Ross had made the change when the relief load kept rising, with resulting increased unrest.

I wrote short articles for release to Idaho newspapers and found that the two Boise dailies, the *Capitol News* and the *Idaho Statesman*, would welcome illustrated feature articles on relief projects. Then, Jacomini, the State Administrator's Assistant, started holding up my news releases.

One day, Pearl Meredith called me. In his office, he showed news stories and letters from newspaper readers, "Giving me hell." "There must have been 300 in the mob down there," he said, pointing to the street below his office in the Yates Building. "Can't you do anything to counter-attack all this stuff appearing in the papers?"

I had come prepared and showed him carbon copies of my recent news stories. The state welfare boss read a few. "Fine, Thompson, get them to our print shop right away!"

At that point, I laid my job on the line with, "My news would have been in the press regularly, if Jacomini hadn't held them up."

Meredith was furious. "We'll see about this; come with me!"

Jacomini uncovered my stuff and, a little chagrined, blamed it on being swamped with "more pressing matters." That didn't satisfy his boss, who said, "Okay, from now on, Thompson, I'll look at your news!"

Jacomini called me into his own office a little later. He was really angry. "I could go to the relief board and have you fired!" he stormed.

Sure of my own position, I retorted, "Why don't you try!" and left his office.

Pete Cohn, busy working with the governor on some reorganization plans, was actually State Director of the I.E.R.A. Transient Program and I was on his payroll. He chuckled when I told him about my run-in with Jacomini. "Don't worry, Ray, your job is a lot more secure than his!" That was comforting, but I wondered what change, or changes, lay ahead.

One of the controversial issues involved seasonal field work in the farms in the Boise and Payette river valleys. Critics of the I.E.R.A. maintained there was plenty of work, if a man wanted to look for it. One news item claimed "Pea Pickers make up to $11.00 a day — no need for relief."

I talked to Pete Cohn about a plan I had to refute such unfair statements. I would take my wife and children into the field and pick peas alongside migrant workers and thus learn the truth. Pete thought it an excellent idea.

I had acquired a photographer, E. L. "Shorty" Fuller, an unemployed truck driver and, as it developed, a real good amateur with a camera. With Pete Cohn's help, we had I.E.R.A. funds for setting up a dark room. I had a camera and Shorty went to work, traveling with foremen of various projects, to get his photos of I.E.R.A. men and women at work.

Our venture into the pea picking business paid off. About 30 miles northwest of Boise, we read "Pea Pickers Wanted" on a sign and just beyond, a field where over 50 men, women and children were picking peas.

I got a ticket from the man in charge and he gave us hampers and pointed to a section of the field. "You bring the hampers back here, I'll punch the tickets and you get paid at quitting time."

So, that was the secret of the $11.00 per day, per picker. One ticket for a whole family!

By sheer good luck, my camera man located some workers who knew about the false report. "That would be Lopez! He has two women and six kids and is a real professional in this business," I was told. So, instead of one man, a whole family had made $11.00 per day, as every hamper full of peas was checked in, on one ticket!

Pea picking, by hand, is a back-breaking job and the afternoon Ruby, the kids and I tried it, was an experience not readily forgotten.

It was on a Saturday, so the kids didn't miss school. Anna, talking about it these many years later, remarked, "I think I made about 35 cents that afternoon, as the pay was only 7¢ per hamper." The discouraging task was filling the pea hamper which was cone shaped and seemed never-ending as you neared the top.

With Shorty Fuller's photos, I was able to get some good feature stories in the Boise papers. One story showed how I.E.R.A. workers were tanning hides in a building Henry Ford had erected for a car assembly plant. The Depression caused Ford to drop the plan, and several fine relief work projects found space in the abandoned building. One was a leather garment making project and Shorty, in taking pictures of the women at work there, confessed to me that, "There's one widow I'm real interested in. She has three kids, though, and my $69.00 a month isn't much to offer a woman."

Shortly after this, in a sudden change, the I.E.R.A. was replaced by the Work Progress Administration, later called Work Projects Administration (W.P.A.) and a relief work, state certifying agency, Idaho Cooperative Relief Agency (I.C.R.A.).

In the change over, I was ordered back to Coeur d'Alene, "To straighten up a real mess," so Pete Cohn told me. Pete was then State Director of I.C.R.A. So, I lost Shorty Fuller as my camera man and didn't see him until two years later, when I was called back to Boise. It was then that I met Shorty again. He was working for the Associated Press and had married Hazel, his "favorite widow." He now lives nearby and we've enjoyed visiting them through the years.

Later, under W.P.A., with a free hand in selecting subjects, I used some of Shorty Fuller's fine pictures to publicize both I.E.R.A. and W.P.A. projects. Anita Tidball, while State Director of Social Service had started a nursing program that proved to be most acceptable by the general public, and of course, was beneficial to the relief clients who could not afford the home visits of trained nurses.

A typical report follows explaining in more detail, the role of the visiting nurse. Incidentally, the Visiting Nurses Association of the State Welfare agencies, working with Medicare in the Federal Social Security Administration, is the culmination of I.E.R.A. and W.P.A. programs started over 40 years ago.

The following is the verbatim report of an I.E.R.A. nurse, referred to previously.

IDAHO EMERGENCY RELIEF ADMINISTRATION

Yates Bldg.
BOISE, IDAHO
Report on Nursing Program, including supplement of photographs
by
Division of Public Relations
I.E.R.A.

THE E.R.A. NURSE

Cheerful and gay in her uniform blue
Eyes looking ahead, steadfast and true
Wheel in her hand, bag by her side
She's ready to start on her merciful ride.

Answering calls of sickness and need
Going wherever the summons shall lead
Through daylight and darkness, sunshine or rain
She goes on her way, easing sorrow and pain.

Bathing a baby, feverish and ill,
Warming a blanket to ward off a chill,
Advising a mother how a child should be fed,
Teaching another to make up a bed.

Through city and village, o'er valley and hill
The nurse follows duty with love and good will,
Pausing at night, discouraged and tired,
Beginning again when or wherever desired.

9/35

by — Ruth Havenor
Pocatello, Idaho
Bannock County E.R.A. Nurse

Idaho Emergency Relief Administration
Yates Bldg., Boise, Idaho
11/12/35

Relief Nurses Report Unusual Activities

Life is never merely a round of routine duty with the field nurses of the Idaho Emergency Relief Administration, reports to Mrs. Kathryn McCabe, State Supervisor of relief nurses, indicate. For, aside from activities engaged in as regular course, exceptional demands are made upon the field nurse at unexpected moments.

A family that had formerly been under I.E.R.A. care but who had been off the relief rolls because of the fact that the father had been transferred to blister rust work, found itself in unexpected difficulties on account of the sickness of a 12-year-old child. The I.E.R.A. nurse, when contacted, explained their inability to help directly because of the closing of the case. Nevertheless, this same nurse left no stone unturned in an effort to aid the family.

First, a doctor was called who agreed to do what he could regardless of uncertainty of payment. He examined the child and, after making a diagnosis of diabetes, instructed the mother on diet. On a second examination some days later, it was found that the child was unimproved and rapidly losing weight. The need for continued medical care was evident.

The doctor then called the I.E.R.A. nurse, who took up the matter with the Social Service Director. Owing to the comparatively short time since the father had been transferred to the blister rust work and the absolute necessity of medical care for the child, this was allowed until such time as the sufferer could be placed in the county hospital for definite treatment.

In the meantime, the mother was carefully instructed by the nurse as to methods of weighing and measuring the child's food allowance, as well as how to give the hypodermic injections of insulin. The child made rapid progress toward recovery and hospitalization was unnecessary.

This family is typical of many Idaho people who are having an extremely hard time to take care of absolutely necessary demands for medical attention, particularly for the children. The father, previous to blister rust work, had paid for dental work by an exchange of his own labor.

A report from another county I.E.R.A. nurse starts out this way: Sunday morning I crawled out of bed, planning to spend a nice lazy day at home, when one of the doctors called and asked if I would like to do a little "extra" work. He said he had a very bad pneumonia case and he felt that it was going to be a fatal one if he could not secure the services of a nurse to help him out.

"The family is not on relief but very poor," the Doctor reported, so I promised to do what I could.

Conditions in the home were really much worse than those we have to contend with in our regular relief work. And, in addition, the husband was desperately ill, running an extremely high fever and the rate of his respiration was alarming. The bed was filthy and the woolen underwear worn by the poor man was wringing wet with perspiration. The room was hot and stuffy. The wife, of a meek and self-effacing personality, was lying in a small child's bed in the front room. She was suffering with a very bad cold and the Dr. stated she was a "heart" case.

It was essential that they have help immediately. After talking with the woman I found they had only 70¢ in the house and a little money coming in from wood sales.

It happened that I knew a woman who was extremely anxious to work and I

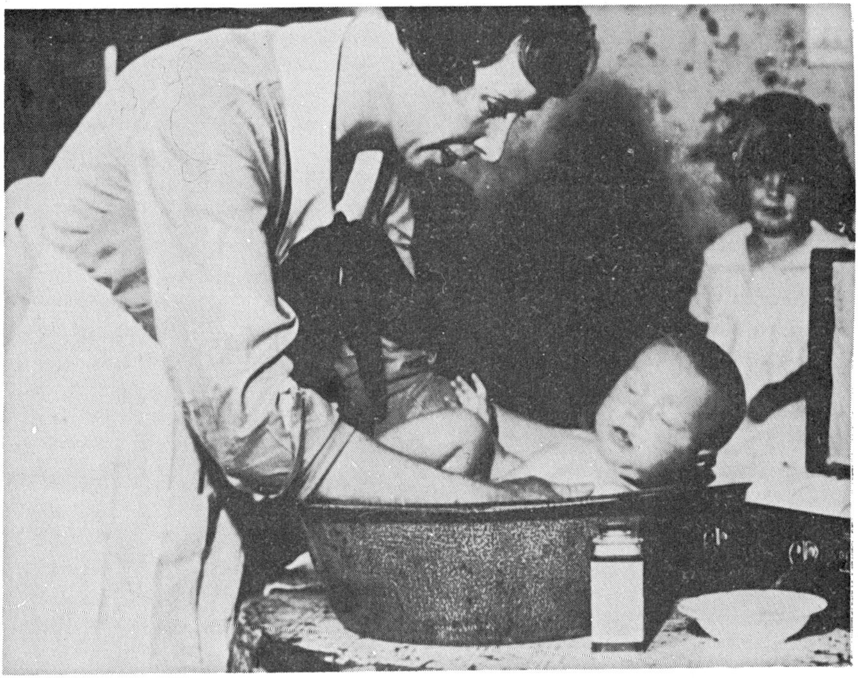

Ada County IERA nurse in a relief home, Boise, Idaho

Nurse Nelson visiting Rock Creek section near Twin Falls. Several typhoid cases added to distress of poverty stricken families of this section.

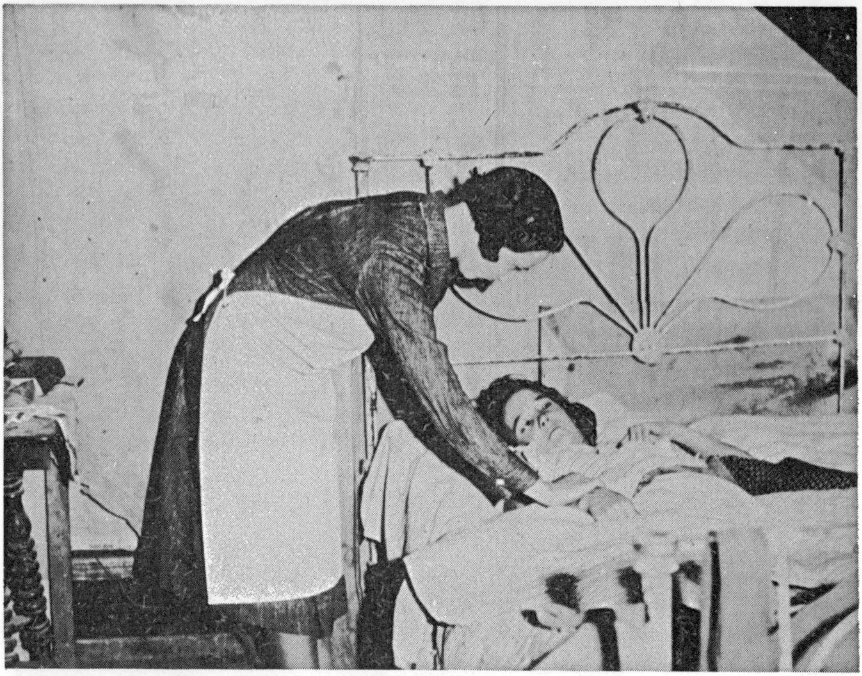

Canyon County nurse caring for a patient hopelessly stricken with cancer. The home consists of a tent with inadequate sanitary facilities.

Typical Rock Creek residence. One old bachelor lives in a rock cave beyond the "home" shown!

went to her home and secured her to help. Together then, we set to work. In addition to taking care of both patients, which included emergency treatment to relieve the condition of the pneumonia patient, warm bath and later a hot foot bath, the application of hot mustard packs, etc., we put clean sheets on the beds and clean papers on the dresser and shelves. The new nurse took hold surprisingly well and when I was finally ready to leave I knew she was responsible and would care for the patients to the best of her ability.

Next morning when I called, it seemed like a miracle had taken place in that house. There was a big washing on the line, and the house was tidy and clean. Both patients were greatly improved and a few days later the Doctor told me he believed the man was out of danger.

I felt that I could not have spent my Sunday in doing anything more worthwhile. I know the Doctor appreciated my help and the patients themselves were very grateful. They are making a hard struggle to get along without relief and I was especially glad for the opportunity to help such deserving people."

And so it goes. In recent months particularly heavy demands have been made upon the I.E.R.A. nurses in certain sections. Typhoid fever, scarlet fever in several different localities, etc., etc., have necessitated the relief nurses visiting the homes of the poor and distressed under most unusual conditions.

It seems to be "all in the day's march," with the public health nurse. Their experiences and particularly their reported findings have gone a long way to acquaint the general public with conditions upon which the same public is prone to close one eye and wink with the other. These untiring women have done much to awaken a public sluggish consciousness to the need of a helping hand where the economic distress has struck deepest — in the homes of the unfortunate. They have done much to show you and me that it is to our interest, to see that such work is kept up, not merely during so-called "emergency" periods, but in normal times as well.

Inaugurated by the Idaho E.R.A. only a little over a year ago, public health nursing on a state-wide scale has made its impression on the serious minded of our state. We sincerely hope and believe it is here to stay.

Backtracking, the "mess" Pete Cohn wanted to straighten up in Kootenai County, was due to pressure from the radicals on the county I.E.R.A. manager, Jim Zornes. Out of funds from the state office, Zornes took it on himself to write grocery requisitions on local stores, with no authority other than his own signature.

I remained County Manager at Coeur d'Alene for several years. C. Ben Ross ran for U.S. Senator in 1936 and Democrat Barzilla Clark was elected Idaho Governor. The Idaho Democrats would not support Barzilla Clark for a second two-year term, instead electing Chase Clark. In the political changeover, I lost my job as Kootenai County Manager of the Idaho Department of Public Assistance (successor to Pete Cohn's I.E.R.A.), but found a much better position in the Federal Work Projects Administration (W.P.A.) and was shortly transferred to the state office in Boise. I worked directly under Dean W. Miller, State Administrator of W.P.A., until near the end of the program. Dean Miller was an able administrator and the finest boss I ever had during 11 years in the Idaho welfare program.

After Pearl Harbor, the W.P.A. closed most non-defense projects, the exception in Idaho, being some schools, including the Boise Junior College, where incidentally, our son, Ray, Jr., got his start in "higher education." U.S. Senator, Frank Church, today a powerful voice in Washington, D.C., was our son's schoolmate.

In summarizing my 11 years with the Idaho Relief program, I can touch only briefly on some of the highlights not previously dealt with, such as the C.C.C. and nursing programs. The Adult Education program was effective, including a Writer's Project under Vardis Fisher. Audrey Arehart had been working on this, but tragically died of a hemorrhage and I was selected to complete her work, later published in book form, as a history of Idaho. Some fine buildings, swimming pools and State Parks facilities were constructed of lava rock in southern Idaho. Under the Federal Surplus Commodity Corporation (a division of I.E.R.A.) thousands of cattle were purchased from ranchers, slaughtered and processed by an I.E.R.A. cannery, the product then distributed to needy families. Many farm-to-market roads were repaired, or extended. I recall one from Oakley, in southern Idaho, to the Nevada border, where ranchers were forced to restrict operations because of annual flooding of their roads. A side road over high country led to the colorful City of Rocks area and on down a valley, where 300 emigrants were ambushed and massacred by Indians in the 1850's. This was on the historic "California Cutoff," up the Raft River, from the Snake River trail.

Ruby accompanied me on a trip covering the Oakley farm-to-market road story and we returned south through the City of Rocks and on down the Raft River road. The City of Rocks is a fascinating place, with hundreds of grotesque shaped rocks. We were unarmed and surprised a cougar, the big predator leaving his spoor in a small stream as he ran down a ravine, just ahead of us. Ruby and I took some good pictures in the City of Rocks, including slides that we value highly. These pictures were also used in a feature story, about the Oakley road, published in the Twin Falls paper. I might add here, that several times when Ruby was with me, we carried dark room equipment and, rented a motel with a bathtub and, of course, running water. We carried a piece of plywood that would be placed on the bathtub for a work table. Developing our own film in this makeshift dark room, we could even make enlargements. Local newspapers always welcomed our news stories, especially if we had pictures.

Other projects I felt were worthwhile were the National Youth Administration, in the I.E.R.A., which taught some shop work, as well as some field projects. Also, after the Japs attacked Pearl Harbor, Welding Schools trained relief workers for jobs in the shipyards. Two airfields were greatly improved. A Scrap Metal program resulted in hundreds of tons of iron and steel being salvaged by W.P.A. workers, chiefly from abandoned mines, although a considerable portion came from worn out farm machinery. I left the W.P.A. with mixed emotions. I felt that some sort of relief program should have been continued, the Welding School project, for example, had proved most valuable.

My personal contact with those on relief, occurred mostly while I was County Manager of I.E.R.A. Many sad cases were brought to my attention. Also, I had to continually check to see that everything was handled properly.

One of Anita Tidball's Social Service plans, included the County Manager's participation, in which he, or she, would make home visits at least once a month with the Social Service "case worker" in each district of the county to which the S.S. Aide was assigned. This proved impractical when I was manager of the I.E.R.A. in Kootenai County. I simply could not spare the time from my administrative duties, to make home visits with all of my eight S.S. Aides.

I did as much as I could, under the circumstances. Samples of the varied type of contacts, follow.

Mary, S.S. Aide for the Post Falls district, needed help. A widower, living alone, retired from sawmill work, was still a strong, aggressive six-foot-180-lb. man with "young ideas."

"He tried to drag me into his bedroom," Mary told me, as we approached the neat, little cottage. I threatened to stop my visits, or go to the county sheriff. Maybe you can set him straight. Mr. James is a very intelligent, lonely old man and doesn't know how to make friends. He's bitter at not being able to work, too!"

The visit paid off. Frank James was all that the S.S. Aide had said. I told him that we would send a male S.S. Aide if he didn't leave Mary alone. He apologized, said he had been an "old fool!" and Mary continued her monthly calls at Frank James' cottage.

I thought the incident closed, but a short time later received the sad news that Frank James had died of a heart attack. Mary and another Aide, cleaning up his little house, found his will, leaving the small home to Mary. We showed the will to a lawyer and his advice was quick and to the point. "Tear that will up — it could mean trouble!" So, Frank James, a lonely, bitter man of 70, died "Intestate."

Another man of 72, was getting a small relief check. Three hundred dollars, in cash, was found in the pocket of his worn jeans. No heirs appeared and Judge Whitney's Probate Court ruled that the money belonged to the I.E.R.A. I received a check for $300 from Judge Whitney, endorsed it and sent it on to the Boise office.

I investigated a rumor that one of our S.S. Aides had added a fictitious old couple to her "case load," collected and cashed a few of the checks and found the "tip off" to be true. I left for Boise shortly after, but heard later that the S.S. Aide involved, had been fired, but escaped prosecution when the money obtained fraudulently, was returned. Her excuse, "My husband needed a serious operation and we were too proud to ask for help."

I learned a lot about human nature visiting homes of the needy, with our Social Service Aides. We really had some hard cases, especially in the larger families on I.E.R.A. rolls. The problem — always the same — not enough money.

With the outbreak of World War II, my office was closed and I went to work at Gowan Field, the largest U.S. Air Force installation in Idaho, which had a large training field and a huge Supply Depot. I edited a civilian personnel publication, "The 14th Sub Depot Sun."

After a few months with the U.S.A.F., in Gowan Field, I quit, leaving Boise, and both Ruby and I helping in the war effort as best we could, worked for the Oregon Shipbuilding Corporation, near Portland, for the balance of World War Two. Our two sons, Ray and Norman, plus our daughter's husband, all saw active duty. We felt fortunate when all three returned safely.

We had been able to carry on our snare business, gradually increasing our shop machinery. Survival kits for our Air Force contained two small snares for catching small game.

In 1936, we had joined my uncle, P. P. Johnson, in building some tourist cabins in Coeur d'Alene. My uncle later added a small store, with living quarters in the rear and above the store. We manufactured our snares in the basement.

When we got into World War II, we thought our snare business would suffer. But Idaho farmers reported heavy loss in sheep from coyotes. Since our self-locking snare was primarily for trapping predators, I applied for a priority license and promptly received authority to purchase steel, including the special stranded steel wire we required and so kept in business. As a matter of fact, the W.P.A. also had a predator (coyote) control program. I made a few trips with W.P.A. trappers and got some good pictures and data for news stories. I even got an illustrated story on predator control in a Spokane farm journal.

EPILOGUE

After the war ended, we moved to Seattle and from there, in 1950, to our present location, about 20 miles north of Seattle and 1½ miles east of the freeway (I-5).

Frances and Doug Sinrud live next door and Fran helps Ruby manage our thriving, although small, manufacturing and publishing business. Anna, married to Jack Voeks, lives about 80 miles north of us. Jack owns an auto repair shop and Anna drives down for a couple days each week, to help care for her "Daddy." Ray, Jr. and wife, Virginia, live about 100 miles from here. Ray says he'll retire from a responsible position with Boeing, in about two years. Norman and wife, Margie, live in California. They have a good landscaping business.

In 1956, we got into the sled dog business, as a sideline. We first started making packs for dogs, then harnesses and sleds. We had become close friends with the (retired) famous sled dog racer, Leonhard Seppala and his wife, Constance. Seppala had turned his Siberian Husky kennels over to Earl Snodie, who ran his Bow Lake Kennels for several years. Wishing to retire, Snodie gave the last of his "Seppala" huskies to Ruby and we were suddenly in the breeding and training of Siberian Huskies.

Ruby got our daughter Frances, interested and, together, they ran the Martha Lake and Paitot Kennels for 10 years. Several of their Siberian Huskies became champions in the show ring and one winter, Fran's daughter, Linda, won the northwestern sled dog race in Oregon, competing with top ranking men drivers.

In connection with our dog kennel operation, we started publishing books on pack and sled dog training; how to make packs; harnesses and sleds, as well as some historical books, including one (two volume) story of Leonhard Seppala and his experiences with sled dogs, in Alaska. I also wrote with Louise Foley, a history of the Siberian Husky. We published *Northern Dog News* for two years, then Frances took it over for several years more. Finally, because it was becoming too much for us, Ruby and Fran quit the kennel operation and we sold our harness dog packs and sled making business. We still publish our books and they are widely distributed, with some sales in Europe. Sometimes, it has been an uphill battle, especially because of my deteriorating health, having to fight Multiple Sclerosis for many years.

We also publish poetry booklets, one collection being my own work. I hoped to encourage unknown writers, one being of special concern to me as she also is a victim of Multiple Sclerosis.

Today, in September, 1979, if you should visit us, you would find everyone busy in a family, neighbor operation. Our daughters, our grandson Pete Sinrud's wife, Chris, a cousin, Judy Walters and, of course, my wife Ruby, run the office, business management and printing, in a shop built on to our home. The basement is part of our snare shop, with two power punch presses and miscellaneous tools. Our main shop is a short distance from the house and this is where we manufacture parts and assemble our Thompson Self-Locking Snare business, with two additional punch presses, cutting torches, etc.

It has been a rewarding life!

Land of Fur and Gold! The "fur" because of my lifetime participation in some phase of the North American fur trade, including many years in Northern Canada, and even after moving to our present location, we leased land and kept experimenting with our snares. One fall, we snared black bears damaging fruit trees and showed farmers how to use our snares.

Gold! The "gold" in my book, is my wife of 61 plus years, our daughters, and sons, and our many wonderful grand and great grand-children.

Ruby is well known and well loved, in our community. She and a few friends, founded the Martha Lake Covenant Mission Church, shortly after we moved to Alderwood Manor. She has also been Precinct Committeeman for several terms.

The press has been kind to us, with several feature articles in the two largest Seattle papers and other stories in the local newspapers. Ours is a rather unique business!

On our walls are several plaques honoring me in the name of American Trappers. One is cleverly shaped like the State of Oregon, with tiny steel traps placed clockwise. It names me as one elected to the Fur Takers of America Trappers Hall of Fame. Another plaque shows that I was elected to a Trapper's Hall of Fame (sponsored by the *Trapper* magazine). A third plaque states that Raymond Thompson is an Honorary Lifetime member of the Wisconsin Trappers Association.

In the sled dog field, I was named to the Alaska Dog Musher's Hall of Fame, in recognition of my "Sled Dog Trails" department, in *Alaska Magazine.*

Actually, my writing has been the keystone to our modest success. When we first marketed our snares, many trappers tried them simply because they liked my stories in many trapper-hunter magazines.

I edited an outdoor-recreation type column in an Edmonton, Alberta magazine, in the 1920's. Later, I edited "Trader and Trapper," a department in Fur Trade Journal of Canada and had my adventure and wildlife articles syndicated in "Western Weekly" a supplement distributed by 65 Canadian papers. While we were in Michigan, I ran a weekly column for the *Detroit Daily*, as Outdoor Editor.

In all this, Ruby has stood by me and has won considerable fame, on her own. Recently, she snared a coyote that was after a neighbor's rabbits. A member of the Washington State Trappers Association phoned and "let the cat out of the bag" by telling Ruby she was to be named "Trapper of the Year" at the upcoming state-wide convention!

In these sunset years, it is good to have such a partner and I often say to myself, "Ray Thompson, you're a lucky man!"

October 31, 19

Dear Mr. Thompson
I hear you are good at trapping Here are some questions: Do you trap with metal springtraps, guns wire traps, or all? What is the fool proof drowner made of? Do you ever catch animals with bows and arrows? What is the largest price you have ever gotten for an animal? What is the lowest Was the depression bad on your business? If you would, please send me back the answers.

16600 S.E.
Blanton Milwaukie
Ore. 97222

Sincerley
Tony Walker

11/29/76

SOUTH EAST TEXAS TRAPPERS ASS'N.

Affiliant of Fur Takers of America

OFFICERS:

PRESIDENT:
Mike Gravis
General Delivery
Evadale, Texas 77615

SEC-TREAS:
Larry Cawley
Star Route, Box 939
Silsbee, Texas 77656

Dear Mr. Thompson,

A letter from the President of the United States could not be prized any more than recieving one from you. Thank you for taking time out to send the information down to us. As yet we don't have a newsletter but hope to have one soon. Please send any and all information about trapping, and we'll get it out.

Sincerely.

Larry D. Cawley

SOUTH EAST TEXAS TRAPPERS ASS'N.

Affiliant of Fur Takers of America

OFFICERS:

PRESIDENT:
Mike Gravis
General Delivery
Evadale, Texas 77615

SEC-TREAS:
Larry Cawley
Star Route, Box 939
Silsbee, Texas 77656

Dear Mr. Thompson,

Sorry to be so tardy about writing. Have recieved your book "Wilderness Trapline Adventures" must thank you very much. Some of the stories sure make a fellow like me do some fancy daydreaming. I probably have seen snow no more than 10 times during my life. The hardships y'all undertook must have been something else. I would like to see you put some of your pictures and stories in "The Trapper" magazine.

Hope this letter finds you & Mrs. Thompson well and will write you again later.

Sincerely,

Larry D. Cawley

October 30, 1979

Dear Mr. Thompson,

Congratulations for winning the Trappers Hall of Fame award. Your great grandson, Shawn brought in the <u>Trapper</u> paper and ~~at~~ our substitute teacher read it to us. I'm not much into trapping, just furs. I wish I could say my great grandpa won a Trapper Hall of Fame award. Shawn's pretty lucky to have a great grandpa thats such a good trapper.

Sincerely
Margo Phillips

LEAVES

A

Collection of Verses

by

RAYMOND THOMPSON

Dedicated

to

His Wife, RUBY,

on

The Occasion of Their

60th

Wedding Anniversary

May 26, 1978

Published by RAYMOND THOMPSON COMPANY
15815-2nd Place West, Lynnwood, WA 98036

THE PATTERN

My dreams disturbed by warning claps of thunder,
One dawn, I rushed outside my cabin door;
I stood, transfixed at heaven's awesome wonder,
It seemed that God himself had gone to war.

I saw the lightning strike and flames start leaping,
Across the canyon was a holocaust;
It was as if all wild things were trapped sleeping,
My precious pines, my firs and aspens lost.

How long the fires blazed, I can't remember,
I crossed the gorge to count each black-robed ghost;
I questioned as I stirred each dying ember,
How God could make a tree His whipping post!

But as I wandered through the blackened spires,
In search of some small lingering sign of life;
I hoped to find amongst the smoldering fires,
An answer to my own discord and strife.

I knelt and prayed that I would find some power
To rise above my bitter loneliness;
They were God's trees, and only for an hour
Could I expect to share His wilderness.

And as I rose my gaze was caused to fasten,
Across the canyon to a verdant hill;
I sensed the trees that God had chose to hasten,
Somehow disclosed the pattern of His will.

Like man, each tree is lost in merging shadows,
Across the great expanse of God's terrain;
The woods, the hills, and even lush green meadows,
Were made to burn, just to be born again.

THE FLOWERS OF MEMORY LANE

The flowers that grow in Memory Lane,
Are the fairest flowers of all,
Our love is the sun and our tears the rain,
That makes them grow so tall!

Yet how bitter the day we leave them there,
Our beloved and precious tots,
E'en though His gardeners tenderly care
For our fragile Forget-Me-Nots.

So we leave our little flowers with God,
Safe in the Master's bed;
And as we turn from this hallowed sod,
We hear Angels softly tread.

FOR RUBY A CHRISTMAS WISH

For us, my darling, at Yuletide,
A room full of memories;
As if they were standing, side by side,
A forest of Christmas trees.

I glance at the clock upon the wall,
And its silent, somber face,
Makes me wish that I might recall,
Another time and place.

I miss the old grandfather's clock,
That seemed so alive, in the hall,
How reassuring that brave "tick-tock"
As if time didn't matter at all.

And if I could only climb the stair,
Though the way to the attic is steep;
I'd bring back Grandma's rocking chair,
And rock us both to sleep.

And I'd pray that Santa would leave a key,
In our special Christmas sock;
To a time rollback for you and me,
And slow that wild "Tick-tock, Tick-tock!"

MY DAUGHTERS

I close my eyes and suddenly your faces
Appear upon my special magic screen,
I see you in the old familiar places,
As babes, as now, and through the years
between.

I see you in your rocking chairs while
holding
Those tattered dolls — to hug so close and tight,
As if you were two little mothers scolding,
Your babes that wouldn't listen to "good night".

I see you as we walked along together —
Hand in hand a father-daughter team;
Laughing, scorning cold and stormy weather —
Remembering it was — a perfect scheme!

How swiftly then the panorama changes
From when you were two toddlers by my side.
How wide the wheel of fortune marker ranges,
How relentless is the flowing ebbing tide.

And now, while Father Time works at erasing
My footprints on the ever shifting sands,
I'll keep on painting scenes of our retracing
The steps we made together holding hands!

MY SONS

When you my sons were little lads,
And I was big and strong and tall;
I was so proud — like other Dads,
Would that I might those days recall.

How swiftly years have come and gone,
My boys long since have grown to men,
Yet precious memories linger on,
In dreams I see my boys again.

For when the clouds seem cold and gray,
And hour-glass sands are running low,
I think of one quite Magic Way,
To stem the tide's swift ebbing flow.

I close my eyes, and in the sky,
A picture flashes clear and strong,
I see my sons there walking by,
And somehow I'll just tag along.

A WISH FOR TODAY

From early morning 'til setting sun
I searched for treasures — not a single one
Could match the sapphires in her eyes;
Could enhance the glory of her hair,
Nor could the reddest rose compare
With cupid's bow that shapes her lips
The tender feel of fingertips,
Far surpasses the velvet touch
Of finest satin and silks so much
I cannot choose a gift today
Except my love — hers anyway!
Perhaps the best of all, I guess,
A kiss and a wish of happiness.

TO A LONE WOLF

Against the backdrop of a frigid moon,
A lone wolf stands in mourning for the pack;
He casts abroad his melancholy tune,
Then waits, but only echoes answer back.

All night he seeks the magic, mystic scent
Of mates who followed him along the trail;
Vague shadows join to mock his wild lament
And winds like voices of the past prevail.

Undaunted still the lone wolf travels far,
Then loping back to reach his lonely den,
To wait until another evening star,
And rising moon shall light his trail again.

But now he dreams, but sleep cannot erase
The scent of game, nor dim the hunting call;
Then rousing from his dream, he leads the
chase,
Returning to his mate at evenfall.

TREE WITH A CROWN
by
Raymond Thompson

The bravest tree I have ever seen
Was a victim of lightning's guillotine
That seared its bole and toppled its head
And left it charred like a tree most dead;
No longer it heeded the warming rains;
No longer the sap stirred in its veins.

It stood with its branches wide apart,
Like a grim outcast in the forest's heart;
No needles or cones its limbs adorned,
By woodsman and timber cruiser scorned.

I, too, spared only a passing glance,
And then I happened to look, by chance,
To the pine tree's top where the fire had scored,
Then I heard a scream as a great bird soared
To swoop back down to the shattered crest,
And there I beheld an eagle's nest.

A nest with thousands of twigs entwined,
And I knew full well that some master mind
Had planted that tree with roots so deep
That it could stand, though fast asleep.

And the eagle's nest was a sort of crown,
That made a king of an awkward clown;
And though years have passed, I know God's hands
Have wrought so well that the tree still stands
As a monument to humility
And a lesson for mortals like you and me.

PRECIOUS HOURS

Oh, Precious Hours that ended all too
soon;
First, magic morn and then enraptured
noon;
And then, to briefly pause in headlong
flight,
Love wrapped its arms around us one
mad night;
Once heaven's gift, now turned to
Satan's spawn,
To haunt me, Precious Hours — forever
gone!

TO RUBY ON OUR 59th

Against the Day when time
runs out —
My Dear, you surely know,
That love is what it's all
about,
And Darling, I've loved
you so!

So, marry me for another
year,
We'll chalk up a full
three-score,
And as the end of that
time draws near,
May God grant us one year
more.

Raymond and Ruby — 50th wedding anniversary

A TRIBUTE TO RUBY ON OUR 60th ANNIVERSARY

One by one, as the years roll by,
Each year adds a priceless treasure,
A treasure that only love could buy,
With a loving cup for a measure.

Some marriages are an ego trip,
Like ships that pass in the night;
But ours has been a partnership,
With bonds holding secure and tight.

The house we've built was made to with-
  stand
The tide with its ebb and flow,
So unlike dream castles in the sand,
We may have dreamed of long ago.

And through the years, among gifts I hold,
You gave me, forever to keep,
Are visions, more precious than finest gold,
Of our babes in their cradles, asleep.

Cherished too are friendships made,
As we've traveled life's corridor.
To our special friends, an accolade,
All for memory's sacred store.

We've managed somehow to survive each storm,
And to skirt the deepest abyss,
Secure in our nest, so cozy and warm,
With for each a goodnight kiss.

The road has been long and often rough
But with you, Dear, by my side,
Our love has always been strong enough,
To stand against the fiercest tide.

So a tribute to Ruby, while counting down,
The years spent in our lotus-land,
I toast the aura she wears like a crown,
With our loving cup in my hand.

SEARCH FOR A STAR

I dreamed that I winged through the Zodiac,
To seek out a magic sign,
That would point the way to a bivouac
With a star that I could call mine.

But the heavens and I were not in tune,
And all I could see from afar,
Was a flash of light on the face of the moon
And the blaze from a falling star.

But a dreamer like me must ever keep on,
For dreams must never be stilled,
In the game of life each dream is a pawn,
We play the way God has Willed.

For additional copies of *Land of Fur and Gold*, please send $5.95 plus $1.00 postage and handling each to:

Land of Fur & Gold
Raymond Thompson Co.
P.O. Box 1745
Bellingham, WA 98225

NO LONGER AVAILABLE

* Washington State residents please add 5.3% sales tax.

NAME ______________________________

Address ______________________________

City ____________ State ____________ Zip ____________

For additional copies of *Land of Fur and Gold*, please send $5.95 plus $1.00 postage and handling each to:

Land of Fur & Gold
Raymond Thompson Co.
P.O. Box 1745
Bellingham, WA 98225

* Washington State residents please add 5.3% sales tax.

NAME ______________________________

Address ______________________________

City ____________ State ____________ Zip ____________

GEOGRAPHICAL NAME CHANGES

Baptiste River - This was the name of the Berland River until 1917.

Jackfish Lake - In 1980 this lake was renamed Sides Lake.

Buck Lake - This lake has been called Smoke Lake since 1960.

Tony River - Today it is called Tony Creek.

Mile 90 - This was stopping place on the Edson-Grande Prairie trail. It was located on a meadow near Tony Creek, approximately 10 miles from where the town of Fox Creek is. This location was usually called Mile 90 but occasionally in other sources it is referred to as Mile 108.